Linking Assignments to Assessments

A Guide for Teachers

Deborah Crusan
Wright State University

Todd Ruecker
University of Nevada, Reno

MICHIGAN TEACHER TRAINING
University of Michigan Press
Ann Arbor

Published in the United States of America
The University of Michigan Press
Manufactured in the United States of America

♾ Printed on acid-free paper

ISBN-13: 978-0-472-03865-7 (print)
ISBN-13: 978-0-472-12937-9 (ebook)

2025 2024 2023 2022 4 3 2 1

Acknowledgments

I am thankful for present and former students from whom I learned the importance of assessment. In particular, thanks to Alaa Bader, Lakmini Grant Siriwardana, Daryl Hausman, Lu He, Jonathan Martinez, Beth Sjostrom, and Shen Yao for their generosity in sharing materials.

Although writing is solitary, I have long written with a group of women in formats both face-to-face and online. Thanks to writing partners Christa Agiro, Jessica Barnett, Shengrong Cai, Carol Mejia-LaPerle, Sirisha Naidu, Nimisha Patel, Marie Thompson, and Sarah Twill. I am particularly grateful to Noeleen McIlvenna for writing sessions in which the two of us spent countless silent but gratifying days together.

I extend thanks to my family (Ron, Leslie, Axel, Sal, Fred, Mark, Kathleen, Nick) for their love and support.

And to Todd—thanks for taking this project on with me. I'm beyond grateful.

—Deborah

I would like to thank the many teachers who have let me visit their classrooms to learn about their work with bilingual language learners. These experiences have been vital in shaping my writing in this book.

I would also like to thank Deborah for inviting me to be part of this project and for being such a fun person to write with, even during a pandemic.

I also thank my family (Brooke, Pingo, and Clementine) for their love and support.

—Todd

Contents

Introduction

We have written *Linking Assignments to Assessments: A Guide for Teachers* with the goal to make assessment accessible and practical. While assessment should be part of every classroom, many teachers feel they are not "good at assessment." This book helps address teachers' concerns by impressing upon readers the idea that no teacher creates any activity without assessment in the background—that is, when teachers create activities for their students, they consider the kinds of information that will result from that activity. We also invite teachers to consider how that information will inform their teaching and what it can reveal about their students' abilities and language proficiencies. In keeping with that stance, this textbook provides ideas for assignments with accompanying information on how to develop rubrics and other assessment tools for assignments, showing the inextricable link between the activity and the assessment and that, in fact, they are actually one and the same.

This text has been primarily designed for a few different audiences. The first is teachers who are training to get their master's in TESOL programs (or earning TEFL certificates) who hope to work in dedicated ESL classrooms in U.S. PreK–12 schools or teach in intensive English programs (IEPs) or English for Academic Purposes (EAP) programs at the university level or in another type of language school. Another audience is future PreK–12 teachers who will face a growing number of English learners (ELs) in their classrooms. The book will also be useful to any practicing instructor who has had little or no preparation to work with ELs, sparse knowledge about language assessment (and quite possibly assessment in general) and language acquisition, and little time to acquire that knowledge, even though assessment knowledge remains one of the keys to successful classroom practice. Both new and experienced teachers will appreciate the book's practicality, its guidance in developing assessment skills and strategies, acquiring assessment literacy, and enhancing student learning.

What's in This Book?

Linking Assignments to Assessments: A Guide for Teachers, which strives to transform teaching and learning, combines foundational information about assessment practices and incorporates extensive step-by-step instructions for teachers to effectively integrate assessment into their classrooms.

Chapter 1 begins by explaining what assessment literacy is and why it is important, especially for teachers working with ELs. We contextualize this in broader political/ social contexts of achievement gaps and explain how focused instruction and assessment can help teachers help students make gains in the classroom. We then provide accessible introductions to commonly used principles in assessment.

Chapter 2 reviews the basics of what we know about language acquisition. We show how this knowledge illustrates how teachers need to have patience in the way they assess their ELs or former ELs, helping them build proficiency while not overly penalizing them because of unrealistic expectations. This chapter is included because many teachers do not realize how long it takes students to learn another language, especially in terms of academic proficiency.

Chapter 3 begins by emphasizing the importance of considering context and student backgrounds in effective assessment, which means that teachers will work with their students to meet national standards in different ways as they craft outcomes that may be unique to their classroom, region, and individual students. We then discuss ways to develop goals and learning outcomes for the class, explaining how teachers can develop their own or understand/analyze standards such as those provided by states and organizations.

Chapter 4 then focuses on the key steps of creating effective assessments, including understanding test specifications, writing directions, writing items, creating rubrics, and establishing accommodations. We discuss the differences in how these elements are considered in creating everyday formative assessments as well as more formal summative assessments like tests. In the last part of the chapter, we bring all these considerations together and walk through the process of creating a test.

Chapter 5 begins by defining what we mean by receptive skills: **listening and reading**. The chapter is then divided into two main sections, listening assessments and reading assessments. These sections are organized in similar ways. After giving background on the skill area being assessed, we discuss examples of relevant language standards that reference the skill. We then explore different ways to assess the skill (e.g., controlled, guided, and free—communicative practice—activities) and illustrate the assessment possibilities by sharing a variety of activities and ways to assess them, including sample rubrics.

Chapters 6 and 7 are similarly structured, with the former focusing on productive skills (**speaking and writing**) and the latter focusing on **grammar and vocabulary** assessment.

Even though this is a textbook aimed at the classroom, teachers need to know about standardized testing since it plays an important role in the academic lives of ELs at all different levels, whether they are taking a state test to graduate from high school or taking the TOEFL® to enter a program of study at a U.S. university. In Chapter 8, we point out some of the problems with standardized testing while providing an overview of what teachers need to know about it, including how to interpret scores and how to teach test-taking strategies that help students perform better.

Chapter 9 leads teachers through the process of articulating their ideas, knowledge, and values surrounding assessment and incorporating them in a philosophy that will shape the work they do. We explain the importance of the theory-practice link, summarizing some of the major approaches to assessment described earlier in the book. We provide examples of philosophies and activities around brainstorming the creation of an assessment philosophy.

How to Use This Book

Linking Assignments to Assessments: A Guide for Teachers is intended to be read sequentially as each chapter builds on what has been previously discussed; however, some readers may prefer to jump to a particular section for a quick reference that helps address a problem they are facing in the classroom.

Each chapter ends with a selection of activities and discussion questions. While these are primarily intended for those reading the book in a classroom setting so that readers can engage more deeply with the text and discuss it with other learners, the activities and questions may also be useful for individual readers who want to reflect further on the material.

Both of us (Deborah and Todd) teach MA students. Deborah also teaches the required assessment course in both undergraduate and graduate TESOL programs. Her philosophy of assessment rides on the shoulders of her students and what she has learned from them about how, when, and why to assess.

1

Principles of Assessment and Their Connection to Teaching and Learning

Assessment: **the mere word strikes** fear into the hearts of teachers simply because many teachers, through no fault of their own, lack the expertise to accurately, fairly, and purposefully assess their students' writing. Teachers who are assessment literate understand how to gather reliable evidence of student achievement; they know when to use which methods and how to use them well. They know how to use the assessment process and its results to support learning and to verify that students have learned. Anyone involved in making pedagogical decisions should understand the difference between sound and unsound assessment. Assessment is not something that we tack on to the end of teaching to see if it worked; we can actually make assessment part of the learning experience (Michigan Assessment Consortium, 2014). That's the point of this book: that assessment IS part of the learning experience; in fact, we would further claim that it is inextricably tied to learning.

Formative and Summative Assessment

When teachers hear the A-word, a *summative assessment*—an assessment that happens at the end of something, such as a unit or a term, and offers little to no feedback to students—is usually what first comes to mind. It is little wonder since large-scale standardized tests are primarily constructed as summative assessments. Those end-of-semester exams or essays designed to figure out if a student met required learning outcomes and to assign a final grade are primarily summative. In short, summative assessments tell a teacher what students can (or cannot) do and are used primarily to assign a grade or make some other determination on a broader scale (e.g., placement, exit from a program). However, we are more interested in another type of assessment.

Imagine a week in a 5th grade English classroom. The week starts out with a warm-up activity focused on using vocabulary from the previous week in written sentences. The primary lesson on Monday and Tuesday includes reading a short story. The lesson begins with a short listening activity in which students listen to the author discussing the story and their composing process, followed by an informal comprehension check where the teacher asks students questions orally. Then the students read individually, complete multiple choice responses and a few short answer questions, and engage in further oral discussion about the story with the class. On Friday, the students write a paragraph in which they compare and contrast two characters of their choosing in the story. Which of these mentioned activities is an assessment? The answer: **All of them.**

While we deal with summative assessment in this textbook, we are more concerned with *classroom assessment*; our main purpose in writing this book is to emphasize the point that **every assignment is an assessment**. Assessment does not have to mean a long test or a large formal writing assignment given at the end of a class, year, or set of years in school. For example:

- A worksheet done for homework is an assessment.
- An in-class presentation is an assessment.
- Student participation in peer review is an assessment.
- A quick listening activity with a workbook response is an assessment.

These shorter-cycle assessments are known commonly as *formative assessments*, and they are designed to tell a teacher and student what the student does or does not know and—this is the key—how to change the curriculum to address gaps in student learning. This should be the goal of ALL in-class assessments.

In this classroom, the teacher uses the feedback from those assignments and adapts her teaching all along the way. She may spend more time with listening to the author recording if students were having trouble responding to her questions or create additional character analyses exercises if the student paragraphs at the end of the week focused more on summarizing than on comparing and contrasting. Harlen (2006) compares this process to a thermostat: "Just as feedback from the thermostat of a heating or cooling system allows the temperature of a room to be maintained within a particular range, so feedback of information about learning helps ensure that new experiences are not too difficult nor too easy for students" (p. 89).

The key to formative assessment is that it is focused on improving learning. In the words of Chappuis (2009), "Formative assessment is not an instrument or an event,

TABLE 1.1
Formative and Summative Assessment Comparison

	Pros	Cons
Formative	▪ Can be spontaneous, easily adapted to specific time and student ▪ More manageable to develop and assess ▪ Connected to daily classroom practice ▪ Validity is not as important since it is a series of multiple tests	▪ Not as comprehensive ▪ Can place an extra burden on teacher if not designed and implemented well in a larger curriculum ▪ Only as good as the way it's used; teacher needs to apply it to curriculum improvement
Summative	▪ Bigger-picture view of student's abilities ▪ Given less often, so more thought and time can go into design	▪ Students can often be over-tested, which takes away from teaching and learning time ▪ Not directly connected to instruction and does not help facilitate learning

but a collection of practices with a common feature: they all lead to some action that improves learning" (p. 4). It is the use of information that counts. Because of this confusion, some have gone so far as to recommend we stop using the term *formative assessment*, preferring the term *assessment for learning*. However, our take on terminology is that we can change the term but the meaning assigned can still be problematic. In Table 1.1, we sum up the pros and cons of summative and formative assessment, both of which have a place in the classroom.

Assessment Purposes

Assessment is a critical and often very challenging aspect of teaching. But if teachers do not know **why** they are assessing their students, it's a rather pointless exercise. Deborah always tells her assessment students that assessment is like buying an airline ticket: "If you don't know where you're going, you'll never get off the ground." So it's vitally important to consider several questions:

- Why am I assessing my students?
- What do I want to know about them?
- What will I do with the data I have collected?

Teachers who are able to develop constructive assessments, give corrective feedback, and provide students with second chances to show achievement can improve their instruction and help students learn. Good assessments help teachers make discoveries about their students. Good assessments also help teachers discover ways to improve their own teaching. For example, an item on a test that every student answers incorrectly is often a sign that the material tested with that item might not have been retained by the students or possibly that the material tested was above the level of the students. If that happens often, or if all students do poorly on assignments, teachers quite possibly might need to examine or re-examine their instruction. This re-examination or reflection can often lead to improved instruction, which benefits both the teacher and the students.

Context matters in the assessment process as well. Scarino (2013) provided evidence that the assessment acquisition process and teachers' own professional beliefs, practices, and local context are intertwined and reminds us of the importance of the assessment perceptions teachers bring to the teaching and assessment encounter. These beliefs influence their classroom practices and are sometimes difficult to negotiate. For instance, Deborah was once giving a writing assessment workshop in which a teacher proclaimed that he would never use rubrics to assess his students' writing. When asked why, he answered that he wanted to be able to penalize his students for things that they did or did not do in their papers, and if those things were not on the rubric, then he would not be able to penalize them. Further, contextually, he was a long-time high school English teacher who felt that he knew best since he had been teaching for so long. He commented that "university professors might have to do that rubric thing" in their contexts, but he "didn't have to." So much for accountability.

Scarino (2013) also cited the impact of sociocultural theories of learning on language assessment for teachers—particularly teacher self-awareness and self-reflection, the ability and the motivation to question what they do in the classroom and why they do it, as well as the wherewithal to expand their knowledge base. She referenced the need to reconcile the two differing paradigms of assessment—traditional and sociocultural.

Another important issue to remember is the inextricable bond that assessment and instruction share. In other words, instruction and assessment are one. Every **assignment** that a teacher develops and uses is an **assessment** of the student and their knowledge or ability to perform in some way. The assignment gathers some kind of information about the student. Even if the teacher will not officially grade the assignment, it nevertheless provides evidence of something that the student knows or does not know, can or cannot do. One example of this kind of assessment could be a response or dialogue journal written by the student and read by the teacher, who comments on what the student has to say but does not attach a grade to the writing. Regardless, the teacher is informed by the student's writing, observing any number of strengths and weaknesses, both at the rhetorical and linguistic level and perhaps at the content level as well. As a result of these observations, the teacher might then plan activities that practice skills that need to be developed and/or reinforce skills that allow rehearsal before students are actually graded on similar tasks. In this way, ungraded work filters over to more formalized assessment, teaching, and learning.

Another example of a nonthreatening, low-stakes assessment exercise inseparable from learning is a group reading activity (largely designed for English language learners) in which teachers cluster students in threes or fours and provide a task in which all students in the group are assigned a role in a story; for instance, the assignment might be a medical role-playing activity in which one student is the doctor or nurse, another is the office manager, and still another is the patient. The teacher provides dialogue and then visits each group, listening for issues of pronunciation and recording them. She then lists items on the board (many of the issues will be alike for the students), reviews phonetic and phonemic information about sounds and articulators and, in that way, provides pronunciation guidance without betraying any of her students or embarrassing them. **The activity is an assessment** of students' pronunciation and it provides the teacher information about individual students, but it is a low-stakes assessment and not disconcerting to the students at all. It provides valuable feedback without embarrassment. Students learn and save face all at the same time.

The Effects of Assessment on the Classroom

Assessment can affect a class both negatively and positively. One illustration of assessment's negative effects on the classroom involves teachers' use of assessment as punishment. For example, some teachers employ pop quizzes to discipline students for talking, neglecting reading assignments, being unresponsive in class, or for doing a host of other behaviors. Other teachers test because it's something they have always done—it's Friday, so it's spelling quiz day, no matter what. Although it is arguable that structure helps students learn, this kind of assessment can quickly become unreflective, mechanical, and dreaded by students. These kinds of assessments, or the reasons behind these assessments, rarely serve any purpose other than a castigatory one, and they expose a practice left unexamined by the teacher.

On the other hand, effective assessment is purposeful and reaps positive benefits for the teacher and her students. It can indicate successful teaching and successful learning. Since what happens in the classroom—what teachers and students do—drives learning, teachers should examine their motives for assessing their students. Thus, the first big question teachers need to ask themselves before administering an assessment of any kind is simply: *What do I want to find out about my students*? Or *Why do I want to give my students this assessment?* Then, teachers need to think about ways in which the assessment will improve their instruction or modify their approach to individual students. These formative assessments are ongoing—that is, they happen every day in class. Suffice it to say that these ongoing assessments are important in every classroom, but in the classroom in which ELs reside, these assessments are critical because they provide a more comprehensive view of ELs' skills, abilities, and continuing progress.

Teachers use assessment to gather data about students, what they know, what they can do, what they cannot do. They use it to inform and direct their teaching. Roediger III, Putnam, and Smith (2011) listed these ten benefits of classroom assessment:

- The testing effect: retrieval aids later retention.
- Testing identifies gaps in knowledge.
- Testing causes students to learn more from the next learning episode.
- Testing produces better organization of knowledge.
- Testing improves transfer of knowledge to new contexts.
- Testing can facilitate retrieval of information that was not tested.
- Testing improves metacognitive monitoring.
- Testing prevents interference from prior material when learning new material.
- Testing provides feedback to instructors.
- Frequent testing encourages students to study.

Therefore, within effective assessment, teachers first examine their reasons for testing. What questions need to be answered and how might a test answer them? This is a powerful illustration of how assessment and pedagogy are connected. Again, when teachers decide that they are going to test their students, they must first answer one question: *What is it that I want to know about my students?* When they have answered that question, they can then develop an assignment that will provide data about what they want to know.

Assessment Literacy

More and more is being written about the need for teachers to be assessment literate; in other words, teachers need to understand the "measurement basics related directly to classroom learning" (Malone, 2011, p. 1), and they need to know how to apply these basics to their teaching and why this matters so much. Assessment literate teachers understand why they assess their students and ways in which to use the many forms of data they gather. Robust assessment that has been appropriately employed provides crucial information about the attainment of educational objectives and student learning to teachers, students, parents, and other stakeholders (e.g., Crusan, Plakans, & Gebril, 2016; Plakans & Gebril, 2015).

As noted previously, teachers' classroom assessments provide a variety of information about their students. Currently, however, many teachers who use textbooks in their classrooms expect authors and publishers to include tests with the other teaching materials provided. In fact, publishers often report excessive demands from textbook users who threaten to discontinue use of textbooks unless all teaching materials—lesson plans, handouts, graphic organizers, formative assessments, chapter tests—are provided to them.

For many reasons, scholars have criticized demands for these prepackaged materials, citing the materials' penchant for de-skilling teachers (Shannon, 1987); the de-skilling of teachers transforms teachers into automatons who merely distribute worksheets, canned tests, and assignments rather than their once carefully crafted materials. When teachers are forced to employ prepackaged curriculum using publisher-created assessments, it can create a classroom devoid of context and unable to meet the needs of the students in that class, needs that may be decidedly different from those in a classroom across town or across the state. Although often ignored in current education policy, no other person knows the education needs of her students more than that teacher who meets with them every day, so it is critical that she creates assessments that meet their needs and that provide current and ongoing information. It is critical that she and her colleagues develop assessment literacy and know not only how to create assessments but also what to do with the information resulting from administration of the assessments. Of course, the surrounding politics at play certainly lead to this de-skilling, especially in the current climate of high-stakes testing and teacher accountability (for things that are impossible to control in their classrooms), where teachers are very often overworked, teach in overcrowded classrooms, and have little time to devote to building expertise.

In assessment, as in all teaching, context reigns as one of the most important variables. What works in one context often will not be the most productive strategy in another context. Some groups of students perform well on dictation exercises; however, another group may resist this kind of assessment. In that same vein, what works in one class of students may not work for another class, even in the same school. For example, suppose a teacher created a rubric (see Chapter 3) for a writing task that she assigned in one of her classes. Along with the assignment, the teacher, following Deborah Crusan's (2010) rules of ethical and transparent assessment, developed an accompanying scoring rubric and used the rubric to assess the writing of students in her class. However, the results were not what she expected. Except for a very few students, everyone received an A on the writing assignment. Clearly, the rubric was unable to effectively discriminate between performances of different quality; in other words, the rubric—because it might not have been specific enough—was unable to recognize a distinction between one paper and another. This is problematic because one of the hallmarks of a valid assessment instrument lies in its ability to discriminate.

Rubrics generally improve the validity of assessments by keeping the assessor's perceptions and biases in check; however, a poorly constructed rubric that assesses points that are not on the assignment or does not provide clearly articulated terminology and expectations is not an effective assessment tool. Again, teachers must first ask themselves exactly what they want to find out about their students from the assignment and then go about judiciously fashioning an accompanying rubric that mirrors criteria on the assignment. A generic rubric, while possibly a good start for a novice teacher, is no replacement for a carefully crafted and pinpointed assessment instrument. Online programs such as RubiStar (http://rubistar.4teachers.org/) can help newer teachers create assignment-specific rubrics. Programs such as RubiStar can become more useful as they allow teachers to import their own criteria and point systems; in this way, teachers can create custom rubrics using the support of online software. Rubrics are discussed in more detail in Chapter 3.

Assessment Concepts and Terminology

Some broader assessment concepts that are important to know are discussed here, followed by some additional terms that are used throughout the book.

Assessment for Learning vs. Assessment of Learning

Assessment for learning and assessment of learning are both important factors to consider.

Assessment for Learning (AfL) is defined primarily as classroom-based assessment that provides information about students that can serve as an impetus to motivate them to learn more, do more, and progress to the next level. It is largely formative in nature; it helps to form the understanding of students' knowledge and allows for feedback to help students improve, which then allows for changes to happen in students' knowledge and abilities. AfL is underpinned by the philosophy that every student can improve (Lam, 2016; Crusan & Matsuda, 2018) and focuses less on the right answer than on the idea that students are learning to learn, which is particularly important when students come from another culture in which learning and teaching are approached differently. Moreover, students who might not be literate in their first language or who have had their schooling interrupted need to be instructed on how to learn and unlock their learning strategies.

Lam (2016) defines assessment of learning (AoL) as assessment that sums up student learning over a period of time. It is summative in nature and rarely provides any feedback to the student except in a solo score (or grade) that can mean little or nothing to the student, since the score is usually delayed, making it meaningless for any real improvement. This is not to say that AoL is unworthy of consideration. Every teacher knows that grades are an integral, important, and often motivating factor for students, as well as required at the institutions at which we teach. And certainly, standardized assessments of achievement are important in their own right as they offer some evidence of student progress and/or achievement. However, AoL as the only kind of assessment does a great disservice to our students since it can offer them little in the way of feedback for improvement.

Criterion-Referenced vs. Norm-Referenced Assessment

Criterion-referenced tests ascertain whether students have met instructional objectives or criteria that they are expected to know and be able to do at a specific stage of their education. Criterion-referenced tests simply assess how well students are obtaining particular learning outcomes (see Bond, 1996), which can be developed externally by state agencies or internally by the teacher. The latter are more contextualized and focused on what has been happening in that particular classroom.

Norm-referenced tests, on the other hand, compare students to each other. Test takers are typically the same age and at the same grade level. Information garnered from norm-referenced tests estimates students' positions in a population. Scores are usually reported using percentiles, which provide little information for the individual teacher or student except to say that one student ranks better or worse than other students like them; these scores can be useful in determining if students need remedial support or should be placed in an honors track (Bond, 1996).

Focused Instruction

Focused instruction helps teachers help students make gains in the classroom. It goes by a variety of names, including *aligned instruction* and *standards* or *goal-based instruction*. In focused instruction, teachers have clear learning goals in mind and make a plan for how to achieve those goals, continuously evaluating whether or not students are making progress toward them. Due to simplistic teacher evaluation practices involving yes/no questions, (e.g. did teacher make students aware of class agenda?), this type of instruction often gets reduced to blindly writing a standard on the board, leaving it there, and not really meaningfully adapting instruction toward it. Meaningful focused instruction includes careful consideration of the desired learning outcomes throughout the process, from planning the sequence of assignments to more in-depth planning of individual assignments and their rubrics (see Chapter 3).

Validity and Reliability

Validity and reliability are two very important concepts in assessment. For a test to accurately measure individual differences and foster learning, it must be both valid and reliable.

Validity addresses the notion that an examination accurately represents what it claims to test, such as students' ability to meet a particular outcome. For instance, states often require ELs to complete a state mathematics assessment in English right away or a few years after their arrival. Some of the newer Common Core–aligned assessments have begun including more word problems to test students' ability to apply mathematical knowledge in practical situations. These tests claim to measure purely mathematical ability; however, when language (and often cultural knowledge) is an important part of students' performance, then the test is not validly assessing math ability: it is not valid.

Reliability is the notion that tests are consistent in their measurement abilities. In other words, test results must be reliable and repeatable, so that teachers are confident that students' scores are true reflections of their achievements. For instance, assessment of student writing is notoriously unreliable as the evaluation of writing tends to be more subjective than multiple choice assessment. While one may see a student essay as a 5/5, another (perhaps shaped by their working experiences or the types of students they tend to serve) may see the same paper as a 3/5. Or, in thinking of particular students, many teachers go into evaluating an individual student's paper based on what they know about them ("oh she's a good writer"; "oh, this student will have a weak paper"). To address this, many test makers often avoid writing assessments or otherwise pair them with indirect measures of writing, typically a number of multiple choice questions about grammar usage, to improve reliability. Chapter 3 will discuss how rubrics are one way to improve the reliability of student grading because they make assessment criteria more transparent.

Careful test construction that closely adheres to a test plan and other guidelines presented in later chapters increase the probability of gaining repeatable test results that accurately reflect achievement of the course content.

Fairness

Teachers in both U.S. PreK–12 and postsecondary contexts are often careless about fairness and full disclosure. For most people in the U.S., the thought of not knowing why they might have received a poor evaluation at work fills them with repugnance. So adamant are they about fairness that the U.S. has "passed disclosure laws to protect people from surreptitious and unfair judgments" (Hitt & Helms, 2009, p. 1). Nevertheless, U.S. educators consistently make judgments about students with little or no evidence or without disclosing the criteria by which those judgments were made. In the course of our research, we have heard countless stories of students who report receiving a letter grade scrawled on a piece of writing without any idea of how the teacher came up with that grade. These actions are unfair, and this is why we push at every turn for fair assessment that makes evaluation criteria transparent and accommodates students from different backgrounds and with different learning styles. Of course, fairness requirements are not important only in the U.S. but should extend all over the world, wherever students are taught and tested and whether the examiner is the teacher or a large-scale testing company. To be a fair assessor, a teacher must consider these issues:

- Why we are having this test or why are students being asked to write an essay or perform a task?
- How their work will be assessed? What counts? For how much?
- What students are eligible to receive accommodations? What are the parameters as far as time, format, and use of items such as dictionaries, translators, and other aids?
- What does high-quality work (essay, project, presentation) look like? Have I provided students with models and sufficient teaching?
- Do the texts and questions I am using require some cultural knowledge that certain groups of students may be familiar with and others may not? How can I choose texts and questions that are familiar to students from different backgrounds?

In performing these tasks to help inform their students, teachers add to students' assessment knowledge by helping them understand the importance of self-assessment, how to compare their work to the work of others through peer assessment, and how to compare their work against criteria established by the teacher (and maybe established by the class as a whole). Learning about assessment creates efficacy—students feel greater ownership of their learning. It helps with student motivation and engagement—the teacher helps them see that they can have some control and responsibility in the assessment process. When students know themselves and know how to assess capably, they can also provide sounder information to teachers, which in turn presents teachers with clearer ideas about what students need and how teachers might individualize the next round of teaching and learning. Becoming assessment literate leads students on the path to becoming independent learners. And to be an independent learner is the goal of all education (Friere, 1985).

Washback

Classical test theory talks a lot about washback. Messick (1996) defines *washback* as "the extent to which the introduction and use of a test influences language teachers and learners to do things they would not otherwise do that promote or inhibit language learning" (p. 241). Generally speaking, there are two kinds of washback: positive and negative. *Positive washback* refers to the positive changes that happen to classroom teaching and learning resulting from the pressures from a test, either internally or externally imposed. For instance, the idea behind many standardized, high-stakes assessments is that they will pressure teachers and students to be more conscious of aligning classroom work with broader standards and to work harder to meet those standards. At a local level, the pressure of a test at some point during the semester can motivate students to take the time to really learn the material or concepts being tested. On the other hand, we have seen plenty or research on the effects of *negative washback* (e.g., Gilliland, 2015; McCarthey, 2008; Taylor, 2005; Ruecker, 2013; Ruecker, Chamcharatsri, & Saengngoen, 2015). This impact can include the stresses imposed on teachers and their students from externally imposed assessments: too much stress can inhibit learning. Much of this work has focused on how the imposition of external mandates has led to adherence to prepackaged curricula and/or a narrow focus on the genres of writing tested on the state exams.

Positive washback is a valuable function of assessment. The practices described in this book can help facilitate positive washback and limit negative washback.

Practicality

Although *practicality* might seem like a frivolous addition to this list of considerations about assessment in general, it does have some bearing since the demands on teachers are incredibly high. In Deborah's assessment class for future ESL teachers, she often asks them questions about length of time for student completion and how long it might take to assign grades. Her students quickly see the impracticality, especially if they have 180 students (as many high school teachers do) and assign multiple tasks through the week that need to be graded (or at least given feedback) and returned to students. The time it takes to read and comment on all of the tasks is prohibitive, but also it can mean that the students do not receive timely feedback if the teacher has too much to grade.

Additional Terminology

Here's some additional terminology that every teacher should be familiar with.

- **Alternative assessment:** "any method of finding out what a student knows or can do that is intended to show growth and inform instruction" (O'Malley & Valdez Pierce, 1996, p. 1).
- **Authentic assessment:** assessment that requires students to perform real-world tasks to demonstrate application of knowledge and skills. Included in this broad category are performance assessment, portfolio assessment, student self-assessment.
- **Accountability:** two kinds of accountability are important to consider in the context of assessment: the first is of course the accountability movement, in which teachers are held responsible for their students' scores on high-stakes standardized tests and are evaluated using just that one score. A second kind of accountability that we believe to be more crucial is the teacher's accountability to her students to provide fair and ethical classroom assessment.
- **Benchmarks:** identifiable points on a continuum toward a goal or standard. Benchmarks describe standards when interim targets are set with regard to age, grade in school, or developmental level. They are also used to illustrate progress steps; for example, in the training of raters for writing assessment, trainers use sets of papers that have been rated to the scoring scale and provide examples of what writing looks like at each score.

- **High-stakes tests:** tests whose results carry tremendous impact in the lives of the test takers and their teachers. These can be once-a-year tests given in PreK–12 contexts as well as college admissions test such as the SAT® and ACT®, as well as language proficiency tests such as TOEFL.
- **Rubric:** also known as a scoring guide. An instrument used for judging student work that establishes a set of criteria and includes descriptors at various levels of achievement. Two of the most recognized rubrics are the *holistic* and *analytic* rubrics—the former assigns one score based on a list of criteria, while the latter provides more specific criteria-based scores.

In conclusion, additional guidance for readers to begin developing an assessment philosophy based on a sound theoretical foundation is provided in Chapter 9. However, here we want to mention that what is encompassed in the intervening chapters will help you begin this development. We would also like to note that there is a critical need for teachers to develop a strong stance regarding ethical, reliable, valid, practical, and fair assessment, how to do it, what it means, and why every teacher needs to know.

Activities and Questions

Activities

1. Ask three people to give you their definitions of assessment. Create a chart to provide ease of access to your findings. How are the definitions alike? Different? Informed? Misinformed? Reflect on what this mini data-gathering activity has shown you. How might you generalize these findings?
2. List as many reasons as you can for assessing your students' language skills; then explain what you will do with the data you have collected. Share your results with a partner. This activity is adapted from Farnsworth & Malone (2014).

Reasons for Assessing	Explanation

Discussion Questions

1. Reflect on what your own definition of assessment was before reading this chapter. Has it changed? If so, how? What considerations about assessment are new to you?
2. Think of a time when you might have used assessment inappropriately. What did you do? What would you change now to make this assessment more meaningful?

2

Language Acquisition and Assessment

To teach and assess their students better, teachers need an understanding of second language acquisition (SLA) (Li & Peters, 2016). It is vital that teachers understand what kinds of errors students will make and how much progress teachers can expect during a term. While it might take several years of professional development to completely gain in-depth knowledge of SLA, teachers can gain some of the key concepts rather quickly and apply them to their classrooms. These concepts are derived from such fields as linguistics, psychology, sociology, anthropology, and neurolinguistics. We will discuss a few terms associated with SLA and then delineate some of the concepts and theories. Although each of the theories discussed here has been problematized in various ways (in particular Krashen's work), there are bits of truth to each one. The important take-away here is that language, particularly academic language, takes quite some time to acquire. When teachers understand this and the many other processes that come into play in language learning, they are far more apt to be understanding and more than a little empathetic for their English language learners.

Most learners go through similar processes when acquiring a second language. One of those is *interlanguage*, defined by Brown & Eisterhold (2004) as "a language system that differs from both the first (L1) and second (L2) language . It is an approximation, a stage on the way to the second language" (p. 84). Selinker (1972) coined this term as well as the term *fossilization.* Fossilization is much like becoming frozen in the process between the L1 and the L2. Because reasons for learning a second language often center on passing a test or satisfying a prerequisite (Brown & Eisterhold, 2004), learners may stagnate in the language learning process, "frequently at the high beginner/lower-intermediate level" (p. 85).

In SLA, learners progress through a continuum of learning. Krashen and Terrell (1983) identified five predictable sequential stages. The first is usually referred to as *pre-production or silent/receptive,* in which the language learner does not understand much and says less but can nod and point. The second stage is *early production*, in which the learner produces single words, familiar phrases, the present tense, and still has limited comprehension. In the third stage, *speech emergence,* the learner begins to form sentences that contain grammatical errors, but comprehension is improving. The fourth stage is called *intermediate fluency*. The learner makes fewer errors in grammar. Vocabulary comprehension is improving. The final stage is *advanced fluency,* in which the learner acquires near native language skills.

The time frame for passing through each of these stages varies depending on a number of factors, including:

- Intelligence: the ability to acquire and apply new skills.
  Usually measured by tests but the tested intelligence may not be as important in the classroom since the results of IQ tests have been questioned
- Aptitude: general ability to learn quickly. In language learning, this can be the ability to learn new sounds, the ability to understand the function and meaning of new words, and the ability to figure out grammar rules
- Learning styles: this refers to the learner's preferred way of learning. Some learners learn through reading and writing; some are more auditory; still others learn kinesthetically
- Personality: the learner's level of extroversion. Inhibition, anxiety, self-esteem, and empathy play a part in language learning
- Motivation and attitude: learner's needs for learning the language, and the attitude the learner has toward the L2 community
- Identity and ethnic group affiliation: see social distance below
- Age and critical period hypothesis: native-like pronunciation might be more difficult to attain after a certain age. It can become more difficult to fully acquire a foreign language as people age, but this has not been found to be true of everyone.

(Krashen & Terrell, 1983; Lightbown & Spada, 1993; Schumann, 1976; Selinker, 1972)

Social distance (Schumann, 1976) can be defined as the distance between the second language learning group and the target language group. When the learners feel distant from the target language group, they are much less apt to learn the L2. Schumann argued that social distance occurs when the learners are either dominant or subordinate and are in the target language area for only a brief period. A bad language learning situation can also occur when either group is concerned about preserving their intact groups or closing them off, when the learner group is very large and cohesive, and when the two cultures are markedly different and have negative attitudes toward each other.

Theories of SLA include Universalist, Behaviorist, Nativist, Cognitivist, and Social Interactionist as well as Krashen's Five Hypotheses for SLA. *Universalist theories* look primarily at language patterns and language universals (features of language that are common across many languages). In the 1950s, psychology and linguistics were dominated by *behaviorist theories*, which concentrated mainly on stimulus (supplied by the environment) and response (supplied by the learner, in which learners imitate and approximate). *Nativist theories* view language as an innate ability. Chomsky (1965) likened this innate ability to a little black box otherwise known as the Language Acquisition Device (LAD), which has been controversial for years. *Cognitivist theories* insist that the conditions for learning a language are the same as those for learning anything and involve automatic processing and controlled learning (Chamot & O'Malley, 1987). *Social Interactionists* believe that knowledge is socially created. Vygotsky (1930–1934/1978) believed that learners have actual and potential development and called these two levels the *Zone of Proximal Development (ZPD).*

Krashen's five hypotheses include:

- the *Acquisition-Learning Hypothesis,* in which he contrasted language acquisition (a subconscious process) with language learning (what occurs in an academic setting).
- the *Natural Order Hypothesis,* which claims that language parts are acquired in a predictable order; acquisition of the *–ing* ending happens early on while other grammar structures, like the third-person singular *–s,* happen later.
- the *Monitor Hypothesis,* which holds that a monitor or editor functions during conscious language learning to inspect what we have just learned and uses previously learned information to correct the new.
- the *Comprehensible Input Hypothesis*, which states that input to the learner should be at a level that is challenging, so the learner stays engaged, but not too challenging, as the learner would become frustrated and lose interest.
- the *Affective Filter Hypothesis,* which connects emotion with learning. Learners who are made to feel comfortable in class will learn more; their affective filter is lowered.

We are acutely aware of the criticisms of some of the scholars and their work, particularly that of Krashen. These critiques centered on a variety of notions, including the simplicity and inadequacy of key concept definitions, as well as "arguments over theory building and the philosophy of science" (Brown & Lawson-Hall, 2012, p. 39). The criticisms are broad and deep, for example, that Krashen treats language as grammar (Krahnke, 1985). Further, Krashen believes acquisition to be unconscious while others argue that to have uptake, learners must have conscious hypothesis testing (Brown & Larsen-Hall). For an in-depth discussion on the myths of second language acquisition, see Brown and Larsen-Hall (2012).

We believe wholeheartedly that pedagogy and assessment are one and the same; we also believe that it is instructive to have even a slight background in language acquisition, so that teachers understand what to expect of their learners and when to expect it, which informs both their teaching and their assessment practices (Ruecker & Crusan, 2018).

The BICS/CALP Distinction

Acknowledging that previous researchers made similar comparisons, Cummins (1980) first introduced a distinction that would shape conceptions of teaching ELs for decades to come: *cognitive/academic language proficiency* (CALP) and *basic interpersonal communicative skills* (BICS). Under Cummins' discussion, BICS include aspects such as one's "accent, oral fluency, and sociolinguistic competence" (p. 177) while CALP includes the development of cognitive/memory skills and more advanced, domain-specific vocabulary. Based on the analyses of over 400 referral forms and psychological assessments in Canada, Cummins reported that students were gaining basic communicative proficiency in English after one to two years in the U.S., but it was taking much longer (around five to seven years) for students to catch up with their peers on assessment performance. He was interested in raising this distinction and claimed that "educators and policy-makers frequently conflated conversational and academic dimensions of English language proficiency and that this conflation contributed significantly to the creation of academic difficulties for students who were learning English as an additional language (EAL)" (Cummins, 2007, p. 72). The consequences for students not performing well on assessments are huge, ranging from being denied graduation to being diagnosed with a learning disability and placed into special education, an identity that may be difficult for a student to move out of. Unfortunately, these practices, as evident in the state policies described, are still evident today. Todd recalls a moment during a visit to a research site when a teacher came up to the ESL teacher lamenting the fact that his EL students' writing was terrible and insisting that some students were faking it and actually knew English because they could speak it just fine.

In this early work, Cummins also made the point that L1 proficiency in CALP would transfer to students' work in their L2. Thus, students who had a strong academic background in their home country/language would likely pick up the academic language in a new schooling system and language and be more likely to make rapid progress in a new context. For students who spend part of their early years learning in one language and then in another, such as when they move to a schooling system like the U.S. that tends to be very English-only oriented, their development of CALP proficiency can be hindered. This is an important rationale behind bilingual education programs (beyond the value of being proficient in multiple languages), in that it's vital to give students access to rigorous academic content and language in key formative stages.

The BICS/CALP distinction quickly caught on as a useful distinction to think about students' ability to learn the language of schooling. However, as Valdés (2004) noted, "Most practitioners who encountered BICS and CALP in their teacher preparation courses accepted it uncritically" (p. 76).

When reduced to quick talking points, one can imagine how it can support a deficit mindset: *It always takes people five to seven years to gain academic proficiency in another language. Since it inevitably takes five to seven years to gain academic proficiency, we should keep these kids in the ESL class until they are ready to handle the mainstream work.*

Ensuing scholars have criticized the BICS/CALP distinction in various ways, especially in how it can ignore language's contextualization in social practice and power relations, its propensity to reinforce a deficit model of EL students, and its tendency to be oversimplified and not useful in developing curriculum (Bunch, 2006; Cummins, 2007, 2016; Enright, 2011; Schleppegrell, 2004; Valdés, 2004). Schleppegrell (2004) and de Oliveira have more recently adopted the terms *everyday language* and *academic language*. Norris and de Oliveira (2013) explain this difference:

> Academic language is the kind of language students learn at school and is different from ordinary language for communicative purposes (Schleppegrell, 2001, 2004). Academic language is generally learned in school from teachers and textbooks, and only with proper instructional support (Fillmore & Snow, 2000; Schleppegrell, 2004). Academic is used differently in each one of the content areas. For instance, mathematics has its own way of meaning-making that makes it different from history. (p. 108)

Despite these critiques, Cummins (2016) stands by the constructs and their use, arguing that the "role of social and educational factors in determining underachievement has always been explicitly acknowledged" and that "the BICS/CALP distinction and the interdependence hypothesis focused on specific issues in particular contexts and (as I have argued) clarified these issues in an evidence-based way that contributed to more effective educational practice" (p. 943).

What This Means for Assessing Language Learners

While we acknowledge that the BICS/CALP distinction has been oversimplified and often misused, and that terms such as *academic language* and *communicative language* may be more accessible and flexible, we agree with Cummins (2016) that the overarching construct remains useful in our work in teaching and assessing language learners and can be used positively to speak out against school and state policies that require learners to test too soon in an L2 and consequently contribute to labeling them as deficient. When discussing language acquisition with colleagues or policy makers, we still use the "five to seven years" figure but always pair it with an acknowledgment that every learner learns at different rates so they should be treated and assessed as individual learners with unique characteristics.

In developing outcomes and assessments, we find it vital to consider individual students' language proficiency and the speed at which they're acquiring English in developing assessments (see Chapter 3). Creating assessments and rubrics that are too easy means the differentiating and motivating ability (think positive washback) of these assessments can be lost. Creating assessments that are too difficult can lead to students becoming demotivated in another way—they internalize the repeated failure label they receive. The state policies described at the beginning of this chapter, in which ELs are expected to test at a high school level in English after a year or two in the U.S., is a key example of this negative effect. For instance, less than 10 percent of ELs tested in New Mexico after the rollout of the Common Core–aligned exam were deemed proficient (Burgess, 2016). Todd has been in classrooms where test results have been delivered and has witnessed the demoralization on students' faces.

How might tailoring assessments to student proficiency levels work in practice? Let's take a look at a few Oral Communication–Speaking outcomes of the University of Arizona's Center for English as a Second Language Intensive English Program:

- On successful completion of this course, students in level 4 Oral Communication will be able to give short presentations on unfamiliar topics allowing for focus on accuracy (minimum 5 minutes).

- On successful completion of this course, students in level 7 Oral Communication will be able to give presentations on academic topics allowing for focus on public speaking skills with appropriate language for the context and rhetorical strategies (minimum 8 minutes).

While students are often placed in different classes based on their levels, the reality is not always so neat with ESL classes in small schools, language programs home to a variety of language proficiency levels, or ELA classes with a number of fully proficient English speakers and only a few immigrant students of varying proficiencies. A look at these two outcomes is useful for illustrating how a common assignment, a student presentation, may be adapted and evaluated based on the proficiency of different students. In this case, we could provide and adapt our presentation prompt, with higher-level students being asked to use academic language to present on an academic topic, and newer ELs allowed to use more informal language on a new topic for them, albeit one not explicitly academic. While teachers should always consider and respond to the content of student work at different levels, they might place a greater emphasis on accuracy at certain levels (such as if the primary goal is for a student to demonstrate their language proficiency) but then include additional skills at other levels as students become more comfortable with the language work (such as general presentation skills, making eye contact, and varying the tone of voice). The differentiation between different students should be considered in the development of outcomes, assessments, and any associated rubrics.

Activities and Questions

Activities

1. Develop a demographic questionnaire that asks students how long they have been learning English, how comfortable they feel speaking and writing in English, and other important details that could inform your teaching.
2. Write about your own experiences in language classes, if any. Reflect on the different levels of fluency in the classes you have taken. How did your teachers teach toward different language levels, if at all?
3. Find an example of a language placement exam used at the institution where you teach or study. Does it seem tailored to students who learned the language in a particular setting or particular way? Does it seem aligned

toward the BICS or CALP end of the spectrum? The everyday or the academic language? Do you think that students of different levels could demonstrate their knowledge through the exam?

4. Look through the websites of several intensive English programs and explore how they differentiate between different levels of students. What types of classes are offered? Is there an indication that different goals are covered in the different classes?

Discussion Questions

1. What did you know about language acquisition before reading this chapter? Was there anything that was surprising to you in this chapter?
2. What pressures do you or your current/future students face or anticipate facing in terms of time available for students to learn English? How do you think these pressures might shape assessment in the classroom?
3. How are students placed into classes in your context or anticipated working context? Do you feel this system works well, or do you consistently end up with a wide variety of abilities?

3

Understanding Context and Standards

When many think of assessment, the first thing that comes to mind is high-stakes standardized tests designed by an organization far removed from a particular classroom or school. The divide between some tests and test takers is especially evident when one takes a critical look at the test content. For instance, a sample passage from Elizabeth Gaskill's *Cranford* used on a Common Core–aligned standardized test reads:

> For keeping the trim gardens full of choice flowers without a weed to speck them; for frightening away little boys who look wistfully at the said flowers through the railings; for rushing out at the geese that occasionally venture into the gardens if the gates are left open; for deciding all questions of literature and politics without troubling themselves with unnecessary reasons or arguments; for obtaining clear and correct knowledge of everybody's affairs in the parish; for keeping their neat maid-servants in admirable order.

When reading this passage, Todd thinks of students he has worked with in rural New Mexico, far removed from the manicured garden and lawns of estates in 19th century England. They might have a hard time imagining *trim gardens full of choice flowers*, a rare sight in a desert climate. They might wonder what the heck are *maid-servants* or a *parish*. Elsewhere, we and others have written about this systematic pattern of bias on standardized tests, which helps in part explain why students from particular backgrounds (e.g., geographic, economic, ethnic/racial, linguistic) perform better on them (e.g., Ruecker, Chamcharatsri, & Saengngoen, 2015). In addition to texts biased toward a certain demographic, other testing bias issues that arise include upsetting content (for instance, certain animals and certain colors have strong negative connotations in some cultures) and the ability for those with means to "game" the test through hiring individualized test-preparation help.

It is evident that the tests are not fair for students from every context. This reveals both the limitations of large-scale standardized tests as well as another important lesson: context matters in assessment. This chapter will focus specifically on the latter, helping teachers ask the right questions or make the right considerations about context when developing assessments for their learners. As we and others have emphasized elsewhere (Crusan, 2010; Huot, 1996; Ruecker, Chamcharatsri, & Saengngoen, 2015), the best assessment is context specific and shaped by those who know their students best: teachers. In some places, such as in the southwestern U.S., the vast majority of language learners in PreK–12 schools are from Spanish-speaking backgrounds, often immigrants from Mexico. Teachers in other contexts, such as an intensive language program, may see students from dozens of different language backgrounds. It is for that reason that this textbook does not provide readers with a stack of premade tests that they can take directly to their classrooms without any work developing and revising them to meet the needs, levels, and backgrounds of their students. Instead, we take aim at the de-valuing and de-skilling of teachers through the rise of prepackaged assessments that claim to be more appropriate for assessing student learning than those familiar with working with students all day, every day. We agree with Cummings (2000), who said standardized tests "are reliable and efficient to administer" but "typically reflect only a narrow band of easy-to-test curriculum objectives" (p. 16). We aim to make every teacher an assessment expert, sharing basic principles and steps to guide everyday classroom assessment as well as the creation of end-of-semester tests.

Some Background

Assessment specialists have long written about the importance of localized assessment practices (e.g., Crusan, 2010; Hamp-Lyons, 2003; Huot, 1996; Yancey, 1999). For instance, Hamp-Lyons (2003) has written about assessment that takes into account "who the learner is, the context the learner has come from, and the context in which the learner must work toward educational success" (p. 168). Huot (1996) has argued that writing assessment needs to be locally controlled. While we might take issue with some aspects of Huot's arguments in that all teachers will not have complete control over their assessment work in an era when computerized assessment, including machine-scoring of writing, doesn't seem to be going away, we agree that the best and most important assessment in terms of promoting student learning is locally designed and implemented. Instead of providing data points for administrators and policy makers, we emphatically argue that the primary role of assessment should be to improve teaching and learning.

Understanding and Crafting Learning Standards

Effective assessment practices are outcome driven. Teachers should know what they want their students to achieve and take steps along the way and at the end of a particular lesson cycle to determine that students are meeting those goals. In that sense, any good assessment begins with an articulation of what students should learn in the classroom. It is vital that *student learning outcomes* (SLOs) set high expectations for **all students**. Too often, researchers have found that language learners are surrounded by low expectations, in part because teachers and administrators have conflated their linguistic and cognitive abilities (e.g., Irizarry, 2012; Suárez-Orozco & Suárez-Orozco, 2001). In one high school Todd visited, the administration told teachers not to assign homework because students had complicated lives outside the school. Research has shown that students rise to the level of expectations. Low expectations in SLOs for particular student groups help perpetuate achievement gaps among different student populations (Callahan, 2005). Language learners have the same cognitive capacity as non–language learners and can rise to the same level as other students; however, they may need additional scaffolding and support to do so.

For teachers in U.S. PreK–12 schools, SLOs may be already defined for them via state-specific standards, the Common Core State Standards (CCSS), and the WIDA standards. In these instances, it is important for teachers to develop strategies to analyze and dissect particular standards to figure out what they are asking. However, even while working with broadly adopted standards such as the CCSS, teachers are still encouraged to develop additional standards/outcomes to meet the needs of their students, as CCSS are not able to capture all the expectations for students. For instance, teachers should consider developing standards that recognize the diversity of languages and cultures in their classrooms, as advocated by bilingual education experts such as García (2011). Those teaching in private schools and IEPs sometimes have a lot more flexibility to develop their own goals for students. With these different contexts in mind, as well as the general assumption that one who knows how to craft effective SLOs can more effectively analyze and use existing ones, we would like to talk a bit about the process of developing effective SLOs.

When first developing SLOs, teachers shouldn't initially get caught up in precise wording but rather should engage in some exploratory brainstorming to figure out what students in the classroom need to learn or know. Teachers should also consider their own values. Questions like these might be useful:

- What strengths do my students bring to the classroom?
- In what areas does their previous instruction seem lacking?
- What are the constraints on the SLOs I develop? Am I required to meet particular externally imposed SLOs/standards?
- What do I value as a teacher?
- What do my students value?
- How much time do I have to work with these students? What is feasible in that amount of time?

Teachers might engage with these questions in their heads or via freewriting, writing down ideas of various SLOs while not thinking too much about wording or limitations, but just getting ideas flowing.

A commonly used framework for writing SLOs is based around the acronym SMART, originally developed by Peter Drucker in the 1950s to introduce outcome-driven management practices. It states that SLOs should be: specific, measurable, attainable, results-focused, and time-focused (Drucker, 1954), . Let's break these down in more detail.

- **Specific**: SLOs should typically be tailored to your students and your particular context rather than be defined for a broad population. Even national or international standards group students into different grade or proficiency levels, defining standards based on these smaller subsets of learners. Similarly, outcomes that are too broad, say ones that focus on too many skills at once, may seem overwhelming to the teacher and/or students. For instance, an SLO that reads "Students will improve their English abilities" is not helpful. Instead, it is important that each SLO is narrow enough to be accessible and to determine whether or not learners are meeting it. For instance, one IEP had this SLO for "Level B" students in listening and speaking: "Respond in short and complete sentences to a variety of prompts (e.g., yes/no questions, ordering food, talking to a doctor, describing the weather, telling the day and date, etc.)."

- **Measurable:** We have often run across SLOs that are vague and appear hard to measure, in part because they depend on very abstract verbs to define student learning. These outcomes include wording such as "students will understand..." or "students will appreciate..." without giving a clear sense of how teachers will be able to measure students' understanding or appreciation of a particular topic. Here's an example of a vague SLO: "Students will be able to appreciate language varieties." It is important to keep in mind the idea that students will need to demonstrate their learning in some form and that teachers will have to assess the quality of that learning, meaning that outcomes need to be clear and focused enough to do that. In a class focused on writing, this SLO may be better worded as "Students will be able to analyze and describe the value of incorporating various languages, dialects, and registers in their own and others' texts."
- **Attainable:** This connects with the idea we touched on earlier: teachers need to know where their students are and set goals for them that are attainable within the span of the planned assessment. Otherwise, students will lose morale if they are repeatedly marked as failing without being given the appropriate time to learn what is expected of them. This is unfortunately a problem endemic with policies governing the use of many high-stakes standardized tests (e.g., states requiring immigrant students to take a test at their grade level in English within a few years of arriving in the U.S.). While problematizing time to proficiency in more recent work (e.g., MacSwan & Rolstad, 2003) as something that varies among individual students and learning contexts, researchers have traditionally pointed out that it often takes five to seven years to gain academic proficiency in another language (e.g., Cummins, 1981); however, many local and national policies ignore this reality and set students up for failure (e.g., school grading systems that set unrealistic benchmarks for passing students out of an EL designation). Let's take a quick look at aligning outcomes with learner levels. The University of Arizona Intensive English Program has one of the following outcomes for students in grammar classes: "Strengthen their knowledge of complex sentences using adjectives and adverb clauses as well as reducing them to adjectives and adverb phrases." This is an unrealistic goal for students in a lower-level language class. Instead, the following goal in their program would be more appropriate: "Learn how to form simple sentences and questions in basic verb tenses, such as the simple present, present progressive and simple past, using appropriate spelling of *–s*, *–ing*,

and *–ed* forms, irregular verbs and time expressions." At the same time, we agree that outcomes need to be ambitious, set high standards for students, and push them to new levels of language proficiency.

- **Results-Focused**: Effective outcomes need to focus on what students can do or accomplish and they tend to be oriented around the ability of a student to demonstrate learning through language such as "Students will be able to...." The outcomes don't specify the process of getting there; they focus on the end result. The process is left to the teacher and students to determine. For instance, "Students will engage in a variety of cloze activities" focuses on the process but does not state the end goal. In this case, the relevant SLO might focus on improving reading comprehension: "Students will be able to demonstrate their ability to understand a variety of academic texts."
- **Time-Focused**: While keeping in mind the attainable aspect, outcomes should keep time in mind as well. For instance, are teachers expecting students to demonstrate proficiency in a certain area by the end of a few weeks, a month, a semester, or a year? In addition to goals for individual lesson sequences, teachers will likely be working with outcomes for a course and a program. Focusing only on longer-term goals is not wise as it is important for both teachers and students to be able to keep track of development and continue to have new goals to strive for. Sometimes the differences between shorter- and longer-term outcomes might focus on gradations of proficiency or ability. For instance, this SLO from the University of Arizona IEP is an example of a longer-term goal for more advanced students: "Learn to read extensively with good comprehension and continue improving skimming and scanning skills in longer texts." A shorter-term goal for a section of a course might be more focused: "Students will improve their ability to skim and scan for information in news articles."

In addition to considering the general SMART characteristics when working on SLOs, writers of outcomes often refer to Bloom's taxonomy (see Figure 3.1), which helps them think of action-oriented verbs that center around different levels and types of learning. This oft-referenced taxonomy categorizes educational goals along a continuum from simpler to more complex and/or abstract, including the following: **knowledge, comprehension, application, analysis, synthesis, and evaluation**. For instance, a simple knowledge-based task might require a student to recall something they learned,

FIGURE 3.1
Bloom's Taxonomy (Vanderbilt University Center for Teaching)

Cognitive Function: Students at all levels of English language proficiency ANALYZE universal themes of literature.						
	Level 1 Entering	Level 2 Emerging	Level 3 Developing	Level 4 Expanding	Level 5 Bridging	Level 6 - Reaching
Listening	Select illustrations depicting literary characters, themes, and plots based on oral statements using environmental print (e.g., posters about character types and themes)	Select illustrations depicting literary characters, themes, and plots based on oral descriptions using environmental print	Classify examples of literary characters, themes, and plots based on oral descriptions with a partner	Find patterns related to literary characters, themes, and plots using graphic organizers with a partner	Predict the evolution of literary characters, themes, and plots	
Topic-Related Language: Students at all levels of English proficiency interact with grade-level words and expressions, such as: universal theme, character type, allegory, mythology, protagonist						

such as the ability to identify a past-tense verb form. At a higher level, rather than simply recall, students would be expected to create knowledge as they function in a variety of communicative situations rather than analyze or use language in restricted situations.

Using these taxonomies in developing and writing outcomes helps teachers think about what type of learning they expect their students to be demonstrating, whether it is simply remembering and demonstrating knowledge of a set of facts (e.g., vocabulary words) or the more advanced work of analyzing a text or creating new work. Take a look at a few different outcomes and figure out where they factor in to Figure 3.1:

1. Capitalize holidays, product names, and geographic names. (Common Core Grade 2 Language Standard)
2. Overarching outcome: "English language learners communicate for Social and Instructional purposes within the school setting." Adapted outcome: Students

> "Compose scripts about emotions and decisions influenced by peer pressure." (WIDA [2020] English Language Development Standard 1, adapted for Grade 7 Example Topic: Peer Pressure)

At this time, we would like to bring up one final point about working with standards/outcomes—namely, making students aware of them and how to understand them. There is some debate regarding how to provide this information to students. Some argue that standards should be translated into language easily understood by students, with the rationale that standards were written for teachers and administrators and not students. We support translating and/or offering a simplified version for students at lower proficiency levels so that they can understand the goals of the lesson or the larger class along with other students—simplified versions of standards might also be helpful for parents. However, we also advocate connecting students with the actual language of standards and taking time in class to unpack them because access to this meta-language helps students more productively reflect on and transfer their knowledge to other contexts (Yancey, Robertson, & Taczak, 2014). For instance, one of the CCSS (2015) Anchor Standards for Reading (www.corestandards.org) reads, "Integrate and evaluate content presented in diverse formats and media, including visually and quantitatively, as well as in words" (p. 35). By being able to explicitly discuss what it means to *integrate* and *evaluate*, learners will be more aware of how well they perform in these areas. Not giving language learners access to the richer, more complex vocabulary included in outcomes and standards denies them access to the language they will need to be successful later in their academic careers as they are asked to perform some of these advanced skills without always being given sufficient information about what it means to "evaluate" a source.

Analyzing and Understanding Existing Standards

As previously mentioned, teachers are often handed a set of standards to work with in their classrooms instead of given the opportunity to develop them themselves, especially in the era of standards-based education and standardized testing. With this in mind, it's important for teachers to be able to analyze these standards, adapt where needed, and translate them into what works for their students and classrooms. Let's do this using Bloom's taxonomy and the SMART lens with examples from different groups of standards: the Association of Language Testers in Europe (ALTE) standards, the American Council on the Teaching of Foreign Languages (ACTFL) Proficiency Guidelines, the CCSS, and the WIDA standards.

Through Bloom's Taxonomy

The ALTE standards are phrased as can-do statements, indicating what a learner can accomplish in a particular skill area (listening/speaking, reading, and writing) at a particular level. They provide overall summaries of each level by skill area while providing more detailed statements for different content areas, such as social and tourist, work, and study areas. For instance, under Work, Level 1 in Listening/Speaking, the statement reads:

- CAN take and pass on simple messages of a routine kind, such as "Friday meeting 10 a.m."

Under Work, Level 4, the statement reads:

- CAN contribute effectively to meetings and seminars within own area of work and argue for or against a case.

While Bloom's taxonomy was not primarily written to address the needs of language learners, we can still see its applicability when looking at standards such as these. For instance, the ALTE Level 1 statement could be placed comfortably at the bottom of the pyramid depicted in Figure 3.1, as learners only need to recall facts and basic concepts, words, and phrases they have learned in terms of pronunciation and writing, and then pass them on. We could also say that they might reach Bloom's Apply skill level at this point, as they need to learn how to apply knowledge from class contexts to new situations (e.g., meetings scheduled on a different time or day or another type of message). By the time a learner reaches ALTE Level 4, they are able to achieve the higher-level goals in their new language, comprehending fully enough to analyze and evaluate complex arguments and create knowledge by contributing their viewpoints to meetings and seminars.

The differences among these levels may be better illustrated by turning to the ACTFL Proficiency Guidelines. At the Novice level, speakers "can communicate short messages on highly predictable, everyday topics that affect them directly. They do so primarily through the use of isolated words and phrases that have been encountered, memorized, and recalled." Here, we see that Novice learners are able to stick to a script of remembering, understanding, and applying existing knowledge but are not at the stage where they feel comfortable creatively interacting in unfamiliar situations by moving outside memorized knowledge.

Through the SMART Lens

Under the CCSS (2015), students in 6th grade are expected to be able to

> Compare and contrast the experience of reading a story, drama, or poem to listening to or viewing an audio, video, or live version of the text, including contrasting what they "see" and "hear" when reading the text to what they perceive when they listen or watch. (37)

In the 11 and12th grades, they are expected to be able to

> Analyze multiple interpretations of a story, drama, or poem (e.g., recorded or live production of a play or recorded novel or poetry), evaluating how each version interprets the source text. (Include at least one play by Shakespeare and one play by an American dramatist.)

Table 3.1 analyzes these learning outcomes through the SMART lens:

TABLE 3.1
Sample SMART Analysis

	Grade 6	**Grades 11 and 12**
Specific	Describes the types of texts expected of students, although not too narrowly; simpler task than 11th and 12th grade learning goal asking students to compare their own experiences with different types of texts; more concrete.	Describes the types of texts expected of students, going as far as to specify the author or author background based on what is expected to be covered in a high school ELA class (Shakespeare and an American dramatist); more complex task than expected of 6th graders, asks students to look at others' interpretations of different texts; in this sense the task aligns with expectations for 11-12 graders to engage in more abstract work.
Measurable	Uses action verbs to indicate what exactly students are expected to do: *Compare and contrast.*	Uses action verbs to indicate what exactly students are expected to do: *Analyze.*

(*Continued*)

TABLE 3.1 (*Continued*)

	Grade 6	Grades 11 and 12
Attainable	This more personal and less abstract work seems feasible for a student in 6th grade.	While this more abstract work may be feasible for students in the 11th or 12 grade, it assumes language proficiency that all students may not possess.
Results-focused	Specifies what a student will be expected to do at a certain level, although it could be more specific on how they would demonstrate this proficiency (via written, spoken, or other type of product).	Specifies what a student will be expected to do at a certain level, although it could be more specific on how they would demonstrate this proficiency (via written, spoken, or other type of product).
Time-focused	Specifies a particular grade level. However, this may not be appropriate for all students at that grade since students enter the U.S. school system at different ages.	Specifies a particular grade level. However, this may not be appropriate for all students at that grade since students enter the U.S. school system at different ages.

Looking at Table 3.1, we can see that the standards provided differentiate between the different grade levels of students, with the grade 11-12 standard asking more complex work of students in those grades, something to be expected. However, we found fault in these standards (as with the CCSS in general) for not considering the diversity of students, their experiences, their linguistic proficiency, and their time in the U.S., in affecting the ability of students to engage in particular work. For instance, if a student enters the U.S. in 9th grade at a relatively low proficiency level in English, it may take her a few years to be able to have the linguistic knowledge to engage in comparing/contrasting texts in English, even if she might already possess this skill in her L1. However, it is important to also know that students might not have learned a particular skill in their L1 due to transitions between school systems and/or other interruptions to their schooling. In this case, students should be provided the support necessary to undertake the requested tasks.

We now turn to discussing the WIDA standards. The WIDA Standards are a means to better understand the way language development connects to meeting standards like the CCSS. The CCSS Standards were developed without language proficiency as a primary consideration.

Analyzing and Understanding WIDA Standards

For those unfamiliar, the WIDA (2020) consortium is a group of states that share the following mission: "WIDA advances academic language development and academic achievement for linguistically diverse students through high quality standards, assessments, research, and professional development for educators" (https://wida.wisc.edu/). While WIDA was originally started by a few states, it has expanded to include many more states who use the WIDA standards to guide language teaching and use the WIDA ACCESS test to test students out of the English language learner designation. The WIDA standards are focused explicitly on language learners, so they help fill the gap left by the lack of consideration of ELs in the CCSS. With this in mind, it is understandable that language proficiency is a central focus of the WIDA standards and that they have a much more complex understanding of language acquisition than the CCSS do. They also do a better job recognizing the linguistic resources ELs bring to the classroom: "WIDA encourages educators to recognize and maximize the language, knowledge, and skills that students bring from their homes and communities, empowering them to explore their own unique pathways to college and career success" (WIDA, 2020, p. 14). It is then unsurprising that they, like the ALTE standards, take a can-do orientation, emphasizing what language learners at different levels *can* accomplish as opposed to what they *can't* (WIDA, 2020; Chapman et al., 2018).

One defining element of the WIDA framework is a division of language into three levels: discourse, sentence, and word/phrase. This acknowledges that language learners have to know different language structures to engage in a particular task at the larger discursive level than at the individual word level. Another defining feature is that the WIDA framework considers students at different levels of language proficiency:

- Level 1: Entering
- Level 2: Emerging
- Level 3: Developing
- Level 4: Expanding
- Level 5: Bridging
- Level 6: Reaching

As a frame for each standard, WIDA defines the expected cognitive demands for students in a particular standard; however, this standard is then broken down in the levels of language use and language proficiency in what WIDA terms Model Performance

FIGURE 3.2
WIDA Model Performance Indicator

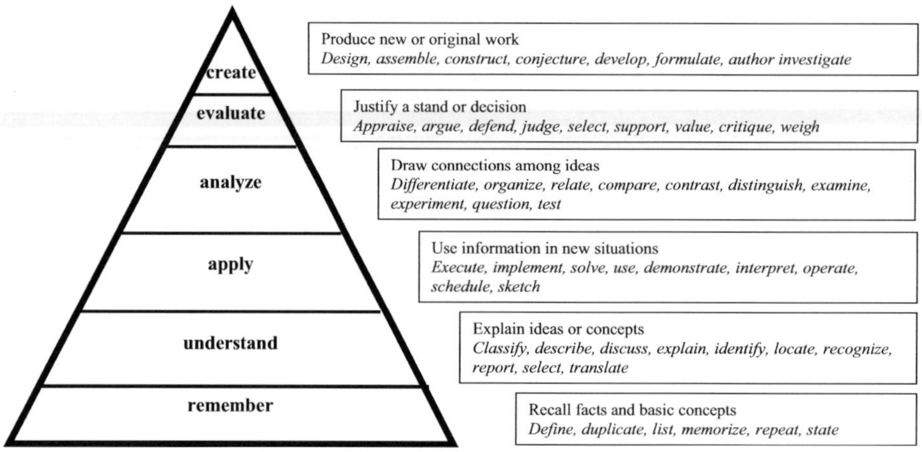

Indicators (see Figure 3.2). This structure recognizes that while students may function on different levels in terms of achieving a particular standard, they are able to achieve the same cognitive goals at different grades, albeit with different proficiency levels.

Let's take a look at the WIDA (2020) ELD Standard 2: The Language of Language Arts, which WIDA connects with the CCSS grade 8 standard for reading literature: "Analyze how a modern work of fiction draws on themes, patterns of events, or character types from myths, traditional stories, or religious works such as the Bible, including describing how the material is rendered new" (p. 38). The Model Performance Indicator is depicted in Figure 3.2.

Under their can-do orientation, WIDA is careful to emphasize that all students *can* achieve the goals set out in the CCSS, albeit at different proficiency levels. At Level 1, students have a beginning grasp of the text and are able to identify basic components such as character or plot descriptions. Nonetheless, they are still engaging in analysis. At Level 5, we see students being able to engage in higher-level work, such as predicting future character and plot development. In Figure 3.3, the WIDA 2020 standards provide even more detail in breaking down what students can do at the different levels, giving examples of their linguistic complexity and calling attention to the language forms and vocabulary they use.

In sum, standards come in many forms. They can be broad or narrow. They can target content or language proficiency. If the former, they may often ignore the needs of language learners, requiring a teacher to make sure that a student's language proficiency is considered when assessing students as they strive toward meeting a particular standard.

FIGURE 3.3
WIDA Detailed Breakdown

	Levels 1–3	Levels 2–4	Levels 3–5	Level 6 – Reaching
Linguistic Complexity Discourse Level	The main character, Loretta, is a heroine. She is not afraid of dragons. She is like the warrior from the other story we read.	In general, Loretta is a strong character. She is both faithful and fearless. She never leaves Sandra's side. Additionally, Loretta challenges the dragon in the magical forest. This is different from how the warrior abandons his horse in the scene of battle.	Obviously, Loretta represents the heroine of the tale. She not only defeats wicked monsters throughout the story, but she also proves herself as a loyal friend. Through overcoming numerous obstacles, she conquers her fears and realizes her own strength. What if Loretta met the warrior from the ancient myth? Would she criticize his actions? Could she offer him some advice?	
Language Forms & Conventions Sentence Level	The main character, Loretta. she is v. she is not	In general, Both ____ and ___ For instance, … never Additionally, different from how	Obviously, Not only…but also Through overcoming numerous obstacles, she… What would… Could…	
Vocabulary Usage Word/Phrase Level	main character hero/heroine afraid dragon warrior other story	strong character faithful fearless ____'s side challenges magical abandons scene of battle	represents defeats loyal friend overcoming obstacles conquers realizes her own strength serve ancient myth criticize offer some advice	

Standards also change over time—by the time you read this, the newer WIDA standards should have been released.

Activities and Questions

Activities

1. Conduct an Internet search for student learning outcomes in a context related to the one you work in (to compare with your own) or find two sets of outcomes for two contexts in which you'd like to work (e.g., PreK–12 context, IEP, language school). In small groups, analyze and discuss them using the SMART framework and Bloom's taxonomy. Is one set stronger than the other? Why?
2. Revise one of the outcomes you worked with in the first activity.
3. Design a classroom activity in which you unpack a standard or set of standards your students might encounter.

Discussion Questions

1. Do you work in a context or program where the learning outcomes are set for you? Are they set at the local level or at a broader level? Do you have any freedom to modify them or create additional ones based on the needs of your students and class?
2. Of the SMART characteristics created by Peter Drucker, which one or ones do you imagine are the most difficult to account for? Are there any you still have questions about?
3. Were you familiar with Bloom's taxonomy before this reading? If so, in what context did you learn about it and what did you remember about it? Did you learn anything new from this chapter's presentation of it?
4. What areas of Bloom's taxonomy do your class or classes most focus on? How do these vary among your classes or the types of students you work with?

4

Creating Effective Assessments

We now turn to some of the key elements of assessment creation, defining each and explaining how it is part of formative and summative assessment:

- creating test specifications
- writing directions
- writing items
- creating rubrics
- implementing accommodation

Creating Test Specifications

Test specifications are often referred to as the *blueprint* for a particular assessment. They generally provide information on **what** information is going to be tested (often specifying alignment with a particular outcome or outcomes), **who** is going to be tested, and **what type of task** the assessment will ask students to complete. Understandably, test specifications tend to be associated with large-scale tests where test makers have the resources (and need) to develop detailed specifications that help a multitude of people collaborate in creating a test instrument that has hundreds of passages and thousands of items in question banks to create different versions of a test. These formal specifications include information about the targeted student population, the type of activities on the test and their alignment with specific standards, and any accommodations associated with them, among other items. Table 4.1 depicts a sample adapted from Tucker's (2014) presentation for the British Council. We share another relatively formal example later in this chapter on p. 67.

TABLE 4.1
Reading test item specification at the B1 level (selections marked in bold)

<table>
<tr><th>Population</th><th colspan="10">Online British Council test takers</th></tr>
<tr><td>Word Count</td><td colspan="10">160–200 words</td></tr>
<tr><td>Domain</td><td colspan="3">Public</td><td colspan="3">Occupational</td><td colspan="2">Educational</td><td colspan="2">Personal</td></tr>
<tr><td>Nature of information</td><td colspan="3">General</td><td colspan="3">Somewhat General</td><td colspan="2">Somewhat Specific</td><td colspan="2">Specific</td></tr>
<tr><td>Lexical Level</td><td>K1</td><td>K2</td><td>K3</td><td>K4</td><td>K5</td><td>K6</td><td>K7</td><td>K8</td><td>K9</td><td>K10</td></tr>
<tr><td>Grammatical Level</td><td colspan="10">CEFR A1-B1</td></tr>
<tr><td>Average Sentence Length</td><td colspan="10">12–15, some longer or shorter</td></tr>
<tr><td>Genres</td><td colspan="10">Instruction guides; product manuals; job adverts (adapted to the specific level)</td></tr>
<tr><td>Task types</td><td colspan="10">Multiple choice: fill in missing</td></tr>
</table>

Test specifications will likely not be as formal for a teacher-designed summative assessment, although it is still valuable to draft them when working on larger assessments over the course of the semester. Here is an example of a more informal set of specifications:

End of Semester Advocacy Portfolio

1. Covers outcomes 1, 2, 7
2. Five weeks to work in this unit
3. Three components: two projects along with a reflection letter
4. One of the projects should be multimodal
5. Approximately 1,200 words total between the three components
6. Prompt should include clear descriptions of each component, including the types of genres that students are being asked to produce and how they'll be evaluated

7. Graded by an analytical rubric, to be included in prompt and focused around four areas: quality of reflection, rhetorical/genre awareness, development of arguments, and style/citation
8. Will include peer review before final submission

When we work with future teachers, we have them create assessment specifications as an assignment. We do this because drafting specifications helps ensure that the test aligns with the standards that one is teaching toward and then actually measures students' progress toward those standards. This refers to **content alignment** and **alignment of question types**, the latter of which ensures that the right type of tasks are being used to determine student progress toward particular outcomes. We address these points in more depth in the "Bringing it All Together: Writing a Test" section later in this chapter.

For ongoing formative assessment in the classroom, specifications play less of an active role, although they should at least be informally considered when thinking of the outcomes and the activities that can help students work toward them. One exercise that has proven useful for Deborah's assessment students asks them to consider general guidelines for the development of their assessments. These guidelines can be in the form of a table that allows her students to construct a test focusing on the key areas and then weights those areas based on importance. The table also provides the teacher with evidence that a test has content validity—that it covers what should be covered. Students should always be reminded that assessment is a constant cycle of improvement and that data gathering is ongoing. Most important to consider is what teachers want their students to learn or to have learned, and they should develop guidelines from there. Considering the goals, standards, and objectives of the course, what kinds of questions/tasks will need to be included? Why? How might these questions/tasks assess the important knowledge and skills gained in the class?

Writing Test Directions

It is essential that the instructions or prompts for any assessment be clearly written so that students are able to understand exactly what they are expected to do. Since instructions are irrelevant to content, that is, they have no bearing on the content of the test and will not affect the test's validity in any way, they should always be written in a simple, straightforward manner so that students, regardless of language proficiency, can understand what is expected of them. In general, instructions should provide students with:

- how they are expected to respond to activities/questions
- how long they will have to respond
- where they are supposed to record their response
- whether or not they can use notes or other resources (legally mandated accommodations may be communicated privately to individual students)

Some principles to guide teachers in ensuring test instructions and items are linguistically accessible:

- **Use frequently used vocabulary and avoid unfamiliar vocabulary.** For instance, "Craft a two- to three-page expository essay delineating the similarities and differences between writing in a first and second language" is an example of prompt language that relies too heavily on potentially confusing vocabulary. Instead, this prompt could be more simply written as "Write a two- to three-page essay comparing and contrasting the differences between writing in a first and second language." (Note: We do recommend that writing prompts, especially for longer pieces, are much more detailed than this example—we will discuss writing prompts in much more detail in Chapter 8). One way to determine the familiarity of particular words is via a publicly accessible corpus such as the Corpus of Contemporary American English (COCA, https://www.english-corpora.org/coca/). For instance, the word *delineate* appears only 633 times in COCA, whereas *compare* appears 14,330 times.
- **Use shorter rather than longer sentences in instructions.** For instance, this example from a TOEFL practice test is long and complex (has a number of components), but it is easier to understand because key words are in boldface and sentences are short:

  On this page, you will listen to a conversation and answer questions about it.

  In the actual test, you will hear the conversation only **once**. You can take notes while you listen and use your notes to help you answer the questions. In the actual test, your notes will **not** be scored. Transcripts are available in this practice test, but not on the actual test. Listen to the conversation by clicking the player under the word "**Listen**."

The questions about the conversation are written below and should also be listened to by clicking the player above the question. In the actual test, you will have **30 seconds** to mark your answer(s) after each question is read.

The questions typically ask about the main idea and supporting details. Some questions ask about a speaker's purpose or attitude. Answer the questions based on what is stated or implied by the speakers. As you're going through the questions, select the appropriate answer or answers for each. (ETS, 2020, https://www.ets.org/toefl)

Trying to combine too many ideas in one sentence, such as in the next example, increases the language demands of the prompt and potentially creates confusion for students: "The questions typically ask about the main idea and supporting details while some questions ask about a speaker's purpose or attitude; either way, strive to answer the questions based on what is stated or implied by the speakers."

- **Use active verbs over passive**. Language learners are always taught the active forms before the passive forms of verbs, in part because they are more commonly used but also because of the linguistic complexity involved in passive language. Compare these two examples:

  1. Each question should be answered by circling the appropriate answer.
  2. Answer each question by circling the appropriate answer.

  The first example has a higher potential to confuse students, meaning that a wrong answer may stem from not understanding the directions, as opposed to not knowing the content.

- **Simplify sentences by limiting conditional clauses, relative clauses, question phrases, abstract concepts, and the number of modifiers before nouns**. Overly complex sentences or examples that are more abstract can be harder for language learners to grasp. Consider this original and revised example in mathematics from Abedi, Lord, and Plummer (1997, p. 29): (1) "The weights of three objects were compared using a pan balance. Two comparisons were made." vs. (2) "Sandra compared the weights of three objects using a pan balance. She made two comparisons." The inclusion of Sandra made this prompt more "story-like" (p. 29) and concrete for readers.

Let us look at some example test instructions and analyze them in terms of their accessibility for students. Read the two example instructions for a 6th grade assignment, and then take a minute to think about which one is more accessible and why.

Example 1:
Read/view the text/video with an analytical mindset, paying attention to your reactions while reading, and after reading, write down your impressions in a way that compares and contrasts your experiences reading the different texts.

Example 2:
Read the story and view the video. Take notes on your reactions to the story and video while reading/watching. Write a paragraph that compares and contrasts your opinions of the story and video.

Hopefully the answer was easy. Example 1 uses an overly complex sentence structure coupled with unnecessarily complex vocabulary (e.g., *analytical, impressions*). It also lacks specificity. What texts? What should the writing do? How long should it be? Some of these concerns overlap with grade-level differences because Example 1 is likely too complex for 6th graders in general, even if it is asking something cognitively appropriate for that grade level. In this sense, the same considerations that a teacher makes for students based on grade level should be applied to language learners. It is important to avoid conflating cognitive and linguistic levels and to maintain the cognitive expectations of a task while making the instructions accessible to students. Example 2 strives to do this. It asks students to do a very similar activity; however, the sentences are short, and the instructions specify the texts that students need to look at, the amount of writing they are expected to do, and what they are expected to do in that writing.

The stakes for writing instructions are higher with summative assessments as there tends to be less room for questions, especially on high-stakes standardized tests. Even when giving an in-classroom assessment—formative or summative—some students may be hesitant to ask for clarification. Some students tend to be shy and do not want to call attention to themselves. For this reason, teachers need to write clear instructions that are likely to be understood by their students; they cannot depend on students asking clarification questions to address the issue of poorly written instructions.

With formative assessments, the stakes for writing instructions tend to be lower as long as teachers are actively checking on students individually and providing feedback as students work on a particular activity. This individual checking in gives students a space to more safely ask questions without fear of drawing attention to themselves in the larger classroom context.

Writing Multiple Choice Items

The discussion on writing items overlaps with the discussion on writing instructions. Principles like seeking clarity and avoiding complex sentence structure still apply, except when the item is trying to test a particular aspect of language proficiency, such as knowledge of advanced academic vocabulary.

Before we continue, it is important to define some commonly used multiple choice item types:

- True/false: consists of a statement and two answer choices; the test taker is asked to choose either true or false
- Odd one out: lists several answers and the test taker is asked to pick one that differs from the others
- Negative questions: these ask the test taker to choose the answer that is **not** correct
- Multiple answer/combined response: these questions have more than one correct answer and may either ask test takers to select all the correct answers or include an option that includes multiple answers (e.g., both A and B; all of the above)

Haladyna, Downing, and Rodriguez (2002) conducted a review of the various guidelines for multiple choice item writing found in 27 textbooks on educational testing and 27 research studies and then developed a revised taxonomy of multiple choice writing guidelines. They divided the 31 guidelines into several different categories: addressing the content, formatting the items, following a consistent style, writing the stem, and writing the answer choices. We have simplified and adapted that list here for readers.

Addressing the Content

1. Focus items on important course content.
2. Use novel language in order to test application and not just recall.
3. Avoid opinion-based or trick items.
4. Use simple vocabulary.

Formatting and Style

5. **Avoid** the complex MC (Type K) format (an example is provided on page 48).
6. Format the item so that the answer options appear vertically and not horizontally on one line.
7. Edit and proof items.
8. Keep items concise.

Writing the Stem

9. Ensure that the directions in the stem are very clear.
10. Include the central idea of the content being assessed in the stem instead of in the choices.
11. Avoid negatives such as *not* or *except*. If used, emphasize them via boldface or capitalization.

Writing the Answer Choices

12. Develop as many effective choices as you can, but three is typically adequate.
13. Include only one correct answer choice and vary the location of the right answer.
14. Keep choices consistent in content, grammatical structure, and length.
15. Avoid *All of the above* and use *None of the above* carefully.
16. Avoid giving clues to the right answer, such as specific determiners including *always, never, completely,* and *absolutely*; grammatical inconsistencies that cue the test taker to the correct choice; or blatantly wrong options.

Let's discuss some of these guidelines in detail. We have already discussed the importance of using simple vocabulary. However, there are important points about avoiding opinion-based questions or trick items, with these issues having extra importance for ELs as questions premised on a trick often depend on close reading of the language of the question. One of the perhaps more confusing items in this section concerns the use of novel language to assess higher-level learning. Here are two examples from Haladyna (2004, p. 101):

Example 1:
Which is the best definition of a metaphor?

A. Metaphors describe something as if it were something else.
B. Metaphors make comparisons to other things.
C. Metaphors are trite, stereotyped expressions.

Example 2:
Which of the following is a metaphor?

A. At the breakfast buffet, I ate like a pig.
B. My cat is a raging tiger.
C. She is like a rose, full of thorns and smelly.

Example 1 is a question that asks students to simply memorize something from a lesson or a book, while Example 2 determines their understanding through application.

Under "Formatting and Style," there are some suggestions focused on ease of reading, careful proofreading (sloppy mistakes can exacerbate misunderstandings and students may be hesitant to question the writing of the teacher), and formatting and structure for ease of reading. Displaying the list of options vertically instead of horizontally also simplifies reading. Look at the following:

Choose the place in the paragraph where the sentence fits best:

a. Option A b. Option B c. Option C d. Option D

Choose the place in the paragraph where the sentence fits best:

a. Option A
b. Option B
c. Option C
d. Option D

While the first example is tempting if one must make paper copies of a test or activity since it is more compact, Haladyna (2004) noted that a horizontal layout can make the answers harder for students to read, especially those suffering from test anxiety. While psychometric experts recommend the use of straightforward true/false, multiple choice, and similar structures, they advise staying away from overly complex multiple choice structures, such as this Type K example:

Which of the following words could be used to complete the sentence below?

The pizza was delivered in a ____ box.

1. dog
2. white
3. school
4. cardboard
    a. 1 and 2
    b. 1, 3, and 4
    c. 2 and 4

One could imagine rewriting this question in a more accessible structure, as we've done below:

Which of the following words could be used to complete the sentence? Choose all that apply.

The pizza was delivered in a ____ box.

1. dog
2. white
3. school
4. cardboard

Under "Writing the Stem," we see additional points that connect with our earlier discussion and make the questions accessible to ELs at the same time that they make them more appropriate for English proficient students as well. These guidelines emphasize the need for writing clear instructions, including the central idea, and—one guideline that might not be so obvious—wording the stem positively, avoiding words like NOT or EXCEPT. This goes back to the earlier point about trick questions, as adding the negative makes the question unnecessarily complex. Compare the following two examples:

Which of the following words is spelled correctly?

A. Parrot
B. Leon
C. Mnkey
D. Girafe

Which of the following words is not spelled correctly?

A. Parrot
B. Leon
C. Mnkey
D. Giraffe

Additionally, the inclusion of Leon, which is lion in Spanish, adds an extra layer of confusion for Spanish ELs. We suggest avoiding language distractions like this.

We believe that writing the choices is the most complex area for consideration. One of the points we'd like to pay attention to is making sure there is only one right answer, which goes back to avoiding opinion-based items. As test writers try to develop multiple choice tests that assess more complex issues such as analytical thinking, they risk erring on this, something Todd experienced when trying NewsELA, a program that aligns questions on articles to particular CCSS standards. One common question is "What option provides the best summary of the reading?" and it allows students to select one correct answer for an arguably subjective question.

Another important, oft-ignored consideration is the use of *none of the above* or *all of the above*, both of which risk being too absolute and verge on the trick question category, potentially making the test more difficult for ELs. Haladyna, Downing, and Rodriguez (2002) found these to be the most disputed recommendations. Most of the other considerations under writing the choices are more obvious, such as making the choices believable and avoiding giving clues to the correct answer, especially when these clues might be misleading (Plakans & Gebril, 2015).

Writing True/False Items

Along with the suggestions above about good test items in general, we need to consider a few other issues when writing true/false test items. While true/false (and yes/no) questions might take less time to create, they can be nevertheless fraught with difficulty. Even though they are easy to grade, some teachers believe that they are not fair indicators of student knowledge as they come with a seemingly high probability of guessing the correct answer. This may not always prove true, as simply relying on guesswork can quickly go south when there are ample test items. Additionally, true/false tests give teachers little feedback into what their students are missing and why they have answered incorrectly. Certainly though, this can be said for many kinds of test items.

Let's have a look at the advantages and disadvantages of the true/false format:

Advantages

- Format allows involvement of a wide skill/knowledge range
- Since questions are often short, the format is not as dependent on test takers' careful reading ability
- Questions can be answered quickly
- Format has positive washback

Disadvantages

- Questions can be simplistic
- Learner understanding is difficult to determine
- There is a 50% chance of guessing correctly
- A true/false-only test must contain a large number of test items in order to be provide germane evidence of learner knowledge

Writing Fill-in-the-Blank Items

Fill-in-the-blank items are another common test question format. They allow for more complexity than true/false or multiple choice questions and can be used to assess language or content knowledge. They can be completely open-ended or can provide students with a word bank for the question set that lets students know if options can only be used once or more than once. Deborah recommends using a word bank with learners at lower proficiency levels. Here's an excerpt from a fill-in-the-blank activity using articles:

Fill in the blank with the appropriate article: *a*, *an*, or *the*. Leave a space empty if no article is needed.

1. I went to ______ theater last night.
2. The teacher lent me ______ pencil because I forgot mine at home.
3. Please pass me ______ piece of pie.

As with the other question types, it is important to pay attention to the unique characteristics of these questions and design them carefully to avoid confusing students. Here are some recommendations:

- Have consistency in the words used to complete the blanks: make it clear in the instructions whether they will be language or content-focused answers and don't mix answer types in one activity. Also, as seen in the example above, the instructions and tasks should focus on a particular skill.
- Allow for only one correct answer: including a word bank helps address this issue by providing clearer guidance, but it's important to ensure that there is only one clear answer choice; otherwise, grading will become more challenging as a teacher encounters technically correct answers that they didn't anticipate.
- Keep sentences simple and clear: even though a sentence may not be grammatically correct or may be missing a particular content detail, make sure that it makes sense even without the blank.
- Limit blanks per item: don't have more than one or two blanks per item. More than that and the task can become overly confusing.
- Keep blanks uniform: don't shorten or lengthen the blanks based on the answer and don't use lines to indicate how many letters the correct answer is—this can make it too easy and focus the exercise on trying to figure out what the answer is based on length. Instead, have one standard-sized line for each answer. In writing the activity above, we copied and pasted the same line into each activity.

As with all the other question types, review carefully and revise tasks as needed to ensure they are clear and accessible to students. It is always helpful to get another set of eyes; however, this is not always realistic with our busy lives as teachers. Consequently, it's important to revise and refine activities over time.

Creating Writing Prompts

(This section is adapted from Crusan (2010) pp. 68–69 and 87–88).

When teachers create writing tasks, they must entertain a variety of considerations, some of which may be more obvious than others. Since they are more complex than the aforementioned question/task types, there is also more room for things to go wrong.

One commonly overlooked consideration concerns issues of bias. Brown (2004) cites this prompt from the International Language Testing System (IELTS®) to illustrate bias in writing assessment:

> You rent a house through an agency. The heating system has stopped working. You phoned the agency a week ago, but it has still not been mended. Write a letter to the agency. Explain the situation and tell them what you want them to do about it.

Brown finds the prompt authentic; that is, the notion that one might have to write a letter of complaint is highly probable. However, he finds problems with the cultural and economic assumptions in the prompt. Will every student reading this prompt understand *rent*? What about *heating system*? Will every student understand the term *phoned*?

It is quite easy to become entangled in bias. One clear example is our tendency to think that our familiar technology is available to everyone. Imagine this homework assignment:

> Go to Google and search for reasons families should take a summer vacation. Write a paragraph that describes the recommendation you found most convincing and the one you found least convincing.

Let's look at the first sentence in our second example. Inherent in these seemingly straightforward 13 words are several major but not necessarily obvious assumptions: that families have access to a computer in their home; that students have access to the Internet; that students understand how the term *go* is used in the sentence; that students understand Google; that students have the economic means to take a vacation.

As this example illustrates, creating explicit, non-ambiguous prompts for writing tasks and timed essay exams can be a daunting task. Here are some steps to help teachers produce good writing prompts for in-class essay exams and for writing assignments outside class:

1. State a context in one to two sentences. Here are two examples:

   Some people believe that a public-school education should include access to extra-curricular activities such as membership on sports teams or the high school marching band with no fees required. Others advocate for a fee schedule to be attached to every non-academic activity in which students wish to be involved.

Many international students studying in the U.S. experience culture shock because of differences in every-day life such as student attitudes toward professors, classroom behavior, food, and perceived large amounts of free time afforded students in the U.S. Other international students take to their new culture more easily and suffer little in the way of culture shock.

2. State the directions in a separate paragraph from the context. These should include genre (e.g., letter, opinion piece, reading response), audience, and topic.
3. Define the mode of the essay using words such as *define, contrast, argue,* and *convince.*

A good prompt includes all the information students need to develop an appropriate response to the assignment, including context and directions that tell the writer the purpose for writing, the audience, and the format of the finished essay.

Here's an example of a well-written prompt:

Context: Many people think that students are not learning enough in school. They want to shorten school vacations and make students spend more of the year in school. Other people think that lengthening the school year and shortening vacations is a bad idea because students use their vacations to learn important things outside school.

Directions: Write a letter [GENRE] to the local school board [AUDIENCE] either in favor of or against [ASSERTION OPTIONS] lengthening the school year [TOPIC]. Give specific reasons to support your opinion that will convince [MODE] the school board to agree with you.

This prompt is strong because it provides a context, states the genre, and defines the audience. The topic and the directions are clear. All the information students need to complete the assignment is included. Further, it is a topic that engages students because it has implications pertinent to their lives. White (1998) reminded us that writing ability will vary according to topic; better results are produced if the writer is interested in what she must write about.

Improperly written prompts can elicit a uniform but unintended response, or students may respond with an unexpected variety of interpretations of the prompt. Poorly written prompts do not specify a context, have vague topics, and are missing the point of the assignment. If we provide an audience for students in our writing assignments, we can help students to move to a more sophisticated level. Examples of ineffective writing prompts:

> Indian armed resistance after 1760 was pointless. Discuss.
> Discuss the use of metaphor in *To Kill a Mockingbird.*
> Discuss the following: *The Prince of Tides* was neither about princes nor tides.

Imagine how these prompts might be interpreted by second language writers. What are the prompts missing? What would it take to improve them?

Like it or not, some teachers often feel obliged to prepare their students for essay tests. While the timed essay has been much maligned for its truncating of the writing process and its promotion of formulaic writing (the five-paragraph essay), many second language writers will be asked to draw on the skill of writing a timed essay. Here are just a few examples of occasions when students need the ability to produce clear, concise essays rapidly: taking the TOEFL, the IELTS, or the Test of English for International Communication (TOEIC®); writing for a test in sociology; taking proficiency tests in settings that are PreK–12 in the United States; and taking the new SAT timed writing test.

Creating Rubrics

Opportunities present themselves in our classrooms to assess our students' production skills. Because multiple choice questions often test more narrowly, focusing instead on the subskills of writing (mechanics, usage, grammar, spelling), it is sometimes necessary to assess students' actual writing skills. When we do that, we need to know how to create the writing assignment and how to create the rubric that we'll use to grade that assignment. Many teachers confess to a love/hate relationship with rubrics, calling them limiting and reductive, and we admit that this can be a problem; however, a well-constructed rubric can make teachers' jobs easier and reduce student questions about grades. Further, if the rubric is pinpointed to one assignment, the narrowing effects disappear. That said, teachers don't have a lot of time to create assignments and accompanying rubrics, which is quite understandable when they are faced with large class sizes, long days, and heavy administrative duties. Of course, canned assignments (and rubrics) exist all over the Internet, and they can serve as jumping-off places. It's just important to remember that canned assignments and rubrics work for few populations because they are not targeted to specific students; nevertheless, they can help teachers.

Materials found online can be adopted and then adapted to specific groups of students. Some helpful sites for creating rubrics are:

- Rubistar (http://rubistar.4teachers.org/index.php). This site allows teachers to find premade rubrics, but even better, teachers can create their own customizable rubrics on the website, save them, and constantly update them. Registration is free.
- Quick Rubric (https://www.quickrubric.com/). Another free website that allows teachers to create their own professional-looking rubrics. There are no premade rubrics, but the site does offer practical tips to writing a strong rubric, including lists of criteria for various kinds of assignments (written, performance, behavior: e.g. Persistence is one of several academic and personal behaviors necessary for student success) and guidance regarding choice of rubric type (holistic or analytic), all while reminding teachers that although rubric creation is often time consuming, rubric use reduces grading time and student angst because students know how and why they will be assessed when rubrics are shared with them.
- Teachnology (http://www.teach-nology.com/web_tools/rubrics/). While this is a paid site, the cost is reasonable and provides unlimited access to countless membership materials, including all rubric makers, lesson plans, graphic organizers, PowerPoint and Word templates, and more for busy teachers. While these materials are canned, teachers can again adopt them and then adapt them to their individual student needs and the context in which they teach.

Even if teachers use rubric creation websites, they still need to know how to create rubrics that meet the needs of the students they see every day in class. The following steps can help:

1. **Define the goal of the assessment.** There are a lot of questions in need of answers here. What do I want to assess? How do I want to assess it? WHY do I want to assess it? Do I want to provide detailed feedback? Are all the tasks in the assignment equally important?
2. **Look at models—review examples of good and poor rubrics.** Teachers can provide their students with models of rubrics. They can then examine them

and analyze them asking very specific questions. Are the rubrics specific enough? Do they ask the right questions for the assignment? Do they reflect observable objectives? What makes the rubrics good? Not so good?

3. **Choose a rubric type.** As mentioned above, the two most common rubrics used in the classroom are the holistic rubric and the analytic rubric. The holistic rubric is "generally a five- to six-point scale that involves ranking a sample of a student's work by matching it with another piece in a benchmark series, scoring it for the prominence of certain features important to that kind of work, and assigning a grade" (Crusan, 2010, p. 44). Holistic rubrics, though, are much better suited to large-scale assessment than they are to classroom assessment, since they offer little in the way of feedback to the developing learner. Table 4.2 is an example of a holistic rubric for a writing class. Notice that it is rather generic, focusing on ideas, coherence, and grammar.

   Perhaps better, especially for in-class use, are analytic rubrics, which "include a more detailed analysis of features selected for evaluation" (Crusan, 2010, p. 46). In the case of writing, those features could be content, organization, vocabulary, language use, and mechanics. The possibilities are endless and depend on the criteria you have set for the assignment; for example, criteria for a summary assignment is different from that of an analysis. Table 4.3 depicts an example of an analytic rubric Deborah uses in her graduate seminar in TESOL.

TABLE 4.2
Holistic Writing Rubric

Excellent 90–100	Ideas are thoroughly explained, highly coherent writing, few grammatical errors
Good 80–89	Ideas are explained, coherent writing, few grammatical errors
Satisfactory 70–79	Ideas are partially explained, somewhat coherent writing, several grammatical errors
Needs Work 0-60	Ideas are poorly explained, incoherent writing, many grammatical errors

TABLE 4.3
English 7500: Writing Assessment Final Paper Rubric

	Missing	Sketchy	Fair	Average	Well Done	Superior
Clear focused topic	0	1	2	3	4	5
Presents a relevant problem	0	1	2	3	4	5
Advocates a position	0	1	2	3	4	5
Supports position with evidence	0	2	4	6	8	10
Effectively communicates both sides of the argument	0	2	4	6	8	10
Provides evidence for both sides of the argument	0	2	4	6	8	10
Adds new knowledge in the form of a question, an insight, a complication, a connection	0	2	4	6	8	10
Is grammatically and mechanically correct	0	1	2	3	4	5
Uses APA/MLA correctly	0	1	2	3	4	5
Cites 10–15 appropriate sources	0	1	2	3	4	5
Column Totals						
Paper Total						

4. **Determine criteria.** What will be used to judge the work? What does good writing include? What are the components of a good presentation? What's most important in this assignment? What is included in a good summary? In an analysis paper?
5. **Create performance levels.** What's the difference between a 1 and a 5? And while we're on numbers for the rubric, always include a zero grade in case the criteria are not present. Write descriptors for each level of performance.

6. **Pilot the rubric.** Use the rubric to grade student work. Is it helpful in providing the feedback that you generally wish to give to students? Do the grades produced align with your general sense of the quality of the assignment? Once you have used the rubric, it will be clear to you what needs to be changed, added, deleted.
7. **Share with students.** Students should always know the criteria by which they'll be judged, so it's important to let them know how, why, how much. It's important to note that some teachers either involve students in the initial creation of the rubric or solicit feedback on the rubric from them at this stage (Chamcharatsri, 2016; Crusan, 2010; Weigle, 2002).

In Deborah's TESOL assessment class as well as in her graduate seminar in writing assessment, students are asked to develop a prompt and rubric. They are then instructed to answer their own prompts. When they have finished writing, they hand the finished product and their rubric to another student to score. After the scoring procedures are completed, students reckon with their successes or failures. Though far from a perfect assignment for many reasons (chief among them that little rater training occurs and the time allotted to materials development is truncated), the exercise still offers insight into the creation, use, and revision of assignments and their accompanying scoring instruments. Students learn so much, especially from their mistakes.

Figure 4.1 depicts a rubric from Deborah's MA program for the final revised seminar paper that students must submit at the culmination of their degrees. What might you include that is not already on the rubric? Could this rubric be transformed for classroom use?

Next, in Figure 4.2 we offer a rubric for an ad analysis assignment in English 1100, the first of two required writing courses for all students at Deborah's institution. Notice the weighting of different criteria. Would you distribute weight in the same way? Could you adapt this rubric for use in your own classroom?

As we have reiterated many times, rubrics are powerful tools when created specifically for each assignment and when students understand why and how they are being used. Andrade & Du (2005) found that "students use rubrics to support their own learning and academic performance … to plan an approach to an assignment, check their work, and guide or reflect on feedback from others" (p. 1). To create even bigger buy-in from students, there are many times when teachers might want to create the rubric for a specific assignment *with* their students. It is a powerful display of both

FIGURE 4.1
MATESOL Revised Seminar Essay Rubric

Note: A paper may not pass with a) a score of 1 in any single category or b) a score of less than 64 for the revised seminar essay.						
	0	**3**	**4**	**5**	**Multiply by**	**Row Subtotal**
Revised Seminar Essay (80% of portfolio score)						
Revised Seminar Essay: Mechanics, proofreading, and discipline-appropriate style are in good order					X1	
Revised Seminar Essay: The essay has a clear and appropriate thesis and places this thesis in the context of its field					X2	
Revised Seminar Essay: The essay maintains focus upon its thesis and offers discussion and analysis of appropriate examples to support the thesis					X3	
Revised Seminar Essay: The essay cites a selection of sources that is appropriate in both size and scope.					X5	
Revised Seminar Essay: The essay engages its sources appropriately, responding to them and engaging the ongoing scholarly conversation rather than merely repeating their points, and appropriately groups and frames arguments of other scholars					X5	
Must score 64 or better to pass (80%)						
Must score 76 or better to PASS WITH DISTINCTION (95%)						
REVISED SEMINAR ESSAY SUBTOTALS (out of 80 possible points)						**70/80**

KEY:
0 = Missing or Egregious (D or F)
3 = Unacceptable (C)
4 = Good (B)
5 = Excellent (A)

FIGURE 4.2
Ad analysis Scoring Guide

CRITERION	Strong 5	Good 4	Adequate 3	Weak 1	Missing 0	Pts.
Introduction—does it grab the readers' attention?						
Thesis—offers a clear interpretation or judgment (multiply by 2)						
Analysis—logical structure, flow, depth, goes beyond surface ideas, supports analysis with examples (multiply by 3)						
Description—accurately describes the ad or song with enough vivid description so the reader does not need to see or hear what the writer is describing (multiply by 2)						
Analysis/Description—should be balanced, one should not overpower the other; should relate directly to your thesis (multiply by 2)						
Word choice—avoid repetition, use vivid adjectives & verbs (multiply by 2)						
Rhetorical situation has been addressed Purpose is clear; draft is focused & doesn't stray from your purpose; audience is clearly defined; you help your readers move through your essay; stance is clear; readers can tell your stance through your tone; stance is consistent throughout the essay (multiply by 2)						
MUGS (mechanics, usage, grammar, spelling)—The essay is clearly & logically organized; sentences are complete & appropriately punctuated (no run-ons), words are spelled correctly; phrasing is appropriate and appropriate for the genre (multiply by 3)						
Conclusion—ends appropriately, restates the thesis & sums up the paper						
Correct MLA format						

Total Score: ____________________

Comments:

(Hausman, 2012)

inclusion and democracy in our classrooms (Crusan, 2010). Aiding in the creation of the means by which they will be assessed helps students recognize skills and illustrates ways in which they might master these skills. The list of creation criteria is basically the same as when teachers create rubrics individually, but there are a few added steps when co-creating a rubric with students:

1. Look at models—examine examples of stronger and weaker work for the kinds for writing your students will be doing.
2. Have students think about how the focus type of writing should be assessed.
3. Elicit criteria that demonstrate effective writing in that genre.
4. Discuss and come to a shared understanding about the criteria.
5. Have students assign a weight or value to those criteria.
6. Have students articulate levels of quality.
7. Draft a rubric and have students comment.
8. Distribute and use the draft rubric; first students will use the rubric on their own work and then they will trade papers and use the rubric on peers' work.
9. After they've piloted the rubric, ask students to write for five minutes on any issues they experienced while using the rubric.
10. Conduct an in-class discussion about ways to solve the issues.
11. Revise and reuse to make sure the rubric is ready for prime time.

These steps can also be useful in developing a rubric that you'll be using with other teachers, such as a program-wide rubric used across shared assignments. It is vital that all the teachers are on board with the rubric and how it defines effective student performances, so the process of developing such a rubric needs to have a similar level of collaboration, ranging from defining the criteria on which writing will be assessed to deciding how important are each criterion and what different levels of performance look like in a certain area, as seen in the example in Figure 4.3, a program-wide rubric for a research paper.

FIGURE 4.3
Research Paper Rubric

CATEGORY	A	B	C	D	F
Relevance of Information: Does it answer the research question(s)? 35 pts.	Information from research clearly and thoroughly relates to the research question(s). It is well-developed and includes several supporting details and/or examples.	Information from research generally relates to the research question(s). It is somewhat developed and provides sufficient supporting details and/or examples.	Information from research sometimes relates to the research question(s). It is under-developed; a few details and/or examples are given.	Information from research generally does not relate to the research question(s). It is under-developed; no details and/or examples are given.	Information is irrelevant to the research question(s).

Implementing Test Accommodation

The underlying principle behind accommodation is to ensure that all students have an equal opportunity to demonstrate their knowledge on an assessment; it's important to remember that rubrics support this goal as they offer ways and levels for each student to succeed. In school settings, providing appropriate accommodations is not optional; it's required by law and can expose a teacher and/or their school to lawsuits if the accommodations are not provided. This is another good reason to use test specifications as they typically take necessary accommodations into account. Whether a student is in an ESL or non-ESL class, they might need some form of accommodation. These accommodations can be required for a variety of learning and physical disabilities and also depending on language learning status. While these have unfortunately been conflated at times in schools, it is important to note that language learners may need accommodations not just related to their language proficiency.

Jamal Abedi is a well-known researcher whose work has focused on testing accommodations for ELs. In a 2004 article, Abedi, Hofstetter, and Lord reviewed the accommodations commonly provided for English learners on large-scale tests and their efficacy. Table 4.4 depicts a brief summary of their findings.

Abedi, Hofstetter, and Lord (2004) provided four guidelines for helping consider which accommodations will be considered by test administrators:

- Effectiveness: What accommodations help language learners demonstrate their abilities while minimizing language-based differences among students' performance?

TABLE 4.4
Abedi et al. (2004) Findings Summary

Accommodation	Pros	Cons
Providing tests and/ or test instructions in students' native languages	▪ Gives students' languages a place in the classroom/ educational context ▪ Relatively straightforward accommodation.	▪ Not appropriate when a test is focused on assessing student's language proficiency in their second language. ▪ Only useful if students have academic fluency in their L1, which many immigrant students may not, depending on when they came to the U.S. ▪ Translation difficulties may mean constructs are not equivalent. ▪ Expensive to translate entire tests, which means students from smaller language groups may be excluded
Linguistic modification of test items (i.e., simplifying tests to "minimize construct-irrelevant linguistic complexity" [p. 11])	▪ Helps reduce performance gap between language learners and non-language learners ▪ Helps ensure that comprehension isn't impeding students' ability to demonstrate their content knowledge in non-English subjects like math ▪ Generally maintains score comparability because it does not inflate the scores of non-language learners	▪ Not always appropriate when measuring English proficiency
Extra time	▪ Logistically uncomplicated; does not require expensive changes to test (which perhaps is why it is the most common accommodation)	▪ Improves the scores of both language learners and non-language learners ▪ Does not reduce performance gap if both groups of students given extra time.

(*Continued*)

TABLE 4.4 *(Continued)*

Accommodation	Pros	Cons
Published dictionaries	▪ Access to word definitions may provide students more accessibility to passages	▪ Dictionaries vary in their content, and some may provide content knowledge being provided on the test ▪ Minimal evidence demonstrating this as a valuable accommodation
Glossary and customized dictionary	▪ Tailored to the test ▪ Helps students overcome lexical challenges in comprehending instructions and content without having to modify test itself ▪ Can be more efficiently provided in computer-based testing, where it has been shown to improve the performance of language learners without threatening the assessment validity	▪ When paired with extra time, improves the scores of both language learner and non-language learners ▪ When not paired with extra time, it may decrease language learners' performance (perhaps due to too much information to process)

- Validity: Do the accommodations reduce the performance differences due to language or do they somehow impact the construct the test is measuring (e.g., simplifying the language on a language proficiency test fundamentally transforms what the test measures).
- Differential impact: Do some students perform better on the tests than others, based on their backgrounds? For instance, if more time benefits fluent English speakers more than ELs, then that becomes problematic.
- Feasibility: Is the accommodation doable given cost, time, staffing, and other constraints, either in a small-scale classroom setting or when administering a large-scale test?

While Abedi, Hofstetter, and Lord's (2004) article focused on large-scale testing, we'd like to take these concepts to the classroom level, thinking about their application by individual teachers. Looking at the options listed in Table 4.3, providing extra time and access to published dictionaries appears to be the easiest options for overworked teachers seeking to support their students. In implementing these accommodations, teachers need to think about how much time is appropriate. Is there a point where the extra time gives a language learner an advantage, especially when the accommodation is paired with a dictionary? For instance, the SAT does not offer students unlimited extra time, with typical time expansions at 150% – 200% of normal test taking time (College Board, 2016). There are also logistical issues such as when this time will be provided. Will a student come in during a free period or after school, or stay longer, taking time away from another class?

Of the linguistic modification options, translating the entire test is probably not feasible for most teachers unless they are bilingual certified in the languages of their students. Computer-based translation programs, while perhaps useful in providing some support, cannot be counted on for providing accurate translations for students and may lead to some performance issues if the translation causes misunderstandings. However, Abedi, Hofstetter, and Lord (2004) found strong evidence in support of linguistic modification of test items, including instructions, to ensure that they are linguistically accessible to all students. They found that this didn't compromise validity and did reduce the achievement gaps between ELs and non-ELs. We will discuss linguistic modification considerations in more depth below.

Bringing It All Together: Writing a Test

We hope the principles we've shared in this chapter have helped make it clear how to create a test. Given all the variables involved, it can at first seem like a daunting task; however, it does not have to be that way and no test is going to be perfect. As a teacher uses a variety of formative and summative assessments throughout the year, the stakes of any individual test are lower, so validity and reliability issues are not going to ruin the assessment as long as the assessment is part of a larger pattern of testing in the course.

In this last part of the chapter, we want to walk through the processes of creating a test. We will go through the following steps:

1. Identifying learning outcomes/standards
2. Creating test specifications
3. Writing directions
4. Writing items
5. Developing a plan for grading
6. Assessing the assessment

Our teaching context for this example will be a 5th grade ELA classroom that includes both EL and English-proficient students.

1. Identifying learning outcomes/standards

We will focus on listening comprehension, which takes us to the 5th grade CCSS standards for Speaking and Listening. We don't expect the test to cover all these standards at once, as that would be too broad and unfocused. With that in mind, we're going to pick two standards:

- CCSS.ELA-LITERACY.SL.5.2: Summarize a written text read aloud or information presented in diverse media and formats, including visually, quantitatively, and orally.
- CCSS.ELA-LITERACY.SL.5.3: Summarize the points a speaker makes and explain how each claim is supported by reasons and evidence.

Turning to the modified Bloom taxonomy (Anderson et al., 2001), we see both standards are primarily dependent on students' ability to understand, which is defined as "Determining the meaning of instructional messages, including oral, written, and graphic communication (p. 215). We also see they are dependent on students' ability to apply, namely to "[carry] out or [use] a procedure in a given situation." They also require students to create, to "[put] elements together to form a novel, coherent whole or make an original product." The second standard requires students to analyze and evaluate as well, with the latter defined as "Making judgments based on criteria and standards." The first standard is focused on simply summarizing, which doesn't explicitly involve judgment. With this in mind, we can see that these standards require rather complex behaviors on the part of students, so we want to ensure that we've prepared them via a variety of formative activities to undertake this work.

Since we have a number of ELs in our class, we want to pay attention to how we can reasonably expect them to perform on the test as well as meet the standards above, which align with the following WIDA (2020) standard: "English language learners communicate information, ideas and concepts necessary for academic success in the content area of Language Arts" (p. 3). We will get into the WIDA standard in more depth when thinking about the rubric.

2. Creating test specifications

Subject: English Language Arts
Grade: 5
Test Description: Mid-term speaking assessment
Standards Tested: 5.SL.2; 5.SL.3

- ❑ Summarize a written text read aloud or information presented in diverse media and formats, including visually, quantitatively, and orally.
- ❑ Summarize the points a speaker makes and explain how each claim is supported by reasons and evidence.

What students need to know/do:

- ❑ Understand a spoken text
- ❑ Write a summary; vocabulary of summary writing
- ❑ Analyze/evaluate an argument

Stimulus materials: Two five-minute audio recordings
How they will demonstrate this knowledge:

- ❑ Multiple response questions: 40%
- ❑ Writing a summary: 30%
- ❑ Writing an analysis 30%

Accommodations for ELs:

- ❑ Five glossed terms
- ❑ One extra chance to listen
- ❑ Extra 30 minutes for completing assessment

3. Writing directions

After developing test specifications, we know generally what is going to appear on the test. The next step is creating the structure for the test in more detail, namely writing descriptions of the tasks students will be expected to complete. In doing this, we want to recall the guidelines we provided earlier, namely that the instructions should be as clearly written as possible because they are not part of assessing students' language proficiency and should not be a barrier for students demonstrating their knowledge. As detailed in the specifications, we have three types of activities, so we need three sets of instructions for students.

For the multiple response we might write:

> You will listen to a five-minute speech by an advocate for laws that require helmet use when riding a motorcycle. Listen carefully and take notes. For each question, circle the correct answer.

This is simple and straight to the point. Keep in mind that additional explanatory information (e.g., "For each answer there is only one correct answer, so keep that in mind when responding") can only serve to confuse students, especially ELs at a lower proficiency level, and will take time away from completing the test. Similarly, let's recall that the answer shouldn't be based on an opinion, so avoid using the phrase "best answer."

Next, let's turn to directions for each of the summaries that students are expected to write. Make sure you capture all the essential information in writing as some students may not listen to or hear orally given instructions; however, since learners have different tendencies, it makes sense to read the instructions out loud, as well. Let's take a shot at writing instructions for each of the summary paragraphs:

1. You will listen to a five-minute speech by an advocate for laws that require helmet use when riding a motorcycle. Listen carefully and take notes. After listening two times, you will write a paragraph-long summary of the author's key arguments.
2. You will listen to the five-minute speech one more time. Then you will write a paragraph-long analysis of two claims that the speaker makes, explaining the evidence used to support each.

In creating the directions for the first written response, note how we opted for the more complex "laws that require helmet use when riding a motorcycle" rather than "motorcycle helmet laws" as we feel that some students may need the additional detail if they are unfamiliar with the concept. We also feel that giving students some context for what they are going to hear will help the EL students, as they can anticipate the topic and be better prepared to listen. Reminding students to take notes and telling them how many times they'll hear the recording are also important details, so they know exactly what to expect.

4. Writing items

Next, let's turn to writing individual items. We've already written the instructions for the writing tasks, so this discussion will focus on writing good multiple choice questions. In doing so, we want to keep in mind the principles we learned earlier: no opinion-based answers; positive, not negative, wording; straightforward question types; plausible options.

The speaker claimed that head injuries on motorcycles lead to how many dollars in medical expenses per year?

A. $150 million
B. $450 million
C. $250 million
D. $590 million

Which of the following states did the author mention in her speech?

A. New Mexico
B. Texas
C. New York
D. California

As seen in the few examples provided above, we avoided the "None/all of the above" options as well the negative structures (e.g., "Which of the following states were NOT mentioned?"), which helps students demonstrate their knowledge rather than be tricked by sentence structure.

5. Developing a plan for grading

How will you grade the test once your students take it? How many points is each item worth? Will you need a key? How will you handle open-ended items in which students have *close* answers? These questions need to be seriously entertained in order to make the grading process as smooth, fair, and equitable as possible.

As noted above, multiple choice questions were worth 40% of the total grade, so these should add up to 40 points on a 100-point assignment. If there were 10 multiple choice questions, we would assign 4 points to each one, the student getting 4 points if correct and 0 points if incorrect.

The writing tasks would benefit from a rubric. We like to align the rubric with the number of points available in order to simplify calculations. For instance, an analytic rubric for the summary portion would include a total of 30 points and might look like the one depicted in Table 4.5.

TABLE 4.5
Analytic Rubric

Characteristic	Description	Points Earned
Overall Summary (up to 15 points)	Accurately captured the content of the speech.	
Details (up to 10 points)	Included some relevant details, including statistics, that the speaker gave.	
Format and Correctness (up to 5 points)	Wrote clearly with minimal errors.	

6. Assessing the assessment

During administration and assessment, it is important to constantly be reflecting on how the instrument is working. Were students given enough time to effectively demonstrate their knowledge? Did it help you learn what you wanted to about your students? What questions arose as students took the test? Did they have difficulties in particular areas? Were some of the items too easy? Too hard? If so, is there value in including them in the future? Did the rubric allow you to identify areas of strengths and weaknesses in student writing? Were there areas it missed? How might the rubric be tweaked? We find it important to take notes so that we can remember what worked and what didn't in future iterations.

In this chapter, we discussed a variety of considerations when developing outcomes and creating assessments based on these outcomes. We have emphasized the importance of considering context when creating assignments and tests for students, ranging from the level of the class, the varying levels of students, students' language backgrounds, the outcomes defined for us, and more. We have provided a few examples along the way. However, context is but one consideration to make when creating assessments. As will be explained in the following chapters, it is also important to integrate assessment of all skills (listening, speaking, reading, writing, and grammar/vocabulary) in a language class.

Activities and Questions

Discussion Questions

1. Do you have any experience working with existing—or creating your own—test specifications? In creating your own, do you anticipate developing more formal or informal specifications?
2. What kind of accommodations are students in your teaching or learning contexts typically provided? Do you feel that students are given sufficient accommodations to accurately demonstrate their knowledge on local assessments and class work? On large-scale, standardized assessments?
3. Have you ever encountered a confusing activity or task on an assessment? What made it confusing? How might it have been improved?
4. For current teachers, what do you consider when writing instructions or prompts for your students? Do you tend to write instructions that conform to the practices we discussed (frequently used vocabulary, shorter sentences, and active verbs)? Do you disagree with any of these suggestions?
5. Which of the items on the "writing items" list were most surprising to you? Why is that the case? Did you disagree with any item on the list? Are you still unclear about any of the items on the list?

Activities

1. Find a poorly designed assessment activity. Work in small groups to improve it using some of the guidance provided in this chapter.
2. Think about two assessments in your own class or in classes you've taken that differ in levels of formality. Develop a less and more formal set of test specifications matching the formality of the assessment. Then reflect on how the formality level changed the development process and what you decided to include.
3. Collect examples of questions you used in your own class or that you encountered in another class. Working in small groups, analyze the questions using the writing items list. Which items on the list seem to be most commonly violated? Practice revising questions based on this analysis.

4. Bring a rubric to class that you developed for an assignment or encountered in another class and be ready to share it with peers. Use the following questions to guide your discussion: Does the rubric seem generic or is it in some way tailored to the specific assignment? If so, how so? Does the rubric illustrate the differences between different levels of performance? If not, how could this be made clearer? Do you anticipate any challenges in using this rubric in your own classroom? If so, what are they?
5. Create your own writing prompt and a rubric to accompany it based on what you learned in this chapter. Then, answer your own writing prompt. When you have finished writing, swap the finished product and rubric with another student to score. After you each complete scoring, discuss what worked and didn't work about your rubrics and how they might be improved.

5

Assessing the Receptive Skills: Listening and Reading

The receptive skills are listening and reading; learners need not *produce* language using these skills; rather, they receive and, with a bit of luck, understand language. In the past, the skills of listening and reading have been referred to as passive skills. However, scholars have long held that listening and reading are far from passive. To further explain the non-passivity of listening and reading, Brown (2011) uses the cognitive model of language processing, which involves both top-down and bottom-up processing. He defines these two modes of processing as "using prior knowledge and experiences" (top-down) and "using information we have about sounds, word meanings, and discourse markers like *first, then,* and *after* to assemble our understanding of what we read one step at a time" (bottom-up) (p. 19). We can see that top-down attends to more global concepts, while bottom-up attends to more local concepts. Both are necessary. And both involve engagement of the listener and reader, not passivity. Engaged listeners listen to learn (informational), listen to evaluate and analyze (critical), and listen to understand feeling and emotion (empathetic). In reading, engagement involves readers taking either an aesthetic approach (living the story) or cognitive method (acquiring factual information) from a reading process.

Hinkel (2006) noted a gradual shift in TESOL pedagogical perspectives over the last 50 years that has profoundly affected classroom instruction and curriculum development. The gradual shift that Hinkel cites is "the decline of methods, a growing emphasis on both bottom-up and top-down skills, new knowledge about English, and integrated and multiple skills taught in context" (p. 110). Therefore, we need to remember that separation of the four skills of reading, writing, speaking, and listening as we have done in this book, whether it is in the teaching of the skills or their assessment, not only flies in the face of current perspectives but is also difficult and artificial. We can never quite achieve that separation. For example, in *any* test, we are always assessing reading.

If students aren't able to read the instructions on the test, they will not be successful; therefore, even if the test is not pinpointed to reading assessment, it is still assessing reading. Nevertheless, we'll attempt a separation, even though "measuring only a single skill (or fewer than four skills) provides a less than adequate estimate of what a person can do in a real-life setting" (Powers, 2010, p. 2).

Why Is Listening Important?

Listening is a crucial activity and the most frequently used communication skill, yet we devote so little effort to improving it. In fact, listening is so common that we tend to ignore it. But that cannot dismiss the fact that listening is the most fundamental component of communication skills. Listening is not something that just happens; listening is an active process in which a conscious decision is made to listen to and understand the message of the speaker.

One very important part of listening is listening discrimination; listening discrimination activities allow students to practice listening to the target language and to discriminate between different sounds at high fluency rates. When creating activities, aim for those that force attention on perception of individual sounds. We will examine this more closely later in the chapter when we discuss activities for the assessment of listening.

We spend a lot of time listening. Emanuel et al. (2008) assessed ways undergraduate college students (N=696) spent communicating and found that 55.4% of students' total communication was spent listening, followed by reading (17.1%), speaking (16.1%), and writing (11.4%). Internet use accounted for some of the listening time, as college students spend as much time listening to media as they do when engaged in interpersonal interactions. Studies also confirm that students are often poor and inefficient listeners, remembering less than 20% of what they listen to in a lecture (Dale, 1969).

A number of research studies demonstrate that listening ability can be taught (and thereby assessed), and EL students can gain positive effects both cognitively and linguistically from training in learning strategies (Huang, 2005 Chien, Kao, & Wei, 2008) One of the most important elements of teaching listening is to impress upon our students the importance of active listening. Active listening requires the listener to fully concentrate, understand, respond, and then remember what is being said. A listener makes a conscious effort to process and understand the complete message rather than just passively hear it. There are many ways to increase effective listening skills. These include understanding why you are listening, taking the time to listen, establishing an environment for listening, letting go of preconceived ideas and listening objectively, watching the speaker's body language, staying alert, keeping to the main points if taking notes, and responding effectively. As we teach these skills, we can also use them to assess our students, as will be shown later in the chapter.

One of the most important aspects of any kind of assessment is that it should inform teachers and students about what students know and don't know and what they can and cannot do. Typical strategies to increase listening comprehension include listening to fluent English, building receptive vocabulary through repetition and schema building, using gestures to show comprehension, and choral reading. Students might read structured dialogues or practice short phrases or sentences repeatedly for fluency. As they build listening comprehension and vocabulary, students can move onto lessons that demand slightly higher levels of interaction, centered on skills such as:

- using common social greetings
- engaging in community-building activities such as describing schedules and pastimes
- discussing current events or pop culture
- expressing an opinion
- explaining why they did something

Again, even as they develop the above skills, students can be assessed as well, evaluating how well these skills are developed and pursuing next steps to making them stronger listeners.

It is important to note here that most standardized listening tests differ a bit from that which was described above; these tests typically resemble reading comprehension tests except that the student listens to a passage instead of reading it. The student then answers multiple choice questions that address various levels of literal and inferential comprehension. Important elements in all listening tests are (1) the listening stimuli, (2) the questions, and (3) the test environment.

Types of Listening

Brown and Abeywickrama (2019) classify four types of listening performance: intensive, responsive, selective, and extensive. As you will see, these four types merge well with the use of controlled, guided, and free activities advocated in this chapter (see in the "Types of Listening Activities" section). Intensive listening is listening discrimination and involves listening for things like phonemes, words, intonation, and discourse markers. Responsive listening involves listening to a relatively short snippet in preparation to respond in kind. Selective listening involves students listening to longer passages and scanning for information. Tasks to assess this skill might include students listening for numbers, dates, names, or certain facts. Finally, extensive listening involves listening to lengthy discourse and deriving specific information, such as the main idea or the ability to make inferences, from it (Brown & Abeywickrama, 2019). Assessment of the extensive skill of listening can take many forms, and the skill is decidedly academic as students spend much time listening to lectures and ascertaining what is important in the lecture.

Listening Assessment Standards

WIDA

WIDA lists the features of academic language in three dimensions: discourse, sentence, and word/phrase, which is a familiar way that teachers think about language.

WIDA's definition of listening can best be accessed by viewing their Can Do statements. WIDA explains that their Can Do statements can be used by educators who work with language learners; the statements can be used to

- differentiate curriculum, instruction, and *assessments* designed in English based on language learners' levels of English language proficiency
- Collaborate and engage in instructional conversations about the academic success of language learners in English environments
- Advocate for equitable access to content for language learners based on their level of language proficiency

(WIDA, 2020 https://wida.wisc.edu)

Although WIDA statements are intended for PreK–12, they can certainly guide those who work with language learners at tertiary institutions as well; they are also valuable in teacher education programs as they make visible important aspects of language learning. Particularly for our purposes in this chapter, the Can Do statements can guide the creation of assignments/assessments in our classrooms because they allow students to tell us what they believe they can and cannot do. The Can Do statements serve as a valuable piece in teachers' judgment of students' abilities and can aid in curriculum planning. Since we believe that one of the cardinal rules of teaching is gauging the needs of our students, these self-assessments can help greatly in this quest.

WIDA includes four key uses for communicative purposes: *recount*, *explain*, *argue*, and *discuss* (WIDA, 2020). For the first three, WIDA includes descriptors for language use in the four skills (reading, writing, speaking, listening). The fourth, *discuss*, is used in the oral domain only. There are six levels of proficiency: Entering (Level 1), Emerging (Level 2), Developing (Level 3), Expanding (Level 4), Bridging (Level 5), Reaching (Level 6). For each of these levels, descriptors delineate what students can do.

Table 5.1 outlines criteria for grades 6–8 for the Developing (3) and Reaching (6) levels in Listening, illustrating what students are expected to be able to do at those levels. Consider the differences between these two levels before continuing your reading.

Consider the processing recounts skill: Reaching students are expected to process more complex information by identifying key ideas and new information. In regard to processing explanations, one example of the differences in levels lies in matching main ideas (Developing students) rather than evaluating ideas (Reaching students). For the

TABLE 5.1
WIDA Key Uses Listening Example

	Process Recounts by	**Process explanations by**	**Process arguments by**
Level 3 Developing	▪ Matching main ideas of familiar text read aloud to visuals ▪ Stating the next event in a series based on clues from narrative or informational oral texts	▪ Matching main ideas of familiar text read aloud with visuals ▪ Showing differences between or among content-related phenomena (e.g., descriptive statistics) described orally	▪ Illustrating claims or reasons from oral narratives ▪ Identifying opposing perspectives (e.g., sides in wars, regimes, or revolutions) from oral text
Level 6 Reaching	▪ Identifying key ideas expressed orally ▪ Identifying new information expressed by others	▪ Evaluating main ideas and supporting details presented in diverse media and oral formats ▪ Developing models from oral discourse and multimedia (e.g., YouTube videos)	▪ Evaluating the soundness of opposing claims presented orally ▪ Identifying bias within claims in oral discourse

processing arguments skill, Developing students are expected to identify opposing points of view while Reaching-level students are expected to evaluate claims and identify bias in them.

CEFR

The Common European Framework of Reference for Languages (CEFR) is an international standard for describing language ability (Council of Europe, n.d.). CEFR uses a six-point scale (from A1 for beginners up to C2 for mastery) with three level descriptors: Basic (PreA1, A1, A2), Independent (B1, B2), Proficient (C1, C2). Teachers and learners can use this information to assess English learner qualifications. According to CEFR, the scale was designed to be instructive, not dogmatic. Its aim is to be comprehensive, transparent, coherent, and open. The CEFR can be used to plan classroom lessons and develop curricula. The CEFR take-away message lies in four principles:

- Adapt the CEFR to fit context
- Focus on the outcomes of learning
- Focus on purposeful communication
- Focus on the development of good language learning skills

CEFR's rich descriptions can aid users in isolating levels necessary to achieve the objectives of the classroom or the language program. CEFR offers global scales, self-assessment grids, and illustrative scales; in terms of listening, scales are provided for very specific activities, including overall listening comprehension, understanding interactions between native speakers, listening as a member of a live audience, listening to announcements and instruction, listening to radio audio and recordings, and watching TV and film.

Table 5.2 outlines CEFR criteria for C2, B2, and A2 levels in overall listening comprehension, illustrating what students are expected to be able to do at those levels. Consider the differences between these three levels before continuing your reading.

Consider the differences between what a student at the C2 level ("has no difficulty") can do in regard to listening with that of a student at the A2 level (understands if speech "is clearly and slowly articulated"). Consider how these differences influence the creation of teaching and assessment materials. C2 students can listen to more information and more complex information easily while A2 students will need to be provided with scaffolds in order to make that leap.

TABLE 5.2
CEFR Criteria Listening Example

Level	
C2	Has no difficulty in understanding any kind of spoken language, whether live or broadcast, delivered at fast native speed
B2	Can understand standard spoken language, live or broadcast, on both familiar and unfamiliar topics normally encountered in personal, social, academic, or vocational life. Only extreme background noise, inadequate discourse structure, and/or idiomatic usage influence the ability to understand.
	Can understand the main ideas of propositionally and linguistically complex speech on both concrete and abstract topics delivered in a standard dialect, including technical discussions in his/her field of specialization.
	Can follow extended speech and complex lines of argument provided the topic is reasonably familiar, and the direction of the talk is sign-posted by explicit markers.
A2	Can understand enough to be able to meet needs of a concrete type provided speech is clearly and slowly articulated.
	Can understand phrases and expressions related to areas of most immediate priority (e.g. very basic personal and family information, shopping, local geography, employment) provided speech is clearly and slowly articulated.

ACTFL

A third set of guidelines, the ACTFL Proficiency Guidelines (2012), call listening an interpretive skill and describe five major levels of proficiency: Distinguished, Superior, Advanced, Intermediate, and Novice; Advanced, Intermediate, and Novice are further divided into High, Mid, and Low. All levels describe what listeners understand from what they hear. I recommend that my students, preservice teachers, become familiar with the guidelines and use them to describe their students' levels because there is so much information provided in the guidelines about what a learner can do within the descriptors of proficiency levels. For example, at the ACTFL Advanced Low sublevel, "Listeners are able to understand short conventional narrative and descriptive texts with a clear underlying structure though their comprehension may be uneven. The listener understands the main facts and some supporting details. Comprehension may often derive primarily from situational and subject-matter knowledge" (ACTFL, 2012, p. 17).

If teachers have students at this level, they can inspect the abilities laid forth in Advanced Mid (e.g., "listeners are able to understand conventional narrative and descriptive texts, such as expanded descriptions of persons, places, and things, and narrations about past, present, and future events") to help them create assignments and assessments that will move students from one sublevel to the next.

The ACTFL Proficiency Guidelines are a handy tool to use in the classroom; Deborah asks her students to use ACTFL to level the learners with whom they work. It allows her students to work with the language of the five levels and enables them to see that language alive in the form of their student. However, for purposes of brevity, in standards discussions for the remaining skills, we will discuss WIDA and alternate between CEFR and ACTFL.

Types of Listening Activities

Anytime we create activities for active listening, we need to remember that they are also assessments. They should have a specific purpose. It is our job as teachers to understand that basic truth and to make sure that we understand the different purposes for assessing listening skills. The objective of listening comprehension practice in the classroom is to enable the students to learn to function successfully in real-life listening situations. Different kinds of listening include listening for gist, main idea, and vocabulary. Listening students need exposure to authentic accents, content, and note-taking situations.

Peachey (n.d.) includes the following elements when developing listening lessons, which of course can be used as assessments, since *all lessons and assignments are assessments.*

His basic framework is divided into three main stages.

- Pre-listening, during which we help our students prepare to listen.
- While listening, during which we help to focus their attention on the listening text and guide the development of their understanding of it.
- Post-listening, during which we help our students integrate what they have learned from the text into their existing knowledge.

These three steps can easily be used in any assessment of listening. Here's an example:

Pre-listening: First, we ask students to activate schemata to help predict content of a listening passage. Then we provide a reason for listening. We can provide these through pre-listening tasks. One pre-listening task uses visuals: students are shown pictures, maps, charts, or graphs that activate schemata and help them guess the content of the listening task. For instance, we can show the students a picture of a runner holding her knee; students can then discuss what theme they think the listening task will be or what they think will happen in the listening passage. Students can also be given a number of pictures and asked if they can make up a story about them.

While listening: The next step is while listening: students listen and try to understand. One excellent option for audio and accompanying scripts is the radio program *All Things Considered* on National Public Radio (https://www.npr.org/programs/all-things-considered/). The excerpts are short; most run for 3–4 minutes and include scripts. Students can listen for the gist or specific information chosen by the teacher, use words in a word bank, or employ any of a number of listening discrimination tasks. One listening example that pairs well with a picture of a runner's injured knee is the *All Things Considered* story "Exercise Studies Find Good News For The Knees" (https://www.npr.org/templates/story/story.php?storyId=112556135).

Post-listening: Post-listening activities help listeners integrate new knowledge into their existing knowledge base. Teachers can promote understanding through a variety of post-listening activities. For instance, teachers can check understanding by asking students to summarize what they've heard. Additionally, students can be asked to write a short essay based on what they've heard. Another effective technique concerns quizzing in which students test their classmates by preparing questions—either multiple choice, short answer, or true/false—that another student will have to answer.

While the vocabulary in the NPR passage above may be at an intermediate (or above) level, the program can still be used with lower-level learners. Teachers would have to provide scaffolding in the way of vocabulary lists and discussions of the topic in more detail. Of course, the post-listening tasks outlined above involve more skills than just listening. Now we consider other types of listening activities/assessments.

Along with Brown and Abeywickrama's (2019) four types of listening performance (intensive, responsive, selective, and extensive), any time we look to assess our students' listening proficiency, or any proficiency for that matter, we should include activities that move from *controlled* to *guided* (semi-controlled) to *free* activities, which can easily provide a framework for lessons/assessment activities.

Controlled activities generally appear at the beginning of the lesson, followed by guided and then free. As the lesson progresses, each type of activity allows increased amounts of creativity, personal relevance, and experimentation with language.

Controlled practice is a stage in a lesson where learners practice new language in a limited form.

- Teacher knows the answer
- There is only one answer

A Controlled Listening Activity

This activity was developed by Alaa Bader (2019a). The teacher directs students as follows:

Listen carefully to each word pronounced then highlight the word. When you highlight words in a line either vertically, horizontally, or diagonally, shout BINGO and win a prize.

Levels: WIDA (Emerging [Level 2], Developing [Level 3]), CEFR (A1, A2), and ACTFL (Novice Low, Novice Mid).

Assessment: The activity is listening discrimination, is an example of intensive listening, and is considered controlled practice. This particular exercise is excellent for Arabic speakers who experience difficulty discriminating between the [p] and [b] sounds in English. Bingo cards can be created to target other sounds based on student needs/L1s. This activity can be tailored to any age group from kindergarten to university. Scoring in the case of Bingo might not be simple since getting Bingo does not necessarily indicate that the winner is listening at a level that other students are not. Instead, Bingo might be used as a fun warm-up for more easily quantified activities. Bingo introduces fun into the classroom, increasing listening ability since there is a repetition of vocabulary

FIGURE 5.1
Bingo Activity

pray	peach	buy	ban	pull
bee	tap	bear	pea	bray
pear	beach	BINGO	bay	bull
pressed	Paul	cup	ball	breast
pan	tap	pay	cub	pie

words. Teachers can tie this activity to more scorable activities. Other possibilities include prefacing this activity with a word list, asking students to define those words and write sentences in pairs, learning their pronunciation (although the teacher's pronunciation of the words is a powerful learning tool).

Other controlled activity examples:

- Vocabulary flashcards
- Crossword puzzles (for other skills, such as reading)
- Fill-in-the-blank listening worksheets
- Sentence unscrambles
- Collaborative dialogue reading (listening to peer)

A Guided Listening Example

This activity was developed by Lakmini Siriwardana (2019a). Listen to the dialogue once through. Then listen again and indicate whether the highlighted lines show *agreement* or *disagreement* by writing A or D in parenthesis. Next, in the space provided, write another phrase that indicates either agreement or disagreement.

A: I was thinking of holding the company retreat in the mountains.
B: I agree, I think that would be perfect! (   )

My new sentence:

____

A: We could plan it for some time in January.
B: That might be a little too cold for some people. (   )

My new sentence:

____

B: What about April? April has good weather that isn't too cold or too hot.
A: Yes, that would work out better. (   )

My new sentence:

____

B: You know, maybe we could take a survey to see how April works for everyone.
A: Or we could set up a Moodle. ( )

My new sentence:

____

Now check your understanding of the conversation by briefly answering the following questions:

1. Where is the company retreat going to happen?

   ____

2. Why is April a good time to hold the retreat?

   ____

3. Why are they going to take a survey?

   ____

Levels: WIDA (Developing [Level 3], Expanding [Level 4]), CEFR (Independent B1, B2), and ACTFL (Intermediate High, Advanced Low). Again, interaction with language is critical for all levels of learners, and adaptation can benefit many levels.

Assessment: Guided (semi-controlled) activities increase freedom, which maintains interest and is a challenge. There is more than one answer, but possibilities might still be limited. Even with this freedom, students are still somewhat limited and can practice new language until it is familiar and they are more confident. This activity fits into the definition of a responsive activity. This activity can be scored in several ways: the most practical way would be to assess the "check your understanding" answers by awarding points for these more concrete answers; additionally, the new sentences indicating agreement or disagreement can be checked for content and grammar, extending the skills assessed.

Other guided activity examples:

- Brainstorming activities
- Short Q & A activities

- Storytelling based on a picture or series of pictures
- Adding to a pre-written dialogue

Controlled and guided activities should offer enough practice to allow the next level—free activities—to be conducted successfully. Also, students can adjust and work within their personal comfort levels, thereby improving student interest. Free activities come last in a lesson; students have complete freedom in the language they produce. Free activities give students the opportunity to personalize the language, experiment, and incorporate previously learned vocabulary, grammar, and other points.

A Free Listening Example

How good is your memory? (Alaa Bader, 2019b)
Warn students that they will be given a group quiz later in the activity.
One student comes to the front of the class. The rest of the class asks questions such as:
What did you have for breakfast?
What is your favorite movie?
What music do you like?
What is your home country?
What is your favorite vacation spot?
What would you like to be when you graduate?
Can you sing (whistle, run, etc.)?

As students quiz each other, the teacher should note some of the answers. Allow half of the students to be interviewed. Then divide students into teams (two to three students per team) and ask them questions such as:

What did Ahmed eat for lunch?
Where did Alaa vacation last summer?
Who wants to be an attorney?

Students should discuss answers quietly in their group and then write the answer. This discussion can lead to learning of new vocabulary, especially if the teacher encourages students at a lower proficiency levels to ask questions and arms those students with the language to do so; examples include language chunks such as "How do you say...", "What does ______ mean?", and things of that nature.

Levels: WIDA (Expanding [Level 4], Bridging [Level 5], Reaching [Level 6]), CEFR (Independent B2, Proficient C1), and ACTFL (Advanced Low, Intermediate High).

Assessment: Again, interaction with language is critical for all levels of learners, and adaptation can benefit many levels; however, in this exercise, more advanced students can set the pace for less proficient students, so the interaction serves as a self-assessment for lower-level students in particular as they are made aware of what they can be capable of. Scoring is simple—the team with the most correct answers gets a prize. In this free activity—which also can be categorized as selective, that is, the student must listen to a longer discourse and scan for information—a weaker student might stick closer to the language targeted in the lesson while a stronger student might use new vocabulary he learned on his own. Both students are working to their potential, feeling challenged and engaged, and building fluency and accuracy. Through the specific order of controlled to guided to free, students can work to their full potential.

Listening Activities for Assessment

Team Refugee

The listening stimuli can be anything to which the student listens. As we mentioned above, *All Things Considered* on NPR is an excellent resource. The short 3–4 minute excerpts come with scripts and provide students with listening opportunities, including listening for the gist, listening for specific information chosen by that teacher, using words in a word bank, or engaging with any of a number of listening discrimination tasks.

Here's an example using an NPR story about an Olympic team made up of refugees:

Introduction of activity: Did you know that a team made up of *refugees* will take part in the 2016 Summer Olympics in Rio de Janeiro, Brazil?

Introduce the discussion questions to think about before watching the video. Of course, the teacher should pre-watch the video and have the answers readily available but should ask students to try to answer these questions as they watch the video rather than give them the answers. This promotes active listening.

- ❑ How many people are on the refugee team?
- ❑ What are a few of the countries that members of the refugee team come from?
- ❑ What are the criteria for being on the team?

Watch: Let's watch the video!
http://www.npr.org/sections/parallels/2016/06/03/480628401/for-the-first-time-a-team-of-refugees-will-compete-at-the-olympics

Read: Now, divide students into groups and take turns reading the script, which is exactly what they've just heard on the video. As they're listening, students should circle any words they aren't sure of. Here's a list of words and phrases that might be new to them and should be glossed on the actual script or provided to students as an additional handout:

- ❑ unusual: adjective—not common or ordinary
- ❑ squad: noun—a sports team or a group of players from which a team is selected
- ❑ made the cut: phrasal verb—successful in making a team or group
- ❑ agile: adjective—quick and well-coordinated in movement
- ❑ relentless: adjective—severe, strict, or harsh
- ❑ perished: verb—died or destroyed by violence

Levels: WIDA (Expanding [Level 4], Bridging [Level 5], Reaching [Level 6]), CEFR (Independent B2, Proficient C1), and ACTFL (Advanced Low, Intermediate High, Intermediate Mid).

Assessment: Teachers can extend this activity/assessment into an integrated skills task by adding Internet searches in which students search for team members for their fantasy Olympic team and by adding a presentation and a writing component.

Teachers can ask students to focus on specific information from the recording. When using the activity above with a group of high school students who were recent arrivals from Dadaab Refugee Camp in Kenya, the teacher asked students to look for specific vocabulary words that are present in the recording and defined for the students on the handout (see list above). Because these particular students were mostly students with limited or interrupted formal education (SLIFE), the teacher provided a great deal of scaffolding in conjunction with individual tutoring and help from prospective TEFL teachers in the class. A listening quiz can be fashioned using multiple choice, true/false, and completion tasks after students have listened to the recording a prescribed number of times. This allows for ease in grading, a matter of practicality for busy teachers.

FIGURE 5.2
Sound Bingo Activity

cat	ball	bow	deed	die
hit	lap	bad	hip	cab
ban	tall	BINGO	pie	lie
mean	leap	fed	peep	bean
need	lab	tie	shed	pow

Sound Bingo

Sound Bingo can be a fun activity for students, and it is also an assessment of their ability to discriminate between sounds either initially, medially, or finally. In Sound Bingo, students listen to recorded sounds and mark their cards. The sounds can be downloaded from the Internet, the teacher can record her own voice, or the teacher can read the words aloud at the time of the assessment. It can be fast-paced, fun, and great for those competitive students in our classrooms. It not only allows teachers to assess students' listening discrimination, but it also raises student awareness of sounds and can be used repetitively to deepen perception of sounds in English. The L1 makeup of your classroom can help determine the selection of sounds for Bingo.

Levels: WIDA (Entering [Level 1] and Emerging [Level 2), CEFR (A1, A2), and ACTFL (Novice Mid, Novice High).

Assessment: No rubric is needed. Of course, cards can be tailored to specific vocabulary being studied at the time. Scoring can be accomplished on a simple point system, depending on the words present on their cards, how many are read by the teacher, and how many correct selections students make. This activity can be tailored for any age, grade, and proficiency level.

Match the Minimal Pair

Another activity that helps students discriminate between two sounds is Match the Minimal Pair. The teacher shows a picture of an item and then pronounces a minimal pair such as park and bark or fan and van. Students have a worksheet and mark the appropriate picture.

FIGURE 5.3
Minimal Pair Activity

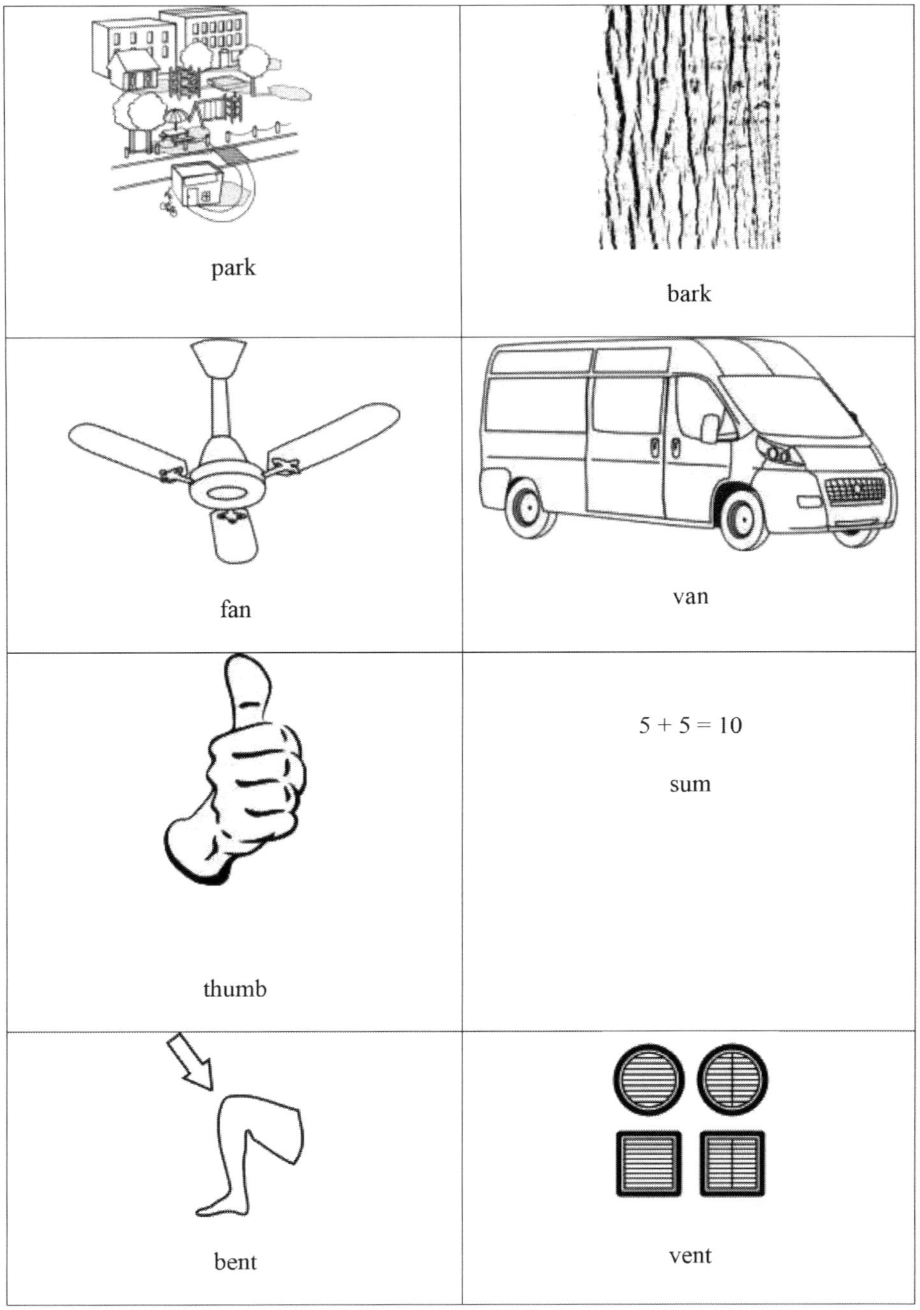

Images from https://publicdomainvectors.org/

Levels: WIDA (Entering [Level 1] and Emerging [Level 2), CEFR (A1, A2), and ACTFL (Novice Mid, Novice High).

Assessment: These are easy to grade as they have only one possible correct answer. The exercise also provides immediate and concrete positive washback. Showing the picture and pronouncing the correct word that goes with the picture can sharpen student's listening skills as well as raise awareness of sounds. Again, this activity can be tailored for any age, grade, and proficiency level.

WANTED

Many activities can be done by students in pairs. For example, in an activity called WANTED, students are given character cards that each include a description of a person. The teacher explains the purpose of the character cards—to give information about a WANTED character. The teacher asks one of the students in the pair to read the first character card.

Here's an example of a character card:

- He has a small round head.
- He has one big eye and one small eye.
- He has short spiked green hair.
- He has big blue lips.
- He has a small round red nose.
- He has a long, pointed chin.
- He has big hairy ears.
- He has a thin black mustache.

The student reads each sentence slowly. After each sentence description, the other student draws what is heard. This process is repeated after all of the descriptions on the card are read and the character is drawn.

Levels: WIDA (Emerging [Level 2] and Developing [Level 3), CEFR (A2, B1), and ACTFL (Intermediate Low, Intermediate Mid). To make this accessible to lower levels, we could simplify this assignment by providing fewer descriptions and/or by adding pictures that students can point to rather than draw.

Assessment: It's easy to see that no scoring guide or rubric is necessary as one can quickly tell if the student understood by looking at the resultant drawing.

Warm-Up Activities

One excellent warm-up activity is very simple and fun. It's called the "ask, answer, add" model of small talk. Someone asks a question (the teacher can start first), and student #1 answers it and adds some extra information before asking student #2 a question based on the first question and the additional information.

An example:

Teacher: What was the most fun activity that you did this weekend?

Student #1: The most fun activity was a canoeing trip Saturday afternoon with my friend. Unfortunately, near the end of the two hours, we got caught in a terrible thunderstorm. Have you ever been caught in a thunderstorm?

Student #2: I have never been caught in a thunderstorm, but just last week the elevator at my job stopped with me in it. It took an hour to be rescued.

Another warm-up activity is dictation, which when used properly is powerful. Dictation provides students with a clear model of pronunciation and allows them to practice their listening (and writing) skills. Initially, dictation might feel a bit cumbersome, but it is a very student-centered strategy that can identify listening issues as well as student issues in vocabulary, grammar, and pronunciation. Dictation is also an effective teaching strategy for recycling vocabulary items or grammar structures. It has many other benefits, as well:

- Dictation is an effective teaching strategy for introducing new language: students can benefit from predicting spelling patterns. If the sound/spelling relationship is weak, dictating a word, letting students attempt to spell it, and then giving them the correct form may prove to be an effective strategy for retention.
- Dictation helps students develop their note-taking ability.
- Although dictation is primarily a listening task, it can also be viewed as an integrated skills task in which students can practice listening, writing, speaking, and even reading.

Why Is Reading Important?

Although this may seem an obvious and even foolish question, it is essential to consider the importance of reading. While our students may conceive of reading primarily in terms of obtaining information about a topic, reading provides mental stimulation, increases knowledge, expands vocabulary, and aids in memory improvement. It also helps us to strengthen analytical thinking skills, makes us more empathetic, improves focus and concentration, and promotes better writing skills.

As we mentioned at the beginning of this chapter, the skills of listening and reading were once thought to be passive activities. Of course, this notion has been proven false. Readers engage actively with text all the time. Witness the last novel you read that moved you to tears or struck horror in your heart or ensnared you with beautiful language. It is most important to remember this active engagement when assessing our students' reading skills. That is, reading is a process that negotiates the meaning between the text and its reader. Key to the assessment of reading, as with the other skills, is the incorporation of performance-based assessment along with assessing the more discreet skills associated with reading.

In order for teachers to be able to teach and thus assess reading—the two are interwoven—they must understand the five "essential elements of reading instruction: phonemic awareness, phonics, fluency, vocabulary, and comprehension" (Irujo, 2007, p. 1). We can also use these essential elements as a framework for reading assessment, along with the notion of controlled, guided, and free assessment. Before we define these five elements, however, let's look at some important concepts in reading and what we can learn from them for developing assessment activities.

These important concepts are (1) **reading as a cognitive process**, which focuses on production and understanding of linguistic communication; (2) **bottom-up processing**, which includes the fundamental mastery of separate letters, words, and phrases; (3) **top-down processing**, in which readers use their knowledge of genre to predict what will be in the text. For example, if a reader chooses a mystery novel, she expects a puzzle or suspense element and then a logical solution; (4) **interactive processes,** in which there is recognition of simultaneous interaction of top-down and bottom-up processing while reading; (5) **schemata or background information and cultural experience processing,** which the reader brings to the act of reading; (6) **genre knowledge,** which encompasses awareness of the discourse conventions of a text. Each text has "its own set of governing rules and conventions" (Brown & Abeywickrama, 2019, p. 196).

Teachers' understanding of these six concepts is crucial for the assessment of reading. Some of the concepts provide a blueprint for the kind of tasks that can be designed and the kinds of knowledge to be tested. The concepts seem to build on one another and although they cannot easily translate into assessment tasks, they do guide us since they show us what is involved when a person reads and what a reader needs to know and be able to do when reading. Of course, it is very difficult to assess process as it is difficult to observe.

As mentioned earlier, the five essential elements of reading instruction include "phonemic awareness, phonics, fluency, vocabulary, and comprehension" (Irujo, n.d., para. 2). Again, we can also use these elements as a framework for reading assessment, along with the notion of controlled, guided, and free assessment. Of course, instruction needs to be adjusted to meet the needs of ELs. Since Irujo (2007) found current research lacking in its definitiveness of the advantages of teaching the five essential elements of reading instruction to ELs (ELs largely benefit from these only when their language skills are on or nearly on par with that of native speakers), she listed the following recommendations when teaching and assessing reading to ELs, initially proposed by the National Literacy Panel on Language Minority and Youth:

- Provide additional work on English phonemes that are not present in the students' native language.
- If students are literate in their native language, focus on differences between that language and English, with less attention given to elements that will transfer.
- Provide extra practice in reading words, sentences, and stories.
- Use cognate words in the native language as synonyms when teaching vocabulary.
- Identify and clarify difficult words and passages.
- Consolidate knowledge of the text through the use of summaries.
- Find appropriate ways to use the native language.

Certainly, as Arujo is quick to remind us, these strategies are not all that must go into a reading program for ELs. She cites the dearth of research but also advances the need to look to what "experienced, reflective teachers of ELs (and observers of those teachers) consider best practices" (p. 2). She recommends looking to the findings of the National Literacy Panel and drawing on information from reliable sources. She claims that the five essential reading elements—phonemic awareness, phonics, fluency, vocabulary, and comprehension—might not be enough for ELs to achieve proficiency in reading for the following reasons. For example, when we consider phonemic awareness, ELs might not be able to distinguish sounds if they do not have enough experience with English. They must receive explicit instruction in the sounds, particularly those sounds that are not part of their L1. If they have developed phonemic awareness in their L1, it is transferrable to English, so it need not be taught. The teacher will need to be able to judge the students' phonemic awareness.

As far as phonics is concerned, ELs often have difficulty discriminating between similar sounds because the English language does not have a regular system of correspondence between letters and sounds.

As Grabe and Stoller (2011) explain, reading is a complex activity that is shaped by the purpose for reading, a number of processes required for fluent reading, different components of reading, and various models of reading from the research perspective: "Reading for general comprehension, when accomplished by a skilled fluent reader, requires very rapid and automatic processing of words, strong skills in forming a general meaning representation of main ideas, and efficient coordination of many processes under very limited time constraints" (p. 8). Of particular relevance for working with L2 learners is perhaps a distinction between lower-level processes (e.g., lexical access and syntactic parsing) and higher-level processes (interpretative skills and use of background knowledge and inferencing). L1 readers typically learn how to read after four to five years of learning the language, so already have 5,000 to 7,000 words when they begin learning reading, a huge advantage over an L2 learner who often learns to read the language as they are learning it. While higher-level reading skills in the L1 can be useful, the Language Threshold Hypothesis, well supported by recent research, asserts that L2 readers need to have a certain amount of linguistic knowledge in the L2 before they can make use of their L1 reading abilities while reading in the L2 (Grabe & Stoller, 2011). In short, if L2 readers are overwhelmed by figuring out the linguistic aspects of the text they are reading, then they have limited cognitive space left for activating higher-order skills. Grabe and Stoller (2011) recommend that "one of the best ways to move beyond heavy L1 interference in L2 reading is to be sure that students are not always reading texts that are too difficult for them; students should be given sufficient opportunities to read texts that are easy to read and enjoyable" (p. 45).

Types of Reading

Although Brown and Abeywickrama (2019) name five types of performance in the skills of speaking and listening, their organization of reading performances in assessment contexts are "derived from the multiplicity of types of texts" (p. 199); they list three genres: academic reading (e.g., textbooks, essays, papers, test directives), job-related reading (e.g., emails, memos, reports, applications), and personal reading (newspapers, schedules, novels, recipes), and four types of reading: perceptive, selective, interactive, and extensive.

Perceptive reading involves "attending to the *components* of larger stretches of discourse: letters, words, punctuation" (p. 199) through bottom-up processing. **Selective** reading involves both bottom-up and top-down processing through such activities as picture-cued, matching, and multiple-choice items. **Interactive** reading includes reading "stretches of language of several paragraphs to one page" (p. 200); interaction with text is important—the reader brings certain knowledge to the text and intake is the product; typically, genres such as anecdotes, descriptions, and short narratives lend themselves to this type of reading. Finally, **extensive** reading involves longer stretches of discourse; assessment "taps into reader's global understanding of the test" (p. 200) and can be accomplished by using items such as multiple choice, matching, and pointing, all of which "capitalize on the uniqueness of the ability to assess extensive reading independently of the other three skills" (p. 201).

Reading Assessment Standards

As with listening, we will begin with WIDA's (2020) Can Do statements, which can serve as a valuable piece in teachers' judgment and can aid in curriculum planning (https://wida.wisc.edu). Table 5.3 clarifies criteria, illustrating what students are expected to be able to do in reading at Level 3 (Developing) and Level 6 (Reaching). Consider the differences between these two levels before continuing your reading.

Consider the processing recounts skill: while developing students are expected to be able to identify some of the main ideas in a text, reaching students are expected to have a more nuanced understanding, such as being able to evaluate the details used to develop key plot elements. In regard to processing arguments, one example of the differences in levels lies in simply identifying opposing points of view (by Developing students) compared to identifying differences between facts and speculation in texts (by Reaching students).

TABLE 5.3
WIDA Key Uses Reading Example

	Process Recounts by	Process explanations by	Process arguments by
Level 3 Developing	▪ Identifying topic sentences, main ideas, and details in paragraphs ▪ Connecting people to actions based on oral descriptions with details	▪ Illustrating relationships between main ideas and details in paragraphs ▪ Sequencing steps or events to describe processes (e.g., solving math problems)	▪ Identifying claims and the reasons for each claim ▪ Identifying opposing points of view
Level 6 Reaching	▪ Identifying a central idea of a text and how it is conveyed through particular details ▪ summarizing text absent personal opinions or judgments ▪ Evaluating how a central event is introduced, illustrated, and elaborated in text (e.g., through examples or anecdotes)	▪ Comparing and contrasting information from experiments, simulations, videos, or multimedia sources with that of text on the same topics ▪ Identifying factors that contribute to phenomena in explanations	▪ Identifying specific evidence to support analyses of content area text Distinguishing among facts, reasoned judgment, and speculation in text

Elsewhere, the ACTFL Proficiency Guidelines (2012) label reading an interpretive skill and provide descriptors for the major levels of proficiency referenced above. For example, "At the [ACTFL] Intermediate Low sublevel, readers are able to understand some information from the simplest connected texts dealing with a limited number of personal and social needs, although there may be frequent misunderstandings. Readers at this level will be challenged to derive meaning from connected texts of any length" (ACTFL, 2012, p. 23). If teachers have students at this level, they can inspect the abilities laid forth in Intermediate Mid (e.g., "readers are able to understand short, non-complex texts that convey basic information") to help them create assignments and assessments that will move students from one sublevel to the next.

Types of Reading Activities

A Controlled Reading Activity

The three passages in Figure 5.4 are similar in structure but are different in various ways. Read them carefully and then identify five ways each one is different from the other. Write words or phrases—complete sentences are not necessary.

Levels: WIDA (Entering [Level 1] and Emerging [Level 2), CEFR (A1, A2), and ACTFL (Novice Mid, Novice High).

Assessment: Instead of simply collecting this informal assignment, many teachers may start by asking students to compare their answers with a partner and then share possible answers with the class. If we were to assess this for a grade, then we would have up to 15 points available for the assignment and deduct a point for each answer that is not correct. Note how we specified that complete sentences are not necessary since this is focused primarily on reading and not writing. It's important to note that this kind of assignment/assessment can be tailored for any level and any age of English learner, but certainly, since it is a test of reading, it would not be best for those who cannot read, no matter what level. For example, in kindergarten, the activity might become more of a listening activity, using less dense text, level-appropriate vocabulary, and level-appropriate concepts.

FIGURE 5.4
Controlled Reading Activity

Over the weekend, Juan went camping with his sister in a national park. They went swimming in a lake and hiking in the woods and had a camp fire at night. The weather was perfect with clear, sunny days and highs around 80 degrees Fahrenheit.	Last week, Lisa went to New York with her friend. They went to Central Park, the Statue of Liberty, and a Broadway show. The weather was okay, cloudy and cool with highs around 50 degrees Fahrenheit.	Last year, Wei went to Disney World with her family. They went to the Magic Kingdom the first day, went on several rides, including Space Mountain and It's a Small World, and ate in the Beauty and the Beast restaurant. The weather hot and humid with highs around 90 degrees Fahrenheit.
1. 2. 3. 4. 5.	1. 2. 3. 4. 5.	1. 2. 3. 4. 5.

A Guided Reading Activity

Now read this extended version of one of the passages that appear in the activity above and answer the questions that follow.

Over the weekend, Juan went camping with his sister in a national park. When they arrived, they set their tent up in a flat spot in site number 75 in the Pine Creek Campground. They inflated their air mattresses and unrolled their sleeping bags. Everyday, they went hiking in the woods in the morning, swimming in the lake in the afternoon, and then read in the shade for several hours before dark. At night, they made dinner over a camp stove and then sat around the camp fire telling ghost stories. The weather was perfect with clear, sunny days and highs around 80 degrees Fahrenheit and lows around 50 degrees.

Where did they put their tent?
What did they do in the afternoon?
How did they cook their dinner?
What did they do around the camp fire?

You will be given credit for responses that supply a correct answer based on the reading, not based on your spelling or grammatical accuracy.

Levels: WIDA (Emerging [Level 2] and Developing [Level 3), CEFR (A2, B1), and ACTFL (Intermediate Low, Intermediate Mid). To make this accessible to lower levels, we could simplify the assignment by adding illustrations and/or by having multiple choice options for the questions after the text.

Assessment: Simple questions like this could be graded in a point/no point fashion, although it is good to let students know how they will be evaluated. For instance, since this activity focuses on reading comprehension, we would likely grade based on whether or not their answers mirror what's in the text. We would also make it clear that they aren't being graded on spelling or grammatical accuracy, something we would be more likely to prioritize if this was a writing assessment. However, even if an aspect isn't being graded it may be useful to provide feedback on the writing to the students. Or, if you are teaching skills in a more integrated fashion, then you might evaluate on multiple aspects.

A Free Reading Activity

Read the first chapter of [include a book appropriate to reading level] and pick out a section of two to three paragraphs that you find particularly interesting. Read through it, looking up and writing down any words you didn't know in your vocabulary journal. Then, write 3–4 sentences that describe this passage and why you liked it.

Levels: WIDA (Bridging [Level 5] and Reaching [Level 6]), CEFR (B1, B2, C1), and ACTFL (Intermediate High, Advanced Low). The level appropriateness of this activity would vary significantly based on the complexity of the text chosen.

Assessment: Compared to the restricted and guided examples, this example gives students the most freedom to select their reading passage, making this more on the free end of the spectrum than the others. Also, the response aspect (in this case writing, but it could be speaking as well) is more open-ended. There is not a clearly defined answer to this task so it requires a more complicated assessment approach than the others. Here's a simple rubric that we might use:

Student accurately understood and retold the important aspects of the passage: /5

Student was able to explain why they found the passage interesting: /5

Total: /10

Again, while writing is an important part of this assignment, this rubric downplays focusing on grammatical accuracy or the need to avoid repeating some of the words in the original text, since our assessment concern here is primarily focused on reading comprehension and personal response to the text rather than abilities as a writer.

Note: If you are having trouble finding level-appropriate readings for your students, you may consider looking at graded reader options, which have selections and adaptations of texts appropriate for particular levels. Some options include:

- Helbing Readers: https://www.helblinglanguages.com/int/en/readers
- Oxford Graded Readers: https://elt.oup.com/cat/subjects/graded_reading/?cc=global&selLanguage=en&mode=hub
- Cambridge Graded Readers: http://www.cambridge.org/gb/cambridgeenglish/catalog/readers
- Penguin Readers: https://www.penguinreaders.co.uk/

Reading Activities for Assessment

Reading Aloud

Reading aloud is a common classroom activity at all different levels. For beginner learners, it is useful in assessing their ability to decode texts to help ensure they are able to recognize the words in the passage. This clearly overlaps with speaking, and many teachers choose to integrate the two, using reading to help improve students' speaking and pronunciation. However, if we are primarily focused on reading, the assessment should focus on students' ability to produce a comprehensible approximation of the words in question—and not necessarily a fully accurate pronunciation—so we know they recognize the words. A caveat: make sure students have been able to practice their read-aloud portion of the text as reading aloud comes with its share of affective notions, including student shyness, fear of mispronouncing words, and other fears.

Begin by choosing an age- and level-appropriate text for the student to read. In order to get the most accurate picture of their abilities, the text should be unfamiliar to them.

Then, have the student read the text to you and follow along with a matching text of your own. Develop a system to track their reading errors as you follow along—remember that this should not assess their pronunciation but rather their ability to recognize particular words.

Levels: WIDA (Entering [Level 1]), CEFR (A1), and ACTFL (Novice Low, Novice Mid). Students at advanced levels may benefit from pronunciation practice through reading more complex words; however, that is not the focus of this activity.

Assessment:

TABLE 5.4
Reading Aloud Rubric

Action	Assessment Mark
Read correctly	Add check mark above word
Missed word	Add X above word
Added word	Add ^ and added word
Unable to read word	Add U above word
Repeated word	Add R above repeated word

As one can imagine, the assessment will go relatively quickly, so it is important to be familiar with whatever system you plan to use before starting the assessment. You may decide to record the session to ensure accuracy, although it is important to realistically recognize whether or not you'll have time to go back and check recordings.

Close Pairs

Write definitions for the following words:

FIGURE 5.5
Close Pairs Activity

Words	Word 1 Definition	Word 2 Definition
pill/pull		
desk/deck		
who/how		
gem/gym		
led/let		
crew/crow		

Levels: Students at the following levels in the three sets of standards outlined earlier might benefit most from this exercise: WIDA (Entering [Level 1] and Emerging [Level 2]), CEFR (A1), and ACTFL (Novice Low, Novice Mid).
Assessment: This is a relatively common activity for beginning learners to help distinguish between words that look alike and may be pronounced similarly. An easy way to assess this would be to give a point for a correct definition, up to 12 points for this activity.

A variation of this activity would be to have these as options in a cloze activity, such as the following example:

Circle the correct word:

She went to the *gem / gym* to play basketball.
She *led / let* the group during the tour.

Multiple Choice

Multiple choice questions are a common way to assess students' reading comprehension and can be a useful way to focus on reading skills as they don't require students to produce written or spoken language. The following example is taken from the Readworks.org website, a free website with tons of reading resources—sites like this abound on the Internet.

Read the passage and answer the following questions:

Devon Miller hoisted the backpack onto his back.

"Did you pack your water bottle?" his dad asked.

Devon nodded. "Yes."

"How about the sandwiches? And the trail map?" Mr. Miller asked.

"I've got everything, Dad," Devon said. "Come on. Let's hit the trail!"

"Okay," Mr. Miller said. He sounded a little nervous. He locked the doors of the car. "Let's go."

Devon couldn't wait to start the hike. He had been waiting all winter to go. Now spring had finally come, and all of the snow had melted on the trails. Devon was ready for a good, long hike. Devon's dad had never been hiking before. His mom usually took him. But she had to work today, and Devon really wanted to go. He had begged and begged until his dad agreed.

"Where do we start?" his dad asked.

"See that tree with the yellow paint mark?" Devon asked, pointing. "That's the start of the trail. We just follow the trail marks. The trail goes in a big circle. We'll end up back here in a few hours."

Mr. Miller tried to smile. "Sounds like fun!"

Devon and his dad began their hike. It was a beautiful day. The weather was cool, but not too cold. Small green plants were peeking up through the dirt. Birds chirped all around them, busy building nests.

They walked and walked. Then they stopped and ate their sandwiches next to a bubbling stream.

Mr. Miller seemed a lot more relaxed. "This is actually fun," he said. "I'll go hiking with you again anytime."

They strapped on their backpacks. They started to walk back to the trail. They stopped. None of the trees had yellow marks on them.

Devon ran up and down the trail. He didn't see any trail marks anywhere. "Uh, Dad," he said. "I think we're lost!"

Questions

1. Which of the following is an example of the climax (most intense/exciting part) in the passage?
   A. They made sure they had water, their map, and sandwiches.
   B. Devon could not find any trail marks.
   C. They got in the car and drove to the trail.
   D. They ate lunch by the stream.
2. In the sentence, "he sounded a little nervous," *he* refers to
   A. Devon's dad.
   B. Devon's grandfather.
   C. Devon's friend.
   D. Devon
3. Devon's dad seems
   A. mad about having to go hiking.
   B. scared something will happen to their car.
   C. worried about Mrs. Miller.
   D. to feel uncomfortable in the woods.
4. The problem in this passage is
   A. Devon's dad was scared to go hiking.
   B. Devon's dad did not want to go hiking.
   C. Devon and his dad got lost.
   D. Devon lost their trail map.

Levels: Students at the following levels in the three sets of standards outlined earlier might benefit most from this exercise: WIDA (Emerging [Level 2] and Developing [Level 3]), CEFR (A2, B1), and ACTFL (Intermediate Mid, Intermediate High). To make this accessible to lower levels, we could choose a simpler text and write simpler questions.

Assessment: Grading multiple choice questions is the easy part—simply give a point for each correct answer. However, as we learned in Chapter 4, developing multiple choice questions can be tricky as there are a lot of aspects to consider. For instance, we learned that it's important to avoid opinion-based or trick items—all the options above seem to avoid these as the answers can be easily obtained from the text. If we look closer, however, we can identify potential problems. For instance, a student might be tempted to answer "A" in question 4 as Devon's dad was scared and that was, in fact, a problem—adding "main" before "problem" might help address this issue. Another recommendation we saw in Chapter 4 was to keep vocabulary simple for the students—if the questions have unnecessarily complex words, then it is important to define them for students so they don't get confused. For instance, if students in your class may not know what a climax is yet, it is important to clarify the term as we did.

Open- and Close-Ended Questions

A popular distinction between different types of reading questions is the idea of thin and thick questions. Thin questions are right there in the text and are pretty easy and obvious to answer. Close-ended questions would arguably fit in the thin category. Close-ended questions involve writing in an answer, although the answer options may be more restricted, like they are in multiple choice questions. For instance, consider an example using the classic text *Swiss Family Robinson*.

We are introduced to several characters in the early chapters of *Swiss Family Robinson*: Father, Mother, Francis, Fritz, Ernest, and Jack. As you read the preface and first three chapters, pay attention to these different characters and their personalities and actions. Each of the sentences below describes one of the characters. Write the name of the character next to each description.

This character was a clergyman. ______________
This character was grabbed by a lobster. ______________
This character narrated the story. ______________
This character disappeared and made the others worried. ______________
This character recovered a box of fishing hooks from the boat. ______________
This character was described as "selfish and indolent." ______________

Levels: Students at the following levels in the three sets of standards outlined earlier might benefit most from this exercise: WIDA (Expanding [Level 4] and Reaching [Level 5]), CEFR (B1, B2, C1), and ACTFL (Intermediate High, Advanced

Low). The difficulty of this activity varies significantly based on the complexity of the text chosen—since it is an older book, *Swiss Family Robinson* has some obscure vocabulary and sentence structures that can make it challenging to follow.

Assessment: This would be a pretty straightforward assessment as each question only has one correct answer—if we think about this assessment in terms of Bloom's taxonomy described in Chapter 3, we are still very low, at the Understanding level. We would give students a point if they included the correct name for a total of 6 points. If you want to make the assignment easier, you might let students know they should only use each answer once, as that will narrow their options as they progress through the questions.

On the other hand, open-ended questions require a phrase, sentence, or multiple sentences to answer and don't necessarily have a clear-cut answer. They likely require more thinking than their close-ended counterparts and possibly involve drawing in information from different parts of a text. In framing an assessment instrument that includes open-ended questions, it is important to let students know what you expect. For instance:

- Do you expect them to answer in complete sentences or will phrases suffice? Do you expect answers to be at least a few sentences? A paragraph?
- Are you going to be evaluating their grammar and mechanics and spelling, or will you be focusing on the creativity of their response or the accuracy of their reading?

Here are some questions focused on another classic text, *The Wonderful Wizard of Oz*.

1. At the beginning of the book, the narrator describes Dorothy's home and the surrounding Kansas landscape in a particular way. Why do you think the narrator describes them in that way?
2. How does the land of Oz compare to Dorothy's home in Kansas? Why do you think she wants to go back to Kansas?
3. Describe the life of the Munchkins.
4. Why do the winged monkeys have to obey the Golden Cap?
5. What are some of the barriers the Wicked Witch of the West puts up to hinder their journey to her castle? Which of these seems the most difficult to overcome and why?

Levels: Students at the following levels in the three sets of standards outlined earlier might benefit most from this exercise: WIDA (Bridging [Level 5] and Reaching [Level 6]), CEFR (B2, C1), and ACTFL (Advanced Low, Advanced Mid). The level appropriateness of this activity would vary significantly based on the complexity of the text chosen and the complexity of the questions. With the possible exception of questions 3 and 4, which are primarily asking for the reader's understanding, most of these questions reach the higher levels of Bloom's taxonomy, asking for some level of analysis and evaluation.

Assessment: Since the questions have multiple components, having a simple point/no point system for each wouldn't work well. Instead, we might have a 1–5 point scale, as included below, to evaluate each question.

1 to 5 point scale:

1: Does not answer the question or reveal any level of comprehension.

2: Answers some parts of the question, although comprehension is limited.

3: Answers most of the question, although some parts of the response may be unclear. Demonstrates comprehension of the text but details may be lacking. Responses to analytical aspects may be missing or unsupported.

4: Clearly answers all parts of the question, demonstrating strong comprehension of the text. Where asked, student provides analysis but analysis may not be fully supported.

5: Clearly and comprehensively answers all parts of the question, demonstrating strong comprehension of the text. Where asked, student provides a logical, well-supported analysis.

We may prefer to reframe this more positively in terms of what students *can do* like we've seen with the WIDA Can Do statements.

1: Student can provide an answer to the question.

2: Student can provide an answer and demonstrate some understanding of the text.

3: Student can fairly clearly answer most of the straightforward aspects of the question.

4: Student can clearly answer all parts of the question and demonstrate a strong comprehension of the text. They can provide some analysis.

5: Student can clearly and comprehensively answer all parts of the question and demonstrate a strong comprehension of the text. They can provide a logical, well-supported analysis.

Activities and Questions

Activities

1. Using the discussions regarding types of listening assessment (intensive, responsive, selective, and extensive) and the flow of assessment (controlled to guided to free), design a listening assessment for your students. Keep in mind their proficiency level, where they might fall on the WIDA, CEFR, and ACTFL scales, and how that assessment can inform your teaching. What do you want to know about what your students can or cannot do?
2. Create a reading assessment using the same criteria as in activity 1. Consider the four types of reading (perceptive, selective, interactive, and extensive), selecting one upon which to focus your assessment.

Discussion Questions

1. The beginning of the chapter has a discussion regarding the integration of the four skills and the difficulty of separating the four skills in teaching and assessing. How might the assessment of listening be separated from speaking? Reading from writing? What steps might be taken to do so?
2. In pairs, discuss three key take-aways from this chapter and how they might influence your listening and reading assessment practices.
3. Above, you were asked to develop a listening assessment and a reading assessment. In pairs, discuss the rationales behind the assessments you created and how they support learning. What are the specific difficulties that students are likely to face in completing the assessment task, and how might a teacher support learning before and after the assessment?

6

Assessing the Productive Skills: Speaking and Writing

The productive skills are speaking and writing; they focus on what output the learner creates rather than their ability to take in new information. As we saw in Chapter 4, however, these two skills are intimately connected with one another and also with reading and listening because we are all situated in social contexts and generally speak and write for an audience beyond ourselves. This is why, as mentioned previously, teacher-scholars such as Hinkel (2006) have strongly advocated for an integrated skills approach. Folse (2006) made this clear in *The Art of Teaching Speaking*: "It is not possible to have a conversation without good listening ability. Without a certain level of listening, a conversation would quickly deteriorate into a series of unconnected questions or statements" (p. 4). As we discuss in Chapter 8, the high-stakes standardized tests our students take are increasingly working from this integrated perspective as well.

As Weissberg (2006) illustrated in *Connecting Speaking & Writing in Second Language Writing Instruction*, a writing classroom based on the latest theories and practices is not a quiet place. With the advent of the shift in applied linguistics and language-teaching that focuses on the functional use of language rather than formalistic approaches and student-focused instruction advocated by writing teachers like Peter Elbow and Donald Murray in the 1960s and 1970s, writing classrooms have become rich in dialogue. These classrooms may involve large group discussions about texts students read, regular rounds of peer feedback on drafts, brainstorming sessions in small groups, debates, and much more. As Weissberg (2006) described it, teachers increasingly "have the option to create within their classrooms a community of writers who, through dialogue, serve each other as tutors, coauthors, sounding boards, and critical readers" (p. 2). This dialogue is "more than a means of livening up the occasional lesson by letting students work together while the teacher enjoys a well-deserved rest" but rather "a general approach to teaching and learning to write in a second language" (p. 4). Literacy scholars have increasingly problematized approaches that see literacy as an autonomous skill, separated from an external social reality—instead, they have argued that literacy needs to always be taught in a social context and with an awareness of the students' goals and communicative needs (Selber, 2004; Street, 1997).

Why Is Speaking Important?

Speaking skills are indispensable for language and literacy development. Although speaking and listening do not present a challenge for some of our students, the mere thought of presenting in front of their peers can be overwhelming to others. This in no way discounts the importance of promoting the teaching of speaking since speaking with adequate pronunciation, fluency, and comprehensibility allows students to convey their wishes in a variety of formal and informal settings. Because oral communication doesn't allow for drafting and revising in the same way that written communication does, students may perceive it as more challenging; however, writing scholars would dispute this notion.

Speaking is often the most desired skill by students although it commonly does not receive sufficient focus in language classrooms, particularly in EL settings, because it can be difficult to focus on speaking skills in large classes. However, it is not impossible. MacDonald & Smith (2010) presented a study conducted in Thailand that focused on teaching speaking to mixed-level learners in very large classes, in some situations with actual physical obstructions in the classroom, such as the room being in an L-shape. Even though the teacher was unable to see all of the students all of the time, speaking activities and assessment still happened through an initiative named Team English. According to the authors, Team English has been successful because it "uses a built-in sports hierarchy, a structure that exists nearly worldwide" (p. 64). Using team colors in sashes, headbands, or placards worn by students and numbers designating proficiency levels, Team English offers a quick way to both heterogeneously and homogeneously group students. Teams are penalized if a member goes off task; further, team formations are more transparent to students, and the buy-in becomes easier as each team is "essentially a small class" (p. 58), promoting cohesiveness. Help to lower-level students is offered by team captains and other members; peer pressure to perform is strong and allows the teacher to be a referee rather than a disciplinarian. Classrooms with upward of 100 students were managed quite successfully with the Team English approach.

Beyond the challenge of teaching speaking in larger classes, another major concern of teachers is classroom support of differing proficiency levels. In this chapter, we will present a series of activities/assessments that can be adapted to different ages, grades, and proficiency levels. We will also consider speaking assessments for a variety of purposes, including placement in intensive English programs, diagnosis, and proficiency. Again, we will use the organizational framework of controlled, guided, and free activities along with the purpose for the assessment, connecting the activities/assessments to standards such as WIDA and CEFR. And as we have asserted many times, we consider every activity to be an assessment; each time a teacher asks a student to do something, it should be for the express purpose of finding out what and how well a student can do and using those findings to guide teaching and learning. That is the most important reason for assessment—assessment for learning in which the first priority is to promote learning

However, this process of assessment can be daunting to teachers unused to the creation and implementation of alternative assessment practices in the classroom, in which students are required to produce language rather than simply react to a stimulus such as a multiple choice item. Lam (2015) problematized the notion of alternative assessment when he cautioned that there may be certain cultural and contextual factors in place that may influence the possibility of adopting alternative assessment practices. That said, whenever possible, especially in speaking, plans should be made to have students use language for communication. Of course, in a speaking class, teachers will also need to give some attention to pronunciation.

Teaching Pronunciation in a Speaking Class

Celce-Murcia, Brinton, and Goodwin (2010) argued that pronunciation should be taught (and assessed) in a speaking class, especially to six groups who need to have a "high level of intelligibility" (p. 8). Those groups are as follows:

1. Teaching assistants
2. Technical and business professionals who work in English-speaking countries
3. International businesspeople and diplomats
4. Refugees wishing to relocate to English-speaking countries
5. English teachers who expect to act as models for their students

6. Tour guides, waiters, hotel personnel, customs agents who use English to communicate with tourists.

It is important to note that the goal is not to achieve "native-like" pronunciation but to be able to communicate clearly and comfortably with intended audiences. Instruction should take a balanced approach that recognizes that an inability "to distinguish suprasegmental features [e.g., stress, intonation]" and "to distinguish sounds that carry a high functional load [e.g., the difference in pronunciation of words like bit and beat]" (p. 11) negatively impacts the oral communication of English learners.

Let us provide an example of a real-life pronunciation story reported to Deborah by a former student who came excitedly to her office one afternoon. It seems that the student's friend had been to Cincinnati and, looking for a parking space, had stopped his car in the middle of the street. A police officer approached and told him to move his car. The student, a native speaker of Arabic, responded, "But officer, I want to *bark." The officer responded, "I don't care if you moo; just move your car!" As many of us know who teach Arabic speakers, Arabic has no [p]; only the [b] sound exists in Arabic. We may know this as language teachers, but police officers likely do not and can respond only to what they hear; therefore, our students need to be made aware of these differences in order to be more comprehensible in the real world.

In order to do so, Celce-Murcia, Brinton, and Goodwin (2010) presented the "Communicative Framework for Teaching Pronunciation" for sequencing activities in pronunciation instruction:

Stage 1: Description and Analysis

The teacher presents a pronunciation feature and the rules of occurrence either inductively or deductively.

Stage 2: Listening Discrimination

The teacher assigns contextualized minimal pair discrimination exercises. In the example below, the speaker reads either sentence a or b, and the listener has to respond with the appropriate rejoinder, for example:

a) He wants to buy my boat.
b) He wants to buy my vote.

Responses:
Will you sell it?
That's against the law!

Stage 3: Controlled Practice

In these activities the learner's attention should be almost completely on forms, limited solely to the explicit focus on language features. Any kind of choral reading can work if the learner's attention is clearly focused on the target feature. Poems, rhymes, dialogues, and dramatic monologues can be used.

Stage 4: Guided Practice

In guided practice the learner's attention is no longer entirely on form. The learner now begins to focus on meaning, grammar, and communication intent as well as on pronunciation. Teachers need to develop a continuum of bridging activities that shift attention gradually to a new cognitive task while the learner attempts to maintain control of the pronunciation target (e.g., memory games).

Stage 5: Communicative Practice

At this stage, activities strike a balance between form and meaning (e.g., debates, role-plays, interviews), but the learner's attention should still be focused on the pronunciation of the target feature.

Celce-Murcia, Brinton, & Goodwin (2010) also provided a list of questions that students can ask themselves about their pronunciation that can be made into a chart of can-do statements (see Table 6.1).

We have included another handy chart in Table 6.2 that describes several domains that are important in pronunciation and speaking in general (ACTFL, 2012).

Teachers should consider these four domains when diagnosing and assessing issues experienced by their students. Note the use of accuracy, extensiveness of vocabulary, and other skills. It is easy to see how this chart might be converted into a rubric for assessing these skills (see Figure 6.1). Of course, the rubric might be best suited for initial proficiency testing and used only by raters who have been trained in the language of the rubric.

TABLE 6.1
Can Do Pronunciation Self-Assessment

	I CAN MOSTLY	I CAN SOMETIMES	I CAN'T DO IT
I notice my issues with pronunciation			
I know that I transfer sounds from my native language			
I hear the difference between target sounds in the L2 and sounds in my L1			
I can produce the difference between target language sounds and L1 sounds			
I can be understood with no problem			
I can produce target language sounds with little effort or concentration			

TABLE 6.2
Pronunciation/Speaking Domains

HOW AND HOW WELL IS THE LANGUAGE LEARNER ABLE TO BE UNDERSTOOD AND TO UNDERSTAND?		
Domain	**What It Answers**	**What It Describes**
Language Control	How accurate is the language learner's language?	Describes the level of control the learner has over certain language features of strategies to produce or understand language
Vocabulary	How extensive and applicable is the language learner's vocabulary?	Describes the parameters of vocabulary used to produce or understand language
Communication Strategies	How does the language learner maintain communication and make meaning?	Describes the strategies used to negotiate meaning, to understand text and messages, and to express oneself
Cultural Awareness	How is the language learner's cultural knowledge reflected in language use?	Describes the cultural products, practices, or perspectives the language learner may employ to communicate more successfully in the cultural setting

FIGURE 6.1
Speaking Rubric

	0 not identified	1 frequent difficulties	2 occasional difficulties	3 rare or non-existent difficulties
Language control				
Vocabulary				
Communication strategies				
Cultural awareness				

Types of Speaking

Brown and Abeywickrama (2019) named five types of speaking performances in assessment contexts: imitative, intensive, responsive, interactive, and extensive. Imitative speaking is typically connected with pronunciation practice as it requires learners to repeat back a word or phrase without being concerned about producing meaning. Intensive speaking involves the production of short oral communications aimed at demonstrating mastery of a particular skill, such as a grammatical point or intonation—examples of this include directed response tasks, passage reading, and dialogue completion. Responsive speaking includes interaction and comprehension but is very constrained, such as a fixed or canned dialogue with just a couple places for brief responses. Interactive speaking differs from responsive in its length and complexity, involving more extended exchanges that may include multiple participants. Finally, extensive speaking is typically more like a monologue in nature; it includes genres like speeches and oral storytelling and often involves more planning.

Speaking Assessment Standards

As in the previous chapter, we will begin with WIDA's (2020) Can Do statements, which can serve as a valuable addition in teachers' judgment and can aid in curriculum planning (https://wida.wisc.edu). As noted, WIDA focuses its expectations around three areas: recounting, explaining, and arguing. Table 6.3 illustrates what students are expected to do in grades 9–12 at Level 3, Developing Level, and Level 6, Reaching

TABLE 6.3
WIDA Key Uses Speaking Example

	Recount by:	Explain by:	Argue by:
Level 3 Developing	Recount by ▪ Posing and responding to questions in small group discussions ▪ Describing the sequence of processes, cycles, procedures, or events with details	Explain by ▪ Connecting causes to effects in a series of statements ▪ Sequencing processes, cycles, or procedures in short extended discourse	Argue by ▪ Stating claims matched to evidence using a series of related sentences ▪ Suggesting details or reasons to reinforce points of view
Level 6 Reaching	▪ Adjusting presentation style, degree of formality, word choice, tone, and information to the context and audience ▪ Presenting information that follows discipline-specific organization (e.g., orientation to topic, sequence of events, conclusion)	▪ Providing precision and accuracy in classifications, procedures, processes, and accounts using abstraction, technical language, and a variety of active/passive verb forms ▪ Following discipline-specific organization (e.g., orienting the reader, details, conclusion) and supporting presentations with graphs, formulas, quotes or other media	▪ Organizing claims and counter claims in debates with evidence from multiple sources ▪ Negotiating differing cultural perspectives in pairs or small groups

level, the highest of all the levels. Take a moment to think about the differences between these two levels before continuing.

If we look at the recounting skill, it's evident more advanced students are expected to more adeptly adapt their speaking to different audiences and contexts by adjusting word choice, tone, and other aspects. Turning to the explaining skill, students are expected to move from "connecting causes to effects" and "sequencing process, cycles, or procedures" to describing procedures and processes with "precision and accuracy" using "abstraction, technical language" and "active/passive verb forms." In both recounting and explaining, advanced students are expected to have knowledge about "discipline-specific organization." For the arguing skill, Developing students are expected to state claims and use evidence while Reaching students are expected to think more carefully about organization, consider counter claims, and draw on multiple sources of evidence. Here, Reaching students are also expected to negotiate "different cultural perspectives," a skill that most certainly draws on more advanced listening skills as well.

As mentioned in Chapter 5, CEFR uses a six-point scale with three level descriptors: Basic [PreA1, A1, A2], Independent [B1, B2], and Proficient [C1, C2]. CEFR provides an overview document that gives a number of illustrative scales based on different communicative activities under a few different areas: Reception, Interaction, and Production. Interaction focuses on comprehension, informal and formal discussions, goal-oriented co-operation, obtaining goods and services, information exchange, and interviews. Production focuses on sustained monologues, public announcements, and addressing audiences. Each section has an overall set of descriptors as well as descriptors tied to specific writing tasks, speaking to the importance of paying attention to how genres change the needed skillset.

Figure 6.2 outlines CEFR criteria for B1 levels in overall spoken interaction and overall spoken production, illustrating what students are expected to be able to do at those levels. Take a moment and note differences between these two skill-level descriptors before continuing your reading.

It is evident that the first descriptor (Overall Spoken Interaction) prioritizes the learner's ability to hold a conversation "spontaneously...on a wide range of general, academic, vocational or leisure topics" without feeling very constrained by their grammatical or lexical knowledge. As might be expected, the production descriptor focuses less on interaction and more on the learner's ability to clearly describe a subject in their field of interest in an organized manner.

FIGURE 6.2
CEFR Criteria Speaking Example

Level	
B1	Overall Spoken Interaction Can use the language fluently, accurately and effectively on a wide range of general, academic, vocational or leisure topics, marking clearly the relationships between ideas. Can communicate spontaneously with good grammatical control without much sign of having to restrict what he/she wants to say, adopting a level of formality appropriate to the circumstances.
	Overall Spoken Production Can reasonably fluently sustain a straightforward description of one of a variety of subjects within his/her field of interest, presenting it as a linear sequence of points.

FIGURE 6.3
CEFR Level Speaking Differences

Level	
C2	Can present a complex topic confidently and articulately to an audience unfamiliar with it, structuring and adapting the talk flexibly to meet the audience's needs. Can handle difficult and even hostile questioning.
A1	Can read a very short, rehearsed statement—e.g. to introduce a speaker, propose a toast.

Under each category, CEFR includes more specific descriptors for specific genres. Under Production, one of the tables provided is Addressing Audiences. If we compare C2 and A1, we see very clear differences (see Figure 6.3.)

With practice, beginning learners are expected to read a short formulaic statement while the most advanced learners can "present a complex topic" adapted to the audience and even handle challenging questions from them.

Comparing these descriptions, there's a clear difference among the range of topics the different level learners can address as well as the topics' complexity. Another aspect that came up under the CEFR standard is that proficient speakers use language to address a wide variety of topics while basic users rely on practiced material that they have learned. As we'll explore more in Chapter 7, learners at different levels will have different levels of lexical and grammatical knowledge.

Types of Speaking Activities

As with teaching the other skills, we find it useful to move from controlled to guided to free activities in our classrooms. Here is a lesson example focusing on word stress that moves from controlled to guided to free; free is also referred to as communicative practice (Celce-Murcia, Brinton, & Goodwin, 2010).

A Controlled Speaking Example

This exercise was developed by Alaa Bader, 2019a.

First, underline the words with more than one syllable that have the **stress on the first syllable**.

For the next part of the activity/assessment, practice reading the passage aloud a few times.

Finally, read the passage, taking care to stress words that convey the meaning of the dialogue. **Your teacher will use the rubric to evaluate each sentence**.

Two students see their friend rushing off…

Bob: Where is Ann going in such a hurry?
Marie: I haven't any idea.
Bob: I hope it is not an emergency.
Marie: Me too. Her grandmother is in the hospital. Do you think it might be that?
Bob: I'm not sure. I did not ask her.

Teachers might also provide the script with stressed words in **BOLD**. That way, students can practice the correct stress before being tested.

Bob: Where is Ann **going** in such a **hurry**?
Marie: I haven't any idea.
Bob: I hope it is not an emergency.
Marie: me too. Her **grandmother** is in the **hospital**. Do you think it might be that?
Bob: I'm not sure. I did not ask her.

Levels: Students at the following levels in the three sets of standards outlined earlier might benefit most from this exercise: WIDA (Emerging [Level 2] and Developing [Level 3]), CEFR (A2, B1), and ACTFL (Intermediate Low, Intermediate Mid). To make this accessible to lower levels, we could simplify this assignment by adding illustrations.

Assessment: Grant (2014) notes that since pronunciation is highlighted more in the contemporary classroom, teachers emphasize elements of pronunciation beyond mere sounds—elements that fit well with a class focusing on communication and extended discourse. These elements include stress, rhythm, and intonation.

In order to assess the stress and intonation of the students, we could use a rubric like the one shown in Figure 6.4.

It's easy to see from this next activity that if we want, we can assess both listening and speaking as students need to listen to the stress as their teacher reads, and they also need to practice reading the dialogue aloud to practice stress, rhythm, and intonation. Listening can simply be assessed by noting if the student underlined the words that have the stress on the first syllable. This immediate feedback to the teacher can inform practice and encourage repetition if needed.

FIGURE **6.4**
Stress and Intonation Rubric

Stress & Intonation	**Poor**	**Fair**	**Good**	**Excellent**
	1	**2**	**3**	**4**
Insert into this rubric the sentence to be evaluated	Flat intonation makes the speaker almost impossible to understand. There is (almost) no attempt to make the key words or stressed syllables prominent.	Inadequate use of intonation makes the speaker very difficult to follow without compensation. There is little effort to make important words or syllables stand out.	Adequate use of intonation, making the intelligibility of the message fairly high, although there are occasional lapses. Intelligibility is sometimes impeded by making the wrong syllables prominent.	Good use of intonation makes the speaker easy to follow. Intelligibility is almost never impeded by insufficient or misplaced prominence.

A Guided Speaking Example

Role-play—what is my nationality?

The teacher and the learner use a dice and a prompting card (see below for an example) to practice saying different nationalities.

1) The student rolls the dice.
2) The teacher asks the question according to the number that appears on the dice (1–6).
3) The student answers the question accordingly.

Example: [Student rolls a 1] Teacher: I came from Morocco. What is my nationality?

Student: Moroccan.

FIGURE **6.5**
Guided Speaking Activity

1) I came from Morocco.	2) I came from Jordan.	3) I came from Germany.
4) I came from Mexico.	5) I came from the USA.	6) I came from Italy.

Levels: Students at the following levels in the three sets of standards outlined earlier might benefit most from this exercise: WIDA (Entering [Level 1] and Emerging [Level 2]), CEFR (A1, A2), and ACTFL (Novice Mid, Novice High).

Assessment: The exercise assesses patterns of speech, applying knowledge of nationality names and the pronunciation of same and can be used as a classroom game. While students answer the question, their use of proper stress can be evaluated. (Did they emphasize the country? E.g., "I came from ITALY.") The exercise can be repeated many times with different questions ("What did you eat for breakfast?" "I ate CEREAL for breakfast." "What time did you go to bed last night?" "I went to bed a TEN.") Points can be awarded for targeted emphasis. This kind of emphasis is important in English since English is a stress-timed language and gains intelligibility with proper stress. Points might be used to acquire a prize, such as a visit to a classroom treasure chest filled with age-appropriate trinkets (candy, pencils, erasers, notepads).

A Free Speaking Example

a) *–ic* is a suffix that is used with adjectives that describe a person.

Example: energetic en·er·GET·ic
It has four syllables. The third syllable is stressed.

b) Choose similar words from the list provided.

c) Create a questionnaire using these related words to interview your co-workers.

Examples: How ro·MAN·tic are you? Are you more op·ti·MIST·ic than your friends?

romantic
optimistic
realistic
economic
allergic
dramatic
artistic
energetic
scientific

TABLE 6.4
Stress Activity

Target word	Stressed correctly	Stressed incorrectly
en·er·GET·ic		
ro·MAN·tic		

Levels: Students at the following levels in the three sets of standards outlined earlier might benefit most from this exercise: WIDA (Emerging [Level 2] and Developing [Level 3]), CEFR (A2, B1), and ACTFL (Intermediate Low, Intermediate Mid). To make this accessible to lower levels, we could gloss the vocabulary in this assignment, allow students to use an online pronunciation app, or make this a pair activity to add a level of scaffolding.

Assessment: This exercise assesses use of the stress patterns in English, something that is quite difficult for English learners. Again, English is a stress-timed language. That means some syllables will be longer, and some will be shorter. The stressed syllables are said at approximately regular intervals, and unstressed syllables shorten to fit this rhythm. Stress-timed languages can be compared with syllable-timed ones, where each syllable takes roughly the same amount of time—has the same length. Some syllable-timed languages are French, Spanish, and Cantonese. Additionally, all Indian languages, such as Hindi, Sanskrit, Tamil, and Punjabi, are syllable-timed languages.

As in the previous exercise, as students answer, their use of proper stress can be evaluated (it's either correct or not), but in this case, teachers might ask pairs of students to answer one another's interview questions and evaluate each other. Students might create a chart with target words listed and check when their partner applies correct (or incorrect) stress (see Table 6.4).

This simple chart can be used as a feedback tool and for awarding points.

Speaking Activities for Assessment

Guided Practice and Feedback for Pronunciation of [æ] and [ɛ]

This activity was developed by Jonathan Martinez (2019).

Check out Jan **[æ]** and Jen's **[ɛ]** itinerary for their trip to California (see Table 6.5). After you've read the itinerary, you will answer the questions that follow aloud.

TABLE 6.5
California Itinerary

Sunday 12/16	Fly from home to San Antonio to Los Angeles
Monday 12/17	Go to the beach in the afternoon, get a tan, collect sand to bring home as a souvenir
Tuesday 12/18	Visit an orange grove, pick oranges, return to apartment, blend oranges with bananas and mangoes to make smoothies
Wednesday 12/19	Visit Hollywood, then drive ten miles to Glendale and then to Santa Ana
Thursday 12/20	Watch the band Panic at the Disco in concert.
Friday 12/21	Visit Jen's uncle Ken at his dairy farm.
Saturday 12/22	Get an autograph from Cher to give to Jen's dad when she returns home.
Sunday 12/23	Try to visit over ten wineries.
Monday 12/24	Start getting ready to head back home.
Tuesday 12/25	Take an early flight to Wisconsin to celebrate Christmas with family.

In complete sentences, answer the questions using information in the table above.

1. What are Jen and Jan's plans for the sixteenth?
2. What are they doing on the seventeenth?
3. What are they planning for the twenty-fourth?
4. What is special about the twentieth?
5. What will they finally do on the twenty-fifth?
6. What are they doing on the eighteenth to make smoothies?
7. Whose dairy farm are they visiting on the twenty-first?
8. Over how many miles will Jen and Jan drive to visit Hollywood and Glendale on the nineteenth?
9. They plan to receive Cher's autograph on the twenty-second. To whom do they want to give the autograph?
10. How many wineries do they want to visit on the twenty-third?

FIGURE 6.6
Pronunciation Rubric

Student Name Here		**1 Emerging**	**2 Near Target**	**3 Target (High Performance)**	**4 Above Target**
Differentiates between the [æ] and [ɛ]					
[Insert words to be assessed (one on each cell)] Jen					
Jan					
seventeenth					

Levels: Students at the following levels in the three sets of standards outlined earlier might benefit most from this exercise: WIDA (Entering [Level 1] and Emerging [Level 2]), CEFR (A1, A2), and ACTFL (Novice Mid, Novice High).

Assessment: Primarily a pronunciation activity, the formative assessment lies in the target sounds of **[æ]** and **[ɛ]** and whether the students can discriminate between the two sounds. The teacher can listen and use a checklist to formatively assess the students' pronunciation using a rubric like Figure 6.6.

Theta [θ]/Eth [ð] Differentiation

This exercise was developed by Lakmini Siriwardana (2019c).

This activity moves through the framework proposed by Celce-Murcia, Brinton, & Goodwin (2010). It's important to remember that although these activities begin with pronunciation, they move toward more communicative activities like creating and giving a speech, participating in role-play, and engaging in other activities that demand more sustained speech production and promote communicative competence, a term in linguistics referring to a language user's grammatical knowledge of syntax (the way sentences are put together), morphology (how words are formed), phonology (the sounds of the language), as well as social knowledge about how and when to use utterances appropriately. It's easy to see the complex issues that make up communicative competence.

Topic: [ð] and [θ] sounds

Stage 1: Description Analysis

The [ð] and [θ] sounds require awareness of tongue placement as well as slight differences in the articulation of the voiced [ð] (eth) (initial sound in the word *they*) and the voiceless [θ] (theta) (initial sound in the word *think*). In order for students to feel this difference, ask them to place the tip of the tongue between the teeth and make the [θ] sound, holding the sound to feel air pushing past the tip of the tongue and the upper teeth. To contrast the voiced [ð] and the voiceless [θ], students can place two fingers on their throats to feel the vibration of the vocal cords (voiced sounds) or the lack of vibration (voiceless sounds). To teach these techniques, guide students through a demonstration video such as one of these:

> "English pronunciation—Comparison—Voiceless [θ] vs. Voiced [ð]—Phonetics—IPA"
> https://www.youtube.com/watch?v=gc14Kc0fFVc
> "TH Sound—Practice Tip—Tom Kelley—Rachel's English"
> https://www.youtube.com/watch?v=lFXzo7Kh8gs

The next step is to show the student where these sounds occur in word initial, middle, and final positions. Using the content in Figure 6.7, ask students first to write in the symbol and then pronounce the words while being conscious of the voiced and voiceless nature of each sound.

Stage 1 can be used for practice and for teaching. For assessment purposes, the rubric can be used to award points for inserting the correct symbol and then for pronunciation of the appropriate sound (either voiced /ð/ or voiceless /θ/).

Stage 2: Listening Discrimination

Instructions: Listen to your teacher as they read the following sentences and underline the word you hear. The first one is done for you.

1. **<u>This</u>/Lis** is my sister and she is a nurse at Kettering hospital.
2. He became **tense/tenth.**
3. The word **"thank"/ "tank"** starts with letter T.
4. My little sister drew a **mouse/mouth**.
5. Wang **taught/thought** creatively.

FIGURE 6.7
Pronunciation Activity

Word Initial			Word Middle		
	Which symbol?	Pronunciation ✓		Which symbol?	Pronunciation ✓
there			toothbrush		
the			toothpaste		
this			athlete		
thorn			python		
think			something		
thunder			birthday		
# symbols correct ____/6 # words pronounced correctly ____/6			# symbols correct ____/6 # words pronounced correctly ____/6		

Word Final		
	Which symbol?	Pronunciation ✓
cloth		
math		
moth		
month		
path		
ninth		
# symbols correct ____/6 # words pronounced correctly ____/6		

6. He was wearing a **thin/tin** hat.
7. These **tree/three** houses are beautiful.
8. It is **sick/thick**.
9. She said the word **"moth"/"moss"** loudly.
10. I saw his **thumb/sum.**

The sheet can then be graded based on an answer key, one point given for each correct answer, helping both the teacher and the student to notice student ability to differentiate between [ð] and [θ] theta and eth.

Stage 3: Controlled Practice

Let's watch a movie!

Choose the correct word from the selection below and fill in the blanks of the dialogue. Once you finish, practice the dialogue with your tutor. Pay special attention when pronouncing words with /ð/ and /θ/ sounds.

than, another, Black Panther, brother, Beth
math, Thursday, theater, then, three

Jacob: I am going to the (1)___ this evening.
Would you like to join me?
Ali: Sure. What movie are you going to watch?
Jacob: I am going to watch (2)____.
Ali: Oh, I watched its trailer last (3) ____. It seems more exciting (4) ____ other super-hero movies!
Jacob: I think so too. (5) _____ of my friends are coming with me as well.
Ali: Do I know them?
Jacob: Yes, you know two of them, (6) ____ and Theodore. My (7) ____ was planning to come, but he has a sore throat.
Ali: Oh I am sorry about it.
Jacob: Thank you. (8) _____ see you in the evening. I have to go to my (9) ____ class now. Let's meet in (10) ____ two hours.

This activity can be used as practice, but it can also be graded by simply checking if the correct word was inserted.

FIGURE 6.8
Guided Pronunciation Practice

A	B
A: I **think** Mr. Shen is going to teach us Chinese **this** semester.	B: It is "**hypothesis**".
A: It is **thundering** and lightening. I don't want to walk in this **weather.**	B: No. Mr. Shen will be in China for the next two months. Our new instructor is Ms. Theresa.
A: What is the noun of **"hypothesize"?**	B: Yes, the **weather** is too bad. Let's call my **mother** and ask her to pick us up.
A: Do you know the **themes** of this novel?	B: **Thank** God!
A: Is your brother in **Thailand** these days?	B: I will! Some **thorns** are really sharp.
A: When is your **birthday**?	B: **Thirteenth** of September.
A: Be careful! There are so many **thorns** here.	B: Yes, the main theme is love. **Another** one is the gap between the **wealthy** and the poor.
A: The police caught the **thief** who stole my wallet.	B: Yes, he went to Bangkok **with** my father on a business trip.

Stage 4: Guided Practice

Build a dialogue by matching a sentence from column A with a sentence from column B. Once you finish, practice the dialogue with a partner. The first one is done for you. Words with /ð/ and /θ/ sounds are highlighted, so you can pay special attention when pronouncing them.

Stage 4 can again be used as practice to raise awareness of sounds. Of course, this practice is both assignment and assessment, as both the student and the teacher can assess where issues lie and work to remediate them.

Stage 5: Communicative Practice

Write a short story of 10–15 sentences using the words below. Choose three or more words from each row to write your story. After you finish, practice reading your story several times before you present it to the class, concentrating on pronunciation and articulation of sounds. Make sure you speak loudly enough to be heard by your classmates and the teacher.

1. thousand, throw, thoroughly, thick, thoughts
2. toothpick, healthy, python, athlete, birthday
3. truth, teeth, south, earth, youth

Levels: Students at the following levels in the three sets of standards outlined earlier might benefit most from the above exercises: WIDA (Entering [Level 1]), CEFR (A1), and ACTFL (Novice Low, Novice Mid). However, students at more advanced levels may also benefit from the pronunciation practice activities/assessments provided above.

Assessment: The above activities move students through very controlled pronunciation practice with a lot of comprehensible input from teacher and online videos as well as definitions, descriptions, and differentiations of sounds.

You will notice throughout the activities that rubrics were created or scoring methods suggested to target skills students were working on concerning the [ð] and [θ] sounds. Some were as simple as noting the pronunciation of a single sound. Others were more complex given the complexity of the task

The rubric in Figure 6.9 is for the final step of the process (specifically for the communicative practice stage), the story in which a bank of words with the sounds of [ð] and [θ] (theta and eth) are given for students to use in their story. Notice that the rubric mimics the criteria supplied to students. The rubric can be used during student presentations by both the teacher and other students—members of the audience. Prior to presentations and in the interest of a more democratic classroom, a discussion can take place in which students and teacher decide what criteria will be on the rubric, who gets to score, what weight teacher scoring and student scoring carries, and other notions of importance to members of the class.

Fun with Idioms

This activity/assessment is good for promoting interaction with people who speak English as an L1. Deborah's speaking and listening students have historically been a bit timid about engaging with this group, so she created this assignment to promote that interaction.

FIGURE 6.9
Story Assessment Rubric

Criteria	3	2	1	0
Story follows guidelines for length	Story has 10–15 complete sentences	Story has 7–9 complete sentences	Story has less than 5 complete sentences	Did not complete assignment
Appropriate number of words from each row	3 or more	2 words	1 word	Did not complete assignment
Pronunciation and articulation	The student makes minor or no errors in pronunciation, with consistent discrimination between /ð/ and /θ/ sounds	The student has errors in pronunciation, some effort in articulation in target language.	Student makes little or no effort to enunciate and articulate in target language.	Did not present
Reading preparedness	Reading is well prepared. Student has practiced often. Volume is always appropriate.	Reading shows some practice. Student is close to prepared. Volume is mostly appropriate.	Reading does not show practice—unnatural and unprepared. Volume not appropriate.	Did not present

The teacher researches and assigns each student three idiomatic expressions. Examples are sayings such as *Let the cat out of the bag*, *it's raining cats and dogs*, *that car costs an arm and a leg*.

The following directions are given to the students:

> Find an English L1 speaker and ask that person to explain these idioms to you. Take notes regarding the explanations so you don't forget what the person told you.
>
> Create a brief recording that will be used to assess pronunciation, fluency, and comprehensibility. Please include the following:
>
> - ❑ your informant's name
> - ❑ the idiom(s)
> - ❑ the meaning of the idiom(s)
> - ❑ whether or not you have similar idiom(s) in your native language

Please upload this recording to (name of course software platform) by (due date).

In addition to your recording, you will be presenting your idiomatic expressions to the class on (name the day). Use the following method:

- write the idioms that you were assigned on the board
- tell who informed you of the meanings of the idioms
- tell what the idioms mean
- tell whether or not you have a similar expression in your native language and explain the similar idiom.

You will receive feedback on your presentation from your classmates (Figure 6.10):

Levels: Students at the following levels in the three sets of standards outlined earlier might benefit most from this exercise: WIDA (Bridging [Level 5] and Reaching [Level 6]), CEFR (B1, B2, C1), and ACTFL (Intermediate High, Advanced Low). The level appropriateness of this activity would vary significantly based on the complexity of the text chosen.

Assessment: Figure 6.11 shows a rubric that we could use to assess the recording part of this activity. In the rubric, the rater places a checkmark next to the statements that most accurately reflect a student's performance.

Note that this rubric is holistic; the teacher will be using the rubric to score students' recording. Usually in Deborah's speaking and listening classes, she uses this type of rubric throughout the semester to grade *recorded* assignments because pronunciation,

FIGURE 6.10
Idiomatic Expression Presentation Audience Feedback Form

Presenter's name: ______________________________

1. Comment on one thing you believe the presenter did well.
2. Comment on one thing you believe the presenter needs to improve.
3. List one thing you learned from this presentation.
4. What word(s) or phrases were difficult for you to understand?

FIGURE 6.11
Pronunciation Rubric Example

Score	Check		
1 2		Pronunciation Fluency Comprehensibility	Consistently interferes with comprehension of the message Even with extraordinary effort on the part of the listener, understanding is difficult The student consistently fails to understand what is being said/asked
3 4		Pronunciation Fluency Comprehensibility	Often interferes with comprehension of the message An effort is required on the part of the listener to understand what is being said The student understands less than half of what is said/asked; repetition and rephrasing are often needed
5 6		Pronunciation Fluency Comprehensibility	Only occasionally interferes with comprehension of the message Ideas are expressed without excessive pauses at a speed that may occasionally distract the listener The student understands most of what is said/asked
7 8		Pronunciation Fluency Comprehensibility	Seldom interferes with comprehension of the message Ideas are expressed with few pauses at a speed that rarely distracts the listener The student has a good overall understanding of what is said/asked
9 10		Pronunciation Fluency Comprehensibility	Very rarely interferes with comprehension of the message Ideas are expressed without unnatural pauses and at a natural speed The student understands virtually everything that is said/asked

Adapted from (http://www.nysed.gov/common/nysed/files/programs/world-languages/lotecassess.pdf)

fluency, and comprehensibility are three important aspects of the class and the recorded assignments are specifically created to target these three aspects. The teacher can then conference with the student and give more in-depth feedback; however, along with the holistic score, Deborah supplies an oral assessment of the strengths and weaknesses of the students' recordings.

While we have repeatedly emphasized that a rubric should be specifically tailored for an assignment, the above rubric is more generic and could be used for multiple presentations, which can free the teacher up to give additional oral feedback and offers the students a familiar set of expectations to aim for in terms of pronunciation, fluency, and comprehensibility.

The teacher could use the rubric in Figure 6.12 to for a pronunciation-focused presentation evaluation.

While the rubric above may seem canned, these are typical definitions of pronunciation, fluency, and comprehensibility that students should learn to be familiar with.

Here's an alternative rubric (Figure 6.13) that has a different focus; the students are graded simply on whether or not they fulfilled the format of the assignment.

FIGURE 6.12
Pronunciation Rubric

	0	1	2	3
English Language Pronunciation (the articulation of sounds)	Speaker makes *frequent* errors and people *often* have trouble understanding.	Speaker makes *frequent* errors and people *sometimes* have trouble understanding.	Speaker made *more than a few* errors, but people can *almost always* understand.	Speaker made *a few* pronunciation errors, but people can *always* understand
English Language Fluency (rate and flow of speech)	Speaker makes *a lot* of pauses and changes in speed that make it *very difficult* to understand.	Speaker often pauses or changes speed, which *sometimes* prevents people from understanding.	Speaker *sometimes* has to make pauses, but they don't prevent people from understanding.	Speech is smooth and effortless.
English language comprehensibility (Can the speaker be understood?)	Speaker has *a lot* of trouble with vocabulary and grammar, *even with simple types of speech.*	*Speaker often* has to search for a word or *often* makes grammar mistakes, and people *often* have difficulty understanding.	Speaker makes *some* errors but can be understood *almost all the time.*	Speaker makes *a few* grammar or usage errors, but they *never* prevent people from understanding.

FIGURE 6.13
Alternative Pronunciation Rubric

	Yes (1)	No (0)
Student wrote assigned idioms on the board		
Student named the informant		
Student defined the idiom		
Student provided and explained a similar expression in the native language or explained that no similar idiom exists		
Score ______/4		

Why Is Writing Important?

As Folse (2006) noted, even in language programs that focus on the four skills of reading, writing, speaking, and listening, there often seems to be an outsized focus on speaking, driven perhaps by students who want to be able to hold conversations in English for a variety of reasons in a variety of contexts. There is also the perception by many learners that writing is an easier skill than speaking because one has time to think through and revise what they're writing as opposed to hearing and responding in the moment of a conversation—however, because of the varieties of genres and the higher expectations for correctness in writing, this myth is simply not true.

A number of scholarly and popular articles have pointed out that writing is becoming increasingly important in this era of electronic communication—emailing, texting, and social media are among a few of the areas where we can expect to communicate in writing electronically (Laurinavicius, 2017). Although many lament that the rise of these technologies, especially texting, has ruined the younger generation's ability to write, the fact is that young people are writing more frequently than their predecessors. While writing classes are increasingly building in multimodal assignments that involve crafting projects like websites and blogs, it is vital in this technology-driven era that language and writing teachers show their students the differences in genres and how students' registers need to change as students transition among genres.

Todd often begins the professional writing classes he teaches at the college level with the National Commission on Writing's 2004 report, *Writing: A Ticket to Work or a Ticket Out*. The report is based on responses from 64 different companies and illustrates the importance of writing in today's workplace. Hiring managers interviewed for the study noted how they took a candidate's writing ability into account when making hiring decisions. Candidates were judged in part by the quality of their application letter and resume—those writing pieces counted for 80% or more of the decision to hire or not in the some of the biggest growth areas for salaried employees (services/finance, insurance, and real estate). As one executive noted, "Applicants who provide poorly written letters wouldn't likely get an interview" (p. 3). This emphasis on writing continued after being hired, as those who could not write well were unlikely to be considered for promotion—half of the executives interviewed considered writing abilities when making promotion decisions. Overall, two-thirds of employees in large U.S. companies were reported to have writing responsibilities, with this number rising to over 80% in some companies. We generally find that our students come to college to improve their career prospects—it is evident from some of these numbers that writing is a vital component of that improvement.

Types of Writing

Over the past few decades, writing instruction has shifted away from modes (e.g. expository, descriptive, narrative, and analytical essays) to genres, although the former is still prevalent throughout writing classrooms informed by more traditional methods and often perpetuated through outdated textbooks or standards. For instance, the Common Core State Standards in the U.S. have been criticized for upholding this modes-based focus (Johnson, 2013). Genres are seen as flexible patterns for composing in a variety of contexts—they are inherently social and tied to discourse communities "whose routine activities influence the kinds of writing that is done and how it is understood" (Hyland, 2004, p. 78). Genres cover a broad range of texts, ranging from movie genres such as comedies and thrillers, journalistic genres such as news articles and opinion pieces, academic genres such as book reports and research reports, and online genres such as blog entries and websites. Tardy (2016) has cautioned that genres can often be seen and taught as rigid templates and formulas:

> I am particularly attentive to critiques of genre pedagogy that caution that genres may be perceived by students (and teachers) as templates or formulas and that conventions may be interpreted as rules; I have seen this potential in my own classrooms as I struggle to engage students in the dynamic, social nuances of a text that they are experiencing out of context and as a graded assignment. Yet, I remain convinced that genre offers a valuable tool for writing students and teachers to explore expected conventions as well as the possibilities for quirky or transformative innovations—that is, the possibilities for real engagement in the processes of written communication. (p. 2)

Genre scholars such as Tardy (2019) have repeatedly pointed out that the five-paragraph essay, commonly taught in U.S. PreK–12 contexts and language classrooms throughout the world, is not a genre. As we have noted elsewhere (Crusan & Ruecker, 2019), the five-paragraph essay might be a useful tool for helping students expediently pass a high-stakes standardized test; however, it is vital that teachers move beyond this rigid formula in order to teach students real-world genres.

In the language teaching realm, Brown and Abeywickrama (2019) classify four types of writing performance: imitative, intensive (controlled), responsive, and extensive. As with speaking, imitative is very much focused on form and most commonly used with early learners—it focuses on mastery over the basic writing conventions, such as appropriately using punctuation and spelling correctly. Exercises at this state may involve copying simple sentences to build comfort over the physical process of writing. Intensive writing, commonly used in assessment contexts, is seen as controlled because it probes learners' ability to use appropriate vocabulary and grammatical structures in different contexts but is at the same time narrowly defined and particularly interested in learners' mastery of form. Next, learners typically progress toward more responsive writing tasks that tend to respond to some kind of stimulus (e.g., students are given data to write a lab report or must describe an image or summarize a text) and advance toward the paragraph level, which means learners start linking sentences together to support and sustain longer stretches of discourse. What Brown and Abeywickrama (2019) refer to as extensive writing "implies successful management of all the processes and strategies of writing for all purposes" (p. 262) and incorporates the whole gamut of genres we referenced above, including writing as comprehensive as a thesis project.

Writing Assessment Standards

As in the previous section, we will begin with WIDA's (2020) Can Do statements, which we noted can serve as a valuable piece in teachers' judgment and can aid in curriculum planning (https://wida.wisc.edu). As we noted, WIDA focuses its expectations around three areas: recounting, explaining, and arguing. Figure 6.14 illustrates what students are expected to do in grades 9–12 at Level 3, Developing, and Level 6, Reaching, which is the highest level. Take a moment to think about the differences between these two levels before continuing.

If we look at the recounting skill, it's evident that students at more advanced levels are expected to write in more complex genres ("research reports") that draw on not just "important information" but "multiple sources of information," an expectation that illustrates the connection between reading and writing well. Turning to the explaining

FIGURE 6.14
WIDA Writing Standards

	Recount by:	Explain by:	Argue by:
Level 3 Developing	▪ Summarizing content-related material ▪ Including important information and related details	▪ Choosing words and phrases to provide precise details, descriptions, comparisons, and ordered procedures ▪ Integrating headings, introductory statements, and other features to organize text	▪ Justifying reasons or opinions with evidence ▪ Summarizing opposing positions with evidence
Level 6 Reaching	▪ Summarizing content-related notes from lectures or readings ▪ Producing research reports using multiple sources of information	▪ Developing ideas about phenomena with relevant and sufficient facts, extended descriptions, concrete details, or quotations ▪ Maintaining discipline-specific patterns that bridge across key uses (e.g., explanation to argument in history, explanation to recount for information reports)	▪ Evaluating positive and negative implications associated with various positions (e.g., historical events, scientific discoveries, individuals) ▪ Organizing information logically and coherently to represent contrasting views

skill, students are expected to move from picking words and phrases to provide "precise details" to drawing in quotes and other details to develop "ideas about phenomena." Similarly, at the more advanced levels, we move from more generic approaches to organization (headings, etc.) to "discipline-specific patterns," that is, patterns that reflect how writing is done in history, science, and other fields. Finally, under arguing, we find that more advanced students have to move from simply justifying an argument with evidence to taking a more nuanced stance toward argumentation as they evaluate "positive and negative implications associated with various positions." It is clear from looking at the more advanced skills why scholars often say that writing and thinking are closely linked (Bean, 2011).

The ACTFL Proficiency Guidelines "describe the tasks that writers can handle at each level as well as the content, context, accuracy, and discourse types associated with the writing tasks at each level" (p. 10). As mentioned in Chapter 5, the guidelines have six different skill levels: Distinguished, Superior, Advanced, Intermediate, and Novice; Advanced, Intermediate, and Novice are further divided into High, Mid, and Low. Similar to CEFR, ACTFL divides its writing guidelines into two areas: presentational, which includes essays, reports, and letters, and interpersonal, which includes instant messaging, email communication, and texting. Compare these descriptions of what writers can do at the Distinguished level and the Novice High level—we bolded some of the language we found important:

> **Distinguished**
>
> Writers at the Distinguished level can carry out **formal writing tasks** such as official correspondence, position papers, and journal articles. They can **write analytically on professional, academic and societal issues.** In addition, Distinguished-level writers are able to address world issues in a highly conceptualized fashion.
>
> These writers can use **persuasive and hypothetical discourse** as representational techniques, allowing them to advocate a position that is not necessarily their own. They are also able to communicate **subtlety and nuance**. Distinguished-level writing is **sophisticated** and is directed to sophisticated readers. Writers at this level write to their audience; they tailor their language to their readers.
>
> Distinguished-level writing is **dense and complex**; yet, it is characterized by an **economy of expression**. The writing is **skillfully crafted and is organized** in a way that reflects target-culture thought patterns. At the Distinguished level, length is not a determining factor. Distinguished-level texts can be as short as a poem or as long as a treatise.
>
> Writers at the Distinguished level demonstrate control of **complex lexical, grammatical, syntactic, and stylistic features** of the language. Discourse structure and punctuation are used strategically, not only to organize meaning but also to enhance it. Conventions are generally appropriate to the text modality and the target culture. (ACTFL Guidelines, p. 4)
>
> **Novice High**
>
> Writers at the Novice level are characterized by the ability to **produce lists and notes**, primarily by writing **words and phrases**. They can provide **limited formulaic information** on **simple** forms and documents. These writers can reproduce practiced material to convey the most simple messages. In addition, they can **transcribe familiar words or phrases**, copy letters of the alphabet or syllables of a syllabary, or reproduce basic characters with some accuracy.

> Writers at the Novice High sublevel are able to **meet limited basic practical writing needs** using lists, short messages, postcards, and simple notes. They are able to **express themselves within the context in which the language was learned**, relying mainly on **practiced material**. Their writing is focused on common elements of daily life. Novice High writers are able to recombine learned vocabulary and structures to create simple sentences on very familiar topics, but are not able to sustain sentence-level writing all the time. Due to **inadequate vocabulary and/or grammar**, writing at this level may only **partially communicate** the intentions of the writer. Novice High writing is often comprehensible to natives used to the writing of non-natives, but **gaps in comprehension** may occur (ACTFL Guidelines, p. 9).

Comparing these two proficiency levels, we see a difference in the formality of writing tasks as well as their complexity. Another aspect that came up under the CEFR standards is that Distinguished writers can write on a wide variety of topics while novice writers rely on practiced material that they have learned. As we'll explore more in Chapter 7, learners at different levels will have different levels of lexical and grammatical knowledge.

Types of Writing Activities

As with the other skills we've discussed, it is important to include activities that move from controlled to guided (semi-controlled) to free activities, which can easily provide a framework for lessons/assessments. Controlled activities generally appear at the beginning of the lesson, followed by guided and then free. As the lesson progresses, each type of activity allows increased amounts of creativity, personal relevance, and experimentation with language. Here's a progression activity surrounding themes from Laura Ingalls Wilder's *Little House* series.

A Controlled Writing Example

Answer the questions associated with the following image. Use complete sentences.

Image credit: Photo by Olivier Guillard on Unsplash.

What color is the cabin?
What is the cabin made out of?
Where is the cabin?
How big is the cabin?
How many windows can you see?

Levels: WIDA (Emerging [Level 2]), CEFR (A1, A2), and ACTFL (Novice Mid, Novice High).

Assessment: Here's a simple holistic rubric we might use for this assignment:

Criteria

Learner consistently used accurate vocabulary in their responses. /5
Learner responded in complete sentences with proper grammar and syntax. /5

Total: /10

While simple holistic rubrics may not be as useful for the student, who might wonder whether their vocabulary, grammar, or syntax was off, it can be useful for overworked teachers as they are easy and quick to use. With this example, it would certainly benefit students to have an additional sentence or two of feedback from the teacher helping them identify where they might have done better. A primary trait rubric is a close alternative to a holistic rubric—instead of giving a single score on multiple traits as the example above does, it focuses on a particular aspect that the teacher wants to emphasize—we have found that a primary trait rubric is more helpful for beginning students and less so for more advanced students.

Other examples of controlled writing:

- Copying sentences from a text
- Circling unfamiliar words and copying them to index cards with definitions
- Listening to speakers and completing missing words in the exchange
- Labeling pictures of items with the correct words
- Grammatical transformation activities (e.g., changing tenses from present to past)
- Ordering words to form grammatically correct sentences
- Completing a form

It is important to note that grammatical transformation activities are commonly used in language classrooms but have minimal utility outside of making sure learners are comfortable using a particular form. As Brown and Abeywickrama (2019) wrote, "[These] tasks are virtually devoid of any meaningful value…If you are interested only in a person's ability to produce the forms, then such tasks may prove to be justifiable" (p. 268).

A Guided Writing Example

In this activity, you will practice paraphrasing and summarizing. A paraphrase typically focuses on a specific passage and involves you rewriting that passage in your own words. The paraphrase may be a similar length to the original. On the other hand, a summary focuses on a longer text and is much shorter than the original.

Take a look at this excerpt from Laura Ingalls Wilder's *Little House in the Big Woods*:

> Laura loved Grandma's house. It was much larger than their house at home. There was one great big room, and then there was a little room that belonged to Uncle George, and there was another room for the aunts, Aunt Docia and Aunt Ruby. And then there was the kitchen, with a big cookstove.

It was fun to run the whole length of the big room, from the large fireplace at one end all the way to Grandma's bed, under the window in the other end. The floor was made of wide, thick slabs that Grandpa had cut from the logs with his ax. The floor was smoothed all over, and scrubbed clean and white, and the big bed under the window was soft with feathers.

The day seemed very short while Laura and Mary played in the big room and Ma helped Grandma and the aunts in the kitchen. The men had taken their dinners to the maple woods, so for dinner they did not set the table, but ate cold sandwiches and drank milk. But for supper Grandma made hasty pudding.

She stood by the stove, sifting the yellow corn meal from her fingers into a kettle of boiling, salted water. She stirred the water all the time with a big wooden spoon, and sifted in the meal until the kettle was full of a thick, yellow, bubbling mass. Then she set it on the back of the stove where it would cook slowly.

It smelled good. The whole house smelled good, with the sweet and spicy smells from the kitchen, and the smell of the hickory logs burning with clear, bright flames in the fireplace, and the smell of a clove-apple beside Grandma's mending basket on the table. The sunshine came in through the sparkling window panes, and everything was large and spacious and clean.

At supper time Pa and Grandpa came from the woods. Each had on his shoulders a wooden yoke that Grandpa had made. It was cut to fit around their necks in the back and hollowed out to fit over their shoulders. From each end hung a chain with a hook, and on each hook hung a big wooden bucket full of hot maple syrup.

Now, paraphrase the second paragraph (starting with "It was fun…") in a few sentences. Next, write a 3–4 sentence summary of the whole passage.

Levels: Students at the following levels in the three sets of standards outlined earlier might benefit most from this exercise: WIDA (Developing [Level 3] and Expanding [Level 4]), CEFR (B1), and ACTFL (Intermediate Mid, Intermediate High).

Assessment: Here's a simple analytical rubric that might be used to evaluate this assignment:

1–5 scale, 5 being the best.

Paraphrase
Captured all the essential details in the third paragraph: /5
Consistently used different language from the original: /5

Summary
Captured the overall gist of the entire passage: /5
Consistently used different language from the original: /5

Total: /20

While simple, note how this rubric clearly identifies what we as teachers will be looking for in evaluating student work, helping them see that accuracy in content and variation in lexicon are the criteria that we'll be examining. It is also clear that we're weighting everything equally. Teachers need to make sure their evaluation aligns with the rubric they share with their students—on this shorter assignment, since we're focusing on the skills of paraphrasing and summarizing, we are not evaluating grammatical correctness and should make that clear to the students. As we will see with the next assignment example, this is a rather simple rubric, albeit one adapted to the task and our goals for it—as we develop more complex, high-stakes assignments, our rubrics typically become more complex too.

Some other guided writing examples:

- Answering questions about a reading.
- Responding to a particular prompt as part of a daily journal
- Completing a semi-open form, such as a table for a lab report

A Free Writing Example

Short Story

(Note that while this prompt provides some expectations and guidance and a theme, students have a lot of freedom compared to the previous activities.)

Laura Ingalls Wilder wrote novels about her childhood that were full of details about daily life and interactions with different family members. Now that we have read part of *Little House in the Big Woods*, you are going to write a short story of your own describing a time you visited your grandparents or another family member's home. Here are some questions to help you think about what to include in your story:

- What did your family members look like? Were they tall? Short? What color was their hair?

- What was their home like? How does it compare to yours? What did you like about it? What didn't you like?
- What did you do while visiting? Did you play games? Eat? Do something else?
- How often did you visit? Did you only go on special occasions like a holiday or for other reasons?

Your story should be at least two pages long and use some of the vocabulary we learned from *Little House in the Big Woods.*

Levels: Students at the following levels in the three sets of standards outlined earlier might benefit most from this exercise: WIDA (Developing [Level 3] and Expanding [Level 4]), CEFR (B1, B2), and ACTFL (Intermediate Mid, Intermediate High). This activity could be made accessible to lower-level students with a more level-appropriate base text and different expectations for their stories, such as shorter length or simply a series of sentences.

Assessment: See Figure 6.15. Rate students from 1 to 5 in each of the listed areas, 5 being the best.

FIGURE 6.15
Story Rubric

	Characteristics of a 1	Characteristics of a 5
Focus (30%)	My story may mention the visit, but it focuses mostly on other topics; it's unclear how most of the story relates to the focus.	My story stays focused on the visit throughout the story; it's clear how everything relates to this focus.
Details (30%)	My story is too short to include enough details; I use boring words that do not help my readers to understand the experience. I use the same words.	My story is at least two pages and includes lots of interesting details; I use a variety of words, including some from *Little House in the Big Woods*, that recreate the visit.
Organization (20%)	My story is difficult to follow because I tell things out of order; I don't transition the reader between ideas.	My story is easy to follow as it has a logical order; I transition the reader between ideas using words such as *then* or *next*.
Conventions (20%)	My story has a number of errors with spelling, punctuation, or sentence structure that make it hard to understand.	My story follows the conventions of the variety of English appropriate to my text.

Note how this rubric is more complex than the one provided for the paraphrase/summary assignment, which makes sense since the assignment would be more complex and heavily weighted in our classrooms. It not only has more categories but weighs each category differently by placing a higher value on the content elements and a lower value on aspects like organization and conventions. As we have repeatedly emphasized, it is also specifically tailored for the assignment. As a rubric gets more complex, it obviously takes more time to develop. For instance, a fully developed rubric could include performance descriptors for each of the point levels. On the other hand, frequently we just define the expectations for top work.

One problem with the rubric above is it could get complicated to calculate a grade with the varying percentages while working with point rankings of 5. Instead of using a standard 5-point scale, we could customize the point levels in each category, perhaps working with a total of 100 points. So under focus and details, we could have up to 30 points each, and under organization and conventions we could have up to 20 points each. A revised rubric might look like the one in Figure 6.16:

FIGURE 6.16
Revised Story Rubric

	Characteristics of a low score	**Characteristics of a high score**
Focus (up to 30 points)	My story may mention the visit but it focuses mostly on other topics; it's unclear how most of the story relates to the focus.	My story stays focused on the visit throughout the story; it's clear how everything relates to this focus.
Details (up to 30 points)	My story is too short to include enough details; I use boring words that do not help my readers to understand the experience. I use the same words.	My story is at least two pages and includes lots of interesting details; I use a variety of words, including some from *Little House in the Big Woods*, that recreate the visit.
Organization (up to 20 points)	My story is difficult to follow because I tell things out of order; I don't transition the reader between ideas.	My story is easy to follow as it has a logical order; I transition the reader between ideas using words such as *then* or *next*.
Conventions (up to 20 points)	My story has a number of errors with spelling, punctuation, or sentence structure that make it hard to understand.	My story follows the conventions of the variety of English appropriate to my text.

Writing Activities for Assessment

Daily Journals

Many teachers like to have students take five or so minutes at the beginning of class to write in an ongoing journal—some tie these into what are often called "bellringers," activities designed to get students warmed up after the first bell. These prompts vary from classroom to classroom and can range from personal writing to a whole-class reading response.

Here's some ideas for personal prompts involving real or hypothetical situations:

Write about the best or the worst day of your life.

Write about your favorite childhood toy.

What would you do if someone just gave you $1 million?

What would you do if you could travel into the future?

There are a lot of sites out there offering ideas for prompts; however, we recommend that teachers think about how writing activities can tie into classroom goals in selecting prompts. For instance, the future-oriented prompt above might be relevant if the class was reading a science fiction story. The toy-oriented prompt might be useful if students were writing instruction sets on how to use a particular toy or game.

Other prompts might have a stimulus that integrates other skills, such as listening or reading. For instance, a teacher can find a short video on a site like YouTube or a news site like CNN or read a short news article or other type of text and have students respond to it using prompts such as the following:

Summarize the video/text in 3–4 sentences.

What did you like about the video/text you just read?

What is one thing you learned from the video/text?

What would you do differently if you were the speaker/writer?

Levels: WIDA (Emerging [Level 2] and above), CEFR (A2 and above), and ACTFL (Novice High and above). In order to journal, students need to have some proficiency in order to write complete sentences; however, the journals can easily be more simple or complex based on students' abilities so can be appropriate for most levels.

Assessment: Typically, the aim of journaling is to help students become more fluent, confident writers, so assessment tends to be pretty simple. In our classes, we typically assess journals on simple scales, such as a check minus, check, and check plus. Or a 5-point scale, with 5 being the best. We tend to reward students based on effort and provide encouraging feedback rather than focus on accuracy. Some teachers treat this kind of assignment as an ungraded one, explaining to their student that the writing done at the beginning of class is done for the student's benefit. Teachers typically find it easier to collect journals after a specific time frame (say two to three weeks) rather than deal with the logistics of collecting and returning them more frequently.

Open-Ended Questions

Open-ended questions are ones that aren't answered with a word or two (*yes*, *no*, a number, etc.) and that give students the opportunity to share their knowledge on a particular point in a short amount of time, with anywhere from a phrase, a sentence, or a paragraph for their response. For instance, the questions provided with the controlled writing example above are close-ended—while we asked students to reply in complete sentences, we were typically looking for a simple one-word answer—for example, *bedroom*, *stressed*. Close-ended questions are commonly used to judge student comprehension of a text, whether read, heard, or viewed. However, in the EL classroom they can also be used to facilitate conversation between students as well, although that is not our focus here.

Take turns with a peer reading out loud the following passage from the website Simple English Wikipedia and answer the questions:

Overview

The Grand Canyon is a famous canyon in Arizona, formed by the Colorado River. It is a UNESCO World Heritage Site,[1] and a National Park of the United States. It is also one of the Seven Natural Wonders of the World.

The Grand Canyon is 277 miles (446 km) long, up to 18 miles (29 km) wide and is over a mile (1.83 km) (6000 feet) deep in places.[2] Nearly two billion years past of the Earth's geological history have been exposed as the Colorado River and its tributaries (smaller rivers) cut their channels through layer after layer of rock.[3]

Evidence suggests the Colorado River established its course through the canyon at least 17 million years ago.[4][5][6] Since that time, the Colorado River continued to erode and form the canyon to the point we see it at today.

"Local erosion in the western Grand Canyon began about 17 million years ago, but a through-flowing Colorado River to the Pacific Ocean did not exist until about 5.4 million years ago… most of the downward cutting has been concentrated in the last 2.5 million years."[7]

Tourism

Many people come from around the world to visit the Grand Canyon. People can also take trips floating on the Colorado River in boats and rafts. Some people like to hike in the Grand Canyon. The land on the north side of the Grand Canyon is called the North Rim. The land on the south side of the Grand Canyon is called the South Rim. There are trails leading from the North Rim and the South Rim to the bottom of the canyon. These trails lead to a place at the bottom of the canyon called Phantom Ranch. Phantom Ranch has a campground and cabins where hikers can spend the night. Some people also ride mules into the Grand Canyon. Most people who visit the Grand Canyon drive in cars to the South Rim and just look at the canyon from the rim and take pictures.

(Source: https://simple.wikipedia.org/wiki/Grand_Canyon)

Discuss the following questions with your partner. Then, on your own, answer them in one to five sentences each:

1. What is the author's main purpose in the first paragraph?
2. How was the Grand Canyon formed?
3. If you've visited the Grand Canyon, describe what you did on your trip. If you haven't visited the Grand Canyon, describe what you might like to do on a trip there.
4. If you visit the Grand Canyon, would you want to visit the North or South Rim and why? Do some quick online research if needed to answer this question.
5. Describe your visit to a national park or a place of natural beauty. Some questions to consider: When did you go? What did you do? What did you like and what didn't you like?

Levels: Students at the following levels in the three sets of standards outlined earlier might benefit most from this exercise: WIDA (Bridging [Level 5] and Reaching [Level 6]), CEFR (B1, B2, C1), and ACTFL (Intermediate High, Advanced Low). The level appropriateness of this activity would vary significantly based on the complexity of the text and the questions, so could be easily adapted for different levels.

Assessment: There are a few different options here. One could have a rubric aimed at student responses as a whole instead of each question. In order to offer students some the specificity lost by not focusing on assessing each question, a multi-section analytical rubric would be better than a holistic one. Such a rubric might look like Figure 6.17.

However, since the questions vary quite widely, with some asking about content from the passage and others asking for a more creative approach, we would recommend assessing each question separately. Here, an analytical rubric would be too time consuming to construct for each, so a holistic rubric would be our choice:

Each question will be ranked on a 5-point scale using Figure 6.18 as guidance:

In drafting this rubric, we started with the top score, our ideal response, and worked down from there, modifying the language as we progressed to account for differences in performance in the primary areas (accuracy, varied language, detail, and grammar/syntax). At the lower levels, we identify the possibility of more serious errors that interfere with understanding.

Timed Writing Assignments

Timed writing assessments are most commonly seen in some kind of standardized exam setting where the goal is to gain a snapshot of a learner's writing ability and then compare that to other students writing under similar conditions. PreK–12 state tests typically have time limits, although they may be for the test as a whole rather than for a particular section. For instance, students have up to 65 minutes to complete the writing portion of the WIDA. For older students, the TOEFL allots 50 minutes total to two writing tasks and the IELTS allots 60 minutes, with test takers encouraged to spend 20 minutes on one task and 40 minutes on another. Timed sit-down essays are sometimes used at a local level for placement purposes. As we explain in more depth

FIGURE 6.17
Short Answer Analytical Rubric

	5	4	3	2	1
Accuracy	The author answered all the questions appropriately and accurately.	The author answered most of the questions appropriately and accurately.	The author answered some of the questions appropriately and accurately.	The author did not answer most of the questions appropriately and accurately.	The author did not answer most or any of the questions appropriately and accurately.
Detail	The author included excellent detail.	The author included sufficient detail.	The author generally included sufficient detail, although it may have been lacking for a few of the questions.	The author did not provide sufficient detail for most of the questions.	The author provided minimal detail for most/all of the questions.
Vocabulary	The author skillfully varied vocabulary throughout.	The author varied vocabulary throughout.	The author used relatively simple vocabulary.	The author used simple and repetitive vocabulary.	The author used simple and repetitive vocabulary and writing may have contained errors in word choice.
Grammar and Syntax	The author made no or very few errors in grammar and/or syntax.	The author made only a few errors in grammar and/or syntax.	The author had some errors with grammar and/or syntax with some unclear parts as a result.	The author had a number of errors with grammar and/or syntax with several unclear parts as a result.	The author had a lot of errors with grammar and/or syntax and the writing was mostly unclear.

FIGURE 6.18
Short Answer Holistic Rubric

5	The author answered the question accurately using their own language and with excellent detail. Their response used varied vocabulary and contained no errors in grammar or syntax.
4	The author answered the question accurately using their own language and with sufficient detail. Their response used varied vocabulary and contained minimal errors in grammar or syntax.
3	The author answered the question accurately using their own language, although details may have been lacking. Their response stuck with relatively simple vocabulary and may have contained a few errors in grammar or syntax.
2	The author did not answer the question accurately and/or used too much original language from the text. Their response contained multiple errors in grammar or syntax that interfered with understanding.
1	The response did not answer the question and/or was not comprehensible.

in Chapter 8, like many writing specialists, we are not fans of timed writing exercises. They ignore decades of research that has helped demonstrate the efficacy of a process approach to writing—the best writing comes from a recursive, multi-step process that includes revision, something not possible in a short time frame. Nonetheless, since timed writing is still common in formal assessment settings, teachers do have a responsibility to familiarize their students with the unique constraints that come with this type of writing, so it may make sense to include it as part of writing in the classroom. In developing timed writing assignments, teachers should learn what kind of timed writing their students will be expected to do and should draw on sample questions from tests or follow other testing guidelines (e.g., Do they have to hand write their response or is it all done on computer? Do they have access to a dictionary or translator or not?) to give students as an authentic experience as possible. Here's a sample from the 4th grade Texas state test:

Read the information in the box below:

> Thomas Edison is famous for inventing many things, including the lightbulb.
> THINK about inventions that you believe are useful.
> WRITE about one invention that is important in your life. Tell what the invention is and explain what makes it important.

Be sure to:

- clearly state your central idea
- organize your writing
- develop your writing in detail
- choose your words carefully
- use correct spelling, capitalization, punctuation, grammar, and sentences

Levels: WIDA (Bridging [Level 5] and Reaching [Level 6]), CEFR (B2, C1), and ACTFL (Intermediate High, Advanced Low).

Assessment: As we recommend with the prompt itself, it is important to learn how student responses will be evaluated on the test. Rubrics for writing portions of tests are widely available and we like to go through them with our students to look at how the expectations vary for the different scores. For instance, a 3 on the Texas STARR grade 4 writing rubric is as follows:

The essay represents a satisfactory writing performance.

Organization/Progression

- The organizing structure of the essay is, for the most part, appropriate to the purpose and responsive to the specific demands of the prompt. The essay is clear because the writer uses organizational strategies that are adequately suited to the expository task.
- The writer establishes a clear central idea. Most ideas are related to the central idea and are focused on the topic specified in the prompt. The essay is coherent, though it may not always be unified due to minor lapses in focus.
- The writer's progression of ideas is generally logical and controlled. For the most part, transitions are meaningful, and sentence-to-sentence connections are sufficient to support the flow of the essay and show the relationships among ideas.

Development of Ideas

- The development of ideas is sufficient because the writer uses details and examples that are specific and appropriate, adding some substance to the essay.

- The essay reflects some thoughtfulness. The writer's response to the prompt is original rather than formulaic. The writer develops the essay in a manner that demonstrates a good understanding of the expository writing task.

Use of Language/Conventions

- The writer's word choice is, for the most part, clear and specific. It reflects an awareness of the expository purpose and establishes a tone appropriate to the task. The word choice usually contributes to the quality and clarity of the essay.
- Sentences are varied and adequately controlled, for the most part contributing to the effectiveness of the essay. The writer demonstrates an adequate command of sentence boundaries and age-appropriate spelling, capitalization, punctuation, grammar, and usage conventions. Although some errors may be evident, they create few (if any) disruptions in the fluency of the writing, and they do not affect the clarity of the essay.

We would read through this with our students and elicit ideas from them on what they need to pay attention to in their writing based on what the STARR rubric values. For instance, we would note that they should outline their writing first, since logical organization is an important part of the rubric. We would also tell them to make sure they have plenty of details to develop their essay and that they should proofread afterward to minimize the number of errors.

Integrated Shorter and Longer Writing Assignments

As part of encouraging learners to adopt a process approach to writing, it is common for writing teachers to use shorter, more informal assignments that lead into longer, more complex ones. The idea is that the short writing assignments are tied in some way to the larger, helping students do some preliminary research or writing to become comfortable with a topic or skill before undertaking more complex tasks. As we saw above with the progression of the *Little House in the Big Woods* assignments, a progression from simpler, more controlled assignments where students gain practice with vocabulary and the topic to a more open, complex assignment in which they write their own story provides support for all learners.

Here is a sample taken from the curriculum in the writing program at Todd's current institution. It starts with a couple connected informal writing tasks, followed by the larger essay, which integrates reading and writing tasks:

Writing Task 1

Practicing Critical Reading

Using the skills explained in the "Explaining Reading Critically" lecture, you will now practice critical reading on your own by picking out points of a common, short, and relatively accessible reading.

Locate this week's assigned reading, read it, and mark up your copy. Underline, highlight, circle—use any method you want to point to specific spots in the text. As well, write margin comments–at least five comments–that show you engaging with the text.

Writing Task 2

Explaining Critical Reading

Working from the mark-up you completed for Writing Task 1–2, you will now summarize and analyze your critical reading by writing a brief description of how and why you annotated. Your explanation should include responses to the following questions:

- What did you mark in the text?
- Why did you mark it?

Assessment: For lower-stakes daily writing tasks such as the two above, we often have a simple scoring scale that we use throughout the semester, as it can be time-consuming for teachers and confusing for students to navigate a myriad of rubrics and scoring mechanisms. One common approach we take is to have a simple 5-point scale for daily assignments with a descriptor for what constitutes a 5, such as the following: student completed the assignment fully and thoughtfully. If you have a common daily assignment, such as a reading response, then you might provide a more specific descriptor for that, such as the following: response addresses the prompt (if given) and is grounded in specifics from the reading.

Essay 1 Summary and Response Paper

Description and Evaluation Criteria

Select one of the three texts we have read as a class and write a paper in which you employ the foundational writing tools explained in these first few weeks' worth of lectures:

- summarizing the author's main claims;
- paraphrasing and quoting selectively; and
- responding to the author by offering your own perspective.

Note: You will be assessed, in part, on the substantial revision and changes you make to improve your essay from the rough draft, if you consider and/or incorporate the feedback you receive from the Writing Center, and on your final version submitted here.

Requirements

Your paper should include the following:

- A cover letter that explains what you learned during your Writing Center visit, what you chose to revise and why, and your strengths and areas for development.
- A 500–600 word section in which you summarize the author's main claims, paraphrasing and quoting selectively—do not repeat everything the author says.
- Another section that is between 500–600 words in length in which you respond to the author by offering your own perspective—agreeing, disagreeing, or a mix of both.

Submission

- Your response should be between four and five pages in length, with double-spaced, size-12, Times New Roman font. Submit the assignment as a single attachment to this assignment (the cover letter must be part of the essay; do not attempt to attach it as a second document to this assignment).

Levels: This is clearly a more advanced activity compared to some of the others, stemming from the fact that it was designed for students in a college writing course. Students at the following levels in the three sets of standards outlined earlier might benefit most from this exercise: WIDA (Reaching [Level 6)], CEFR (C2), and ACTFL (Advanced High).

Assessment: We typically use analytic rubrics for longer essay assignments, but the creators of this assignment included a detailed holistic rubric that explains the various levels of performance they are looking for at different grade levels. Note that the rubric provided here uses letter grades rather than points and is oriented toward variation in language as opposed to a narrow focus on grammatical accuracy, which perhaps stems from the target audience being a writing class primarily serving English L1 learners.

Detailed Holistic Rubric

A range: Students meet the course's highest expectations for quality. For example,

- ❑ Students draw out the implications of their Writing Center consultation and their revision decisions for their development as writers. For example, students may explore the challenges of applying the insights of the consultation to their future composing situations.
- ❑ Students offer a nuanced portrait of a writer's argument. For example, students may explore how underemphasized facets of the writer's argument shift or recast the writer's larger perspective.
- ❑ Students identify significant source material and smoothly employ a full range of the methods described in the textbook. For example, depending on what is appropriate in the context, students may begin sentences with their own words, with quotes, or with a summary.
- ❑ Students articulate why their response to a writer's perspective matters. For example, students may connect their agreement, disagreement, or a combination to a current conversation or issue.
- ❑ Students effectively move back and forth between the global and local levels. For example, elements of students' compositions, like topic sentences and repeated key phrases, may help to gain, sustain, and ultimately fulfill reader interest.

B range: Students meet the requirements of the assignment and address course expectations for quality. But at least one part of this writing can still be improved. For example,

- ❑ Students explore the relationships among their Writing Center Consultation, their revision decisions, and their development as writers. For example, students may discuss how their consultation shaped their revision decisions and what these decisions suggest about their future development as writers. However, students can still engage more fully with the future implications of their experiences.
- ❑ Students represent a writers' perspective adequately. For example, students may attend to the writer's argument as well as the writer's qualifications to this argument. However, students can still explore and explain the nuances of the writer's perspective more fully.
- ❑ Students integrate relevant source material consistently. For example, students may frame their quotations correctly. However, students may not employ a wider range of the methods described in the lectures on summary, quote, and paraphrase.
- ❑ Students respond to a writer's perspective, elaborating on their agreement or disagreement with this perspective. But, students can also state their point of view.
- ❑ Students close most gaps between the global and local levels. However, opportunities for refinement remain. For example, students may build in transitional phrases or tailor word choice to clarify their stance toward a writer's perspective.

C range: Students meet the assignment requirements, but at least one part of their project approaches rather than meets class expectations for quality. For example,

- ❑ Students discuss their Writing Center consultations, their revision decisions, and their strengths and needs for development as a writer, but students may only begin to explore the relationship among these topics. For example, students may emphasize only one facet of their consultation while ignoring other facets that would shed light on their revision decisions and development as a writer.
- ❑ Students represent a writer's perspective, but this representation may be selective. For example, students may emphasize one element of the writer's perspective while ignoring another element important to the writer's overall argument.

- ❑ Students quote, summarize, and paraphrase passages from the reading, but source material may be only partly relevant or integrated unevenly. For example, students may only partly employ the methods described in the lectures on summary, quote, and paraphrase.
- ❑ Students respond to other writers' perspectives, but this response may only begin to develop students' own perspectives. For example, students may stop short of elaborating on their reasons for agreeing or disagreeing with a perspective.
- ❑ Students revise and edit, but gaps may remain between the global and local levels. For example, one part of an essay may need to be revised to reflect changes in the larger argument.

D range: Students do not meet at least one of the requirements of the assignment.
F range: The student did not turn in the assignment.

Portfolios

Portfolios have become increasingly popular for writing assessment in recent years because of their ability to help illustrate writing as a process and capture a more authentic picture of learners' abilities (Crusan, 2010). For instance, the first-year writing program at Todd's former institution required students to pass the final portfolio at the end of the semester to pass the class, regardless of how they did on the previous assignments. Writing portfolios vary in what they include. Some might include just one essay, but with very high expectations for the amount of revision materials included. Others might include multiple essays. Sometimes, students are expected to revise an earlier essay by changing the genre for the portfolio version. Hamp-Lyons and Condon (2000) listed the following as key characteristics of portfolios:

- Collection: includes multiple performances
- Range: includes writing for different audiences and purposes
- Context richness: provides a richer picture of students' work in the learning context
- Delayed evaluation: promotes revision over time and gives teacher an opportunity to evaluate the assignments and not just focus on grading
- Selection: includes a portion of student work from a course, not the whole corpus

- Student-centered control: writer can select which pieces to submit; more control over their performance as they can revise with feedback and time
- Reflection and self-assessment: usually includes some reflective writing (more on this below)
- Growth along specific parameters: teachers can better monitor growth in a specific area over time, such as student ability to organize their essays or their ability to spell more accurately
- Development over time: related to the former, students and teachers can see their progress over time.

As noted above, portfolios typically include some kind of reflective/framing letter, an element we highly recommend, as it helps students think about their process metacognitively and arguably helps support the transfer of the knowledge and skills they learned in the class and through creating the portfolio to other contexts (Yancey, Robertson, & Taczak, 2014). These letters are often focused on the course/student learning outcomes because the aim is to help students reflect on how the course helped them grow as writers. Here's an example of a portfolio assignment Todd has used:

At the end of each semester, each English 101 and 102 student prepares a writing portfolio. This typically includes revised drafts of one or more major writing assignments, the materials used throughout the drafting process for the chosen assignment(s), and a reflective essay discussing the progress the student made toward course goals through the semester. The goal of assembling this portfolio is twofold: (1) to demonstrate that the student advanced as a writer during the course of the semester and (2) to show that the student recognizes how to transfer the learning they took from this course into future writing situations across the university and beyond.

The portfolio for this class should contain the following:

- A reflective essay between 900–1,200 words
- A final revision of one major writing assignment along with the drafts and peer feedback leading up to that assignment

Your final portfolio will be completed and submitted electronically in the form of a wiki page (a site designed for groups of people to share ideas by creating simple pages and linking them together) devoted to your portfolio.

Proposed sections of the page include:

- Title and Name
- Introduction to your portfolio: this should be one or two paragraphs long and should introduce the purpose of your portfolio and guide your reader through viewing it. Where should they start? What should they do?
- Revised essay, process documents, and feedback: post these as .doc/.docx or .pdf files Include the commented documents I turned into you along with any extra written feedback peers or myself provided (these comments can be posted on your Wiki page).
- Reflective essay: post this as a .doc/.docx or .pdf file.

Reflective Essay

Along with revising your chosen essay, this is probably the most time-consuming part of this portfolio assignment. The purpose of this reflection is to identify and explain how you've worked toward the course outcomes. View this reflection as a written argument demonstrating that you have strived to meet the requirements of 101. Format simply with your name and date at the top left and 101 Reflective Essay centered as the title. No APA style required.

Introductory paragraph

A short introductory statement briefly explaining what you intend to discuss regarding your progress as a writer.

Sections 1–5

Pick four different course goals (listed below), focusing each section on a chosen goal. The last section should focus on goal G. Begin each section by explaining/defining the chosen goal in your own words and then use examples from your three major writing examples to explain how you advanced toward that goal. These examples can be anecdotes from the composing process and direct quotes from your writing. Be sure to use both and to reference all three major writing assignments at some point in these sections (note: you don't have to refer to all three in each section).

A. analyze rhetorical situations in terms of audience, context, purpose, and medium in order to improve your reading and writing
B. compose arguments in a variety of genres, using rhetorical strategies, claims, and evidence that are appropriate to the rhetorical situation
C. use research and writing as a means of discovery, to examine your personal beliefs in the context of multiple perspectives, and to explore focused research questions
D. describe the social nature of writing, particularly the role of discourse communities at the local, national, and international level
E. integrate others' positions and perspectives into your writing ethically, appropriately, and effectively
F. use multiple approaches for planning, researching, prewriting, composing, assessing, revising, editing, proofreading, collaborating, and incorporating feedback in order to make your writing stronger
G. **required** ** evaluate how what you've learned about writing in this course can be applied in other contexts and can advance your goals and the goals of your communities
H. characterize your improvement in the dialect of Standardized Written American English at the level of the sentence, paragraph, and document
I. recognize and describe the value of different languages and dialects in your own and others' texts

Conclusion

Summarize your overall progress in the course, what you wish you had done better, and what you plan to take from this class as you advance in your academic and professional career.

FIGURE 6.19
Portfolio Rubric

Points Possible	Points Earned	
50		**Revised essay:** revision quality (Look at both my summative comments and in-document comments and undergo substantial revisions for full credit. If I make a comment at one point, you want to see if it is applicable for other parts in your essay. Don't just revise locally.)
50		**Revised essay:** all process materials included (Items to include are brainstorming materials/lists, annotated bibliographies, all drafts, and peer/instructor comments. The more comprehensive and detailed this section, the higher your score will be.)
50		**Reflective essay:** depth of reflection (The essay should show you carefully considered the goals you chose and took the time to seriously reflect on how you moved toward achieving them throughout the semester.)
50		**Reflective essay:** detail (The essay includes quotes from your major writing assignments and interesting anecdotes or stories to ground your reflection.)
50		**Reflective essay:** all major components covered, clear writing that is largely free of grammar/mechanical errors (The essay discusses all three essays, five major goals including G, and has an introduction and conclusion.)
50		**Wiki page**: formatting (The page includes all the major sections, is easy to navigate, has the same font throughout, and uses emphasis techniques such as bolding and font size appropriately.)

Levels: This is clearly a more advanced activity compared to some of the others, stemming from the fact that it was designed for students in a college writing course. Students at the following levels in the three sets of standards outlined earlier might benefit most from this exercise: WIDA (Reaching [Level 6]), CEFR (C2), and ACTFL (Advanced High).

Assessment: In this assignment, Todd tried to clearly spell out the expectations for his students—note how the analytical rubric provides additional details and examples that aren't found in the body of the assignment. Note that he provides an outline for the reflective letter, which some instructors and students might find too restrictive. He made this choice because he has found that learners often struggle with reflective essays and that a clear organization schema helps them stay focused on what they learned, the primary goal of the assignment, rather than spending too much time thinking about how to structure their reflection. The reflection letter is also organized around the course outcomes, which we stated above is a strategy to help students return to the goals of the course and think about how they progressed toward them. This focus can also be useful for the instructor as he is able to gauge how well students understand and feel they progressed in a certain area—for instance, reading through the reflections might reveal that the class needs to spend additional time on a particular outcome in future semesters.

Activities and Questions

1. Using the discussions regarding types of speaking assessment (imitative, intensive, responsive, interactive, and extensive) and the flow of assessment (controlled to guided to free), design a speaking assessment for your students. Keep in mind their proficiency level, where they might fall on the WIDA, CEFR, and ACTFL scales, and how that assessment can inform your teaching. What do you want to know about what your students can or cannot do?
2. Create a writing assessment using the same criteria as in #1. Consider the four types of writing (imitative, intensive [controlled], responsive, and extensive), selecting one upon which to focus your assessment.
3. Design a short reading test for use with a specified group of students. Explain clearly what the test is assessing, justify its design with respect to the characteristics of good assessments, and include a scoring system.

In pairs, discuss three key take-aways from this chapter and how they might influence your listening and reading assessment practices.

1. Above, you were asked to develop a speaking assessment and a reading assessment. In pairs, discuss the rationales behind the assessments you created and how they support learning. What are the specific difficulties that students are likely to face in completing the assessment task, and how might a teacher support learning before and after the assessment?

7

Assessment of Grammar and Vocabulary

This chapter considers separately the assessment of grammar and the assessment of vocabulary. The grammar portion of the chapter first addresses the idea that multiple choice test questions do not assess student ability to use language authentically, making the point that evaluation must reflect contextualized real-life uses of grammar. The chapter then discusses advantages and disadvantages of assessment methods and elucidates ways that teachers can move through a controlled to guided to free approach when teaching and assessing grammar.

The vocabulary section of the chapter considers both discrete and embedded vocabulary assessment, describing these approaches in detail and considering the advantages and disadvantages to each method. This section will include sample questions for discrete assessment (multiple choice, matching, sentence completion, translation) and embedded vocabulary assessment (in reading, in writing, and in speaking).

Why Is Grammar Important?

Folse (2016) defined grammar as "the set of patterns that holds a language together" (p. vi). Grammar patterns describe how we use words in English. A grammar pattern tells us what words, phrases, or clauses can be used with adjectives, nouns, or verbs. One of the most common sentence patterns in English is noun phrase + BE + adjective phrase (e.g., the dog is furry). In fact, there are number of phrase structure rules in English considered basic, such as noun phrase + verb phrase (e.g., the class studied; the baby cried). Since grammar is useful for communicating and comprehending effectively, those patterns are useful in that they help learners recognize and become familiar with many different sentences.

Despite the fact that grammar is a critical and consequential topic for teachers, grammar is rarely discussed in the major journals in our field today. Work on vocabulary is even rarer. Until the Natural Approach (Krashen & Terrell, 1983) (in which language output is not forced but allowed to emerge spontaneously after students have attended to large amounts of comprehensible language input) took hold, grammar and vocabulary teaching and research were *de rigueur*; following the pedagogical shift as a result of adoption of the Natural Approach grammar never regained its former popularity among researchers. Research into the assessment of grammar and vocabulary is rarer still. Teachers, however, still hold grammar and vocabulary teaching in high regard. Students often care even more about grammar and vocabulary.

For teachers and students, grammar and vocabulary are key components in learning a new language. Folse (2016) aptly encapsulated the historical role of grammar in English language teaching: "Sometimes grammar has been promoted, almost worshipped, in our field, but other times grammar has been completely shunned. Despite the often-predictable swings of the pendulum in acceptable L2 pedagogy, grammar has continued to be central to the teaching of foreign languages" (p. 64).

Grammar is not taught for its own sake; in good language programs, it is taught so students can communicate better. Given this goal, grammar assessments should focus on a student's ability to use the target grammar, not just identify it linguistically (Folse, 2010).

In Chapter 3, we discussed Bloom's taxonomy, reminding readers that the taxonomy presents educational goals along a continuum from simple to more complex and includes knowledge, comprehension, application, analysis, synthesis, and evaluation. Folse's (2010) point that students should be able to use the language incorporates knowledge, comprehension, and, most importantly, application; it is one thing to be able to recognize the past tense in a string of words, but it is wholly another to be able to use the past tense in conversation.

Savage, Bitterlin, and Price (2010) argued that, in teaching, a knowledge-transmission approach to grammar leads to limited language acquisition. Most of us are familiar with the phenomenon of students who know the rules of grammar but who are nonetheless unable to perform a simple task in English, such as asking for directions. As a result of this observed gap between knowledge of grammar and its successful application, there has been a shift in our view of grammar instruction over the last 20 or 30 years. Nowadays, many ESL practitioners view grammar less as a body of knowledge to be studied than as a skill to be practiced and developed; in other words, grammar is an enabling skill, acts as a motivator, promotes self-sufficiency, and provides a resource for learner self-correction.

Grammar is inextricably linked to communicative language learning. It is useless to learn how to read, write, speak, or understand the meaning of words without also learning the underlying syntactical structure of language. A basic knowledge of syntax can change the meaning of isolated words from nonsensical garble to a statement or a question, or from a narrative to a directive. A deeper knowledge of syntax can also enhance how communicators present themselves orally or in written products, giving them a wider range of interaction from casual to formal (Larsen-Freeman, 2014).

It is therefore essential that ESL/EL teachers include grammar skills instruction in their lessons. Constructing meaning is impossible without all elements of understanding: morphology and phonology; knowledge of adequate syntactical structure; comprehensible (not *perfect* or *native*) pronunciation and spelling; a relevant lexicon of second language vocabulary; and decoding skills for input (which is also informed by knowledge of syntax). These aspects of language are inextricably linked to grammar, which is the blueprint for creating meaning in spoken and written form in any language.

Basic Considerations in Teaching Grammar

In order to acquire any knowledge, it is important to first get the learner's attention and interest. There is an acronym commonly used in marketing that we can apply: **AIDA.**

A = Attention I = Interest D = Decision A = Action

Learning will only take place once learners have a reason to apply themselves to it. To inspire the desire to learn, an instructor must learn about the students in order to present skills at the individual and group level through topics and activities that attract **attention**, keep student **interest**, encourage the **decision** to master the skills, and ask students to take **action** freely in speaking, listening, reading, and writing (Sjostrom, 2020). Savignon (2017) has reminded us that grammar is best learned when it is matched with learners' experiences and goals. Consequently, she encourages teachers to focus on communicative concepts such as rules of appropriacy and other broader features of communication rather than sentence-level morphosyntactic features.

Instruction should be as individualized as possible to meet students at their level of linguistic competency in the L1 as well as at their familiarity or inexperience with spoken and written English. In order to maintain interest and motivation for learning when learning becomes frustrating or confusing, teachers need to understand students' reasons for learning English and capitalize on that knowledge, reminding students of their goals. By couching implicit and explicit grammar instruction into relevant content, the significance and use of grammatical skills is more likely to make sense and keep student motivation high (Folse, 2016). Allowing for ample practice in real-world language use with the freedom to create meaning with existing skills—even with errors—helps students gain linguistic competence (and confidence) that can be applied in any situation (Savignon, 2017).

Purposes for learning English will also determine the amount of emphasis on academic grammar vs. competence in everyday communication (Folse, 2016). The need to communicate at an academic level necessitates more rigorous attention to formal, academically relevant grammar along with academic vocabulary and language usage. However, students who are learning English for everyday communication with service providers, employers/employees, or for conversation with friends simply need to learn how to understand and be understood in less formally structured discourse. In this case, vocabulary, idiomatic language, and body language, and an understanding of the differences in structuring questions and statements in relevant situational usage, are more important.

In short, grammar is naturally a part of language learning; however, the depth and type of instruction will be determined by purposes for learning. Teachers can better ensure maximum engagement and application if they teach skills by tailoring topics to the purpose and interests of learners. Teachers can also use direct instruction for remediation of ingrained habits or when students struggle to attain a particular skill, but should only do so for a short, intensive time. Encouraging students to engage freely in discussion or other use of the target language without excessive correction also allows students to learn and gain confidence through natural exploration of and engagement with language.

Grammar Assessment Standards

WIDA

WIDA contains a broad range of oral phrase and sentence patterns and grammatical structures matched to content topics; the grammar standards are mostly intertwined with the four skills of listening, speaking, reading, and writing. For example, in the performance definitions for listening and reading in grades PreK–12, WIDA states, "At each grade, toward the end of a given level of English proficiency, and with instructional support, English language learners will process" these language forms and conventions "within sociocultural contexts for language use" (p. 8). Here are the expectations at various levels:

At Level 1 Entering

- Simple grammatical constructions (e.g., commands, Wh- questions, declaratives)
- Common social and instructional forms and patterns

At Level 2 Emerging

- Compound grammatical constructions
- Repetitive phrasal and sentence patterns across content areas

At Level 3 Developing

- Compound and some complex (e.g., noun phrase, verb phrase, prepositional phrase) grammatical constructions
- Sentence patterns across content areas

At Level 4 Expanding

- A variety of complex grammatical constructions
- Sentence patterns characteristic of particular content areas

At Level 5 Bridging

- Compound, complex grammatical constructions (e.g. multiple phrases and clauses)

It is an easy step to use these descriptions as a set of can-dos; once teachers see what their students can and can't do, the level descriptors can also be used to plan curricula.

CEFR

While CEFR does not offer explicit standards for grammar, you will find lists of grammatical structures expected to be mastered for particular CEFR levels on outside websites, such as Exam English (2020, https://www.examenglish.com/CEFR/cefr_grammar.htm). While not sanctioned by CEFR, resources on third-party websites can be helpful for teachers and students in thinking about what grammar work is important for students at particular levels.

According to Exam English, here's a list of the grammatical structures necessary for CEFR B1:

Adverbs
Broad range of intensifiers, such as *too, enough*
Comparatives and superlatives
Complex question tags
Conditionals, 2nd and 3rd
Connecting words expressing cause and effect, contrast, etc.
Future continuous
Modals—must/can't deduction
Modals—might, may, will, probably
Modals—should have/might have/etc.
Modals: must/have to
Past continuous
Past perfect
Past simple
Past tense responses
Phrasal verbs, extended
Present perfect continuous
Present perfect/past simple
Reported speech (range of tenses)
Simple passive
Wh- questions in the past
Will and going to, for prediction

While CEFR does not provide the level of specificity that the above list does, it provides some general standards in the form of what students should be able to do in terms of grammatical accuracy at each CEFR level.

A1 Shows only limited control of a few simple grammatical structures and sentence patterns in a learned repertoire.
A2 Uses some simple structures correctly but still systematically makes basic mistakes—for example, tends to mix up tenses and forget to mark agreement; nevertheless, it is usually clear what he/she is trying to say.

B1 Communicates with reasonable accuracy in familiar contexts; generally good control though with noticeable mother tongue influence. Errors occur, but it is clear what he/she is trying to express. Uses reasonably accurately a repertoire of frequently used "routines" and patterns associated with more predictable situations.

B2 Has good grammatical control. Occasional "slips," or non-systematic errors and minor flaws in sentence structure may still occur, but they are rare and can often be corrected in retrospect. Shows a relatively high degree of grammatical control. Does not make mistakes that lead to misunderstanding.

C1 Consistently maintains a high degree of grammatical accuracy; errors are rare and difficult to spot.

C2 Maintains consistent grammatical control of complex language, even while attention is otherwise engaged (e.g., in forward planning, in monitoring others' reactions).

Types of Grammar Activities

As we have reminded readers throughout this text, anytime we create activities for grammar, we are creating assessments with specific purposes. Again, we need to make certain that we understand the different purposes for assessing grammatical skills. The objective for grammatical practice in the classroom is to enable students to become successful users of the language in speaking and writing. As in other chapters, we incorporate controlled, guided, and free activities for grammar, although, as we mentioned earlier, grammar is often assessed using discrete activities; assessment at the controlled and free levels necessarily incorporates reading, writing, listening, and speaking. When we assess grammar, it is quite evident that we cannot easily separate the four skills.

Controlled Grammar Activity

Controlled grammar assessment usually takes the form of multiple choice tests or fill-in-the-blank worksheets. Because there is only one correct choice, and because the teacher can immediately review the test, the students can quickly see how well they did and what they might have to work on. It's easy to see how a test of this sort, especially at lower levels of language proficiency, can inform the student of grammar issues and also inform the teacher of what they need to review or what they can omit from their lessons.

Multiple Choice: Past tense verbs—consider the bracketed verb. Which answer is the past tense of that verb? Please circle the letter of the most appropriate answer (answers are bolded):

1. My brother and I _______ [go] to the store.
   a. Went
   b. Gone
   c. Go
2. The horses _____ [run] on the beach in Assateague, Virginia.
   a. Run
   b. Ran
   c. Runned
3. Many of my friends _____ [visit] the beach last summer.
   a. Visiting
   b. Visit
   c. Visited
4. Deer _____ [eat] my flowers last week.
   a. Eat
   b. Eaten
   c. Ate
5. I _____ [teach] online for the first time last spring.
   a. Taught
   b. Teach
   c. Teaching

Fill in the blanks with the ***simple past*** of the verb in brackets [].

1. Two years ago, my parents _______ [buy] a new house.
2. My sister ______ [get] a new job as a nurse.
3. We ________ [drive] to the cabin on the lake last week.
4. Susana and her cousins _____ [travel] to Italy five years ago.
5. I ______ [ride] a horse at summer camp.

6. My grandparents ______ [come] to my birthday party in June.
7. The students _____ [finish] their homework during study period.
8. I _____ [meet] my friends for lunch last week.

Assessment can be accomplished by students scoring their own worksheets or by teachers scoring. Either way is a great form of washback; students scoring their own sheets provides immediate feedback to the students that can be furthered by reviewing answers in class and answering questions about what is correct and why; teachers scoring gives immediate feedback to the teacher and informs her of who got it, who didn't, and what she might have to reteach.

Guided Grammar Activity

This activity was developed by Lakmini Siriwardana (2019b).
The following activity is not fill in the blank or multiple choice; therefore, it leaves a little more to the student, as they need to be able to recognize the form and use of certain grammatical structures, in this case adjective clauses.

> Directions: Find all the adjective clauses in the short paragraph and reduce the adjective sentences that can be reduced. The adjective clauses have been underlined in the following example; one clause has been reduced.

Paragraph:

Mozart, who is one of the most popular composers of all time, is a very talented musician. Mozart showed promise early in life. At an age when most children can only play "Chopsticks," five-year-old Mozart, who was already competent on piano and violin, was performing for royalty. The court musician job for which he was hired at 17 bored young Mozart, who quit the job and traveled, seeking a position that might challenge him. The music that he wrote in Salzburg, and which made him famous, never made him rich. The musical genius who so enriched the world died young, ill, and penniless.

One reduction: Mozart, ~~who is~~ one of the most popular composers of all time, is a very talented musician.

While not controlled, there are only a few options for correct answers.

Free Grammar Activity

Before we outline any free activities, it is important to consider the notion of free. Even when we are creating what we consider to be free test items, we are usually prompting our students with some kind of information that may reduce the free-ness of the activity. For example, writing is most often considered a free activity; however, we most often prompt our students to produce certain kinds of language. Nowhere is that more visible than in grammar. We might ask students to write an essay about what they did last weekend, prompting the use of past tense, and past tense can be expressed in seven ways: simple past (I talked to my friend), past progressive (I was talking to my friend until you called me), present perfect (I have talked to my friend), past perfect (I had already talked to my friend when you said you'd help me), past perfect progressive (I had been talking to my friend for nearly ten minutes when you said you'd help me), used to (I used to talk to my friend), would (I would talk to my friend.) (Folse, 2016).

A difficult concept for students, especially in how they are *formed*, is understanding comparative and superlative adjectives in context, mainly in reading (a *good*, *better*, *best* teacher). A fun activity involves assigning students to first look at advertisements in magazines and then create their own advertisement using comparative and superlative adjectives.

For this formative assessment, gather English-language newspapers and magazines. Ask students to look through them to find instances of comparative and superlative adjectives. Divide students into four groups to create ads; they then present their advertisement to the class. To use the activity as a formative assessment, classmates can vote on which ad they think is best by using a ballot with the following instructions:

Best ad ballot—circle your choice for the best ad

1. Group One
2. Group Two
3. Group Three
4. Group Four

   In one sentence, tell why you voted the way you voted. Example: I voted for group one because they used exciting comparative and superlative adjectives, made the words come alive, and convinced me to buy their product.

Assessment: To make the activity one that teachers can assess, create a rubric using criteria that has been agreed upon by all students. The rubric might look something like the one in Figure 7.1.

FIGURE 7.1
Comparative and Superlative Grammar Rubric

	0 Missing	1 Needs work	2 Satisfactory	3 Exceptional
Correctly *forms* the comparative				
Correctly *forms* the superlative				
Correctly *uses* the comparative				
Correctly *uses* the superlative				

A free type of task uses guided discovery, which requires teachers to plan activities and questions that push students toward the key points of the lesson. Teachers may not explicitly teach about comparatives and superlatives, but through the guided discovery activities and tasks planned, students can work with comparatives and superlatives and pick up on the rules and patterns. This encourages learners to become more autonomous, to achieve a more active role in language learning.

There are quite a few websites that offer a plethora of grammar worksheets and activities. Because many PreK–12 teachers are busy all day long managing a large student population in various classes, a (paid or free) subscription to one or more of these websites (e.g., Teachers Pay Teachers—not a subscription, but teachers pay one another for lessons and activities, BetterLesson, PBS Learning Media) might be beneficial in fighting fatigue and burnout.

Another **free** grammar assessment activity/assessment is to ask students to find examples of certain grammatical structures in authentic writing.

Directions: Read the article below. Choose one paragraph and underline all the nouns. Then, put them in two categories: count and non-count. Then give a reason why you think the noun is either count or non-count. Afterward, as a class, we will check the answers and discuss our answers.

Making the Switch to a Healthy Diet

Switching to a healthy diet doesn't have to be an all or nothing proposition. You don't have to be perfect; you don't have to completely eliminate foods you enjoy, and you don't have to change everything all at once—that usually only leads to cheating or giving up on your new eating plan.

A better approach is to make a few small changes at a time. Keeping your goals modest can help you achieve more in the long term without feeling deprived or overwhelmed by a major diet overhaul. Think of planning a healthy diet as a number of small, manageable steps—like adding a salad to your diet once a day. As your small changes become habit, you can continue to add more healthy choices.

[Excerpted from Robinson, Segal, & Segal (2020).]

Assessment: The chart in Figure 7.2 can be a simple way to assess students' answers. Students list the nouns, whether they are count and non-count, and why students have classified them as either count or non-count. This forced classification reinforces the count/non-count binary. One of the benefits of this chart: students can grade their own work as the teacher and other students call out nouns they underlined. This is one way to provide excellent washback.

In order to address grammatical issues in her second language writing classes, Deborah expects her writers to complete a worksheet before coming to her office for a required grammar conference during many writing assignments. The worksheet presses students to come to terms in many different ways with consistent errors in their writing. Deborah believes, as do others (Ferris, 2011), that self-identification is a powerful tool that promotes autonomy. This is what goes on the worksheet:

Each week, before our grammar conference, you are to fill out this sheet using your most recent writing assignment. *You cannot conference* without first thinking about the errors that are consistent in your writing and making note of them on this sheet. This will help you edit more carefully because you will be forced to look for errors that you might miss otherwise. Please remember that you are in charge of the conference and

FIGURE 7.2
Noun Activity Chart

Noun	Count	Non-count	Why

will do most of the talking. You need to tell me what steps you are taking to make your writing more meaningful.

1. Select three (3) errors that are the most noticeable in this example of your writing. Write the sentences (below) in which these errors occur.
2. Why do you think you made these errors?
3. How can you correct these errors? Correct them here.
4. Grammars errors often interfere with our message. How has your meaning been improved because of the corrections you made?

Why Is Vocabulary Important?

Linguistically, a word is a single distinct meaningful element of speech or writing, used with others (or sometimes alone) to form a sentence and typically shown with a space on either side when written or printed. English has four major word classes: nouns, verbs, adjectives, and adverbs. They have many thousands of members, and new nouns, verbs, adjectives, and adverbs are often created. Nouns are the most common type of word, followed by verbs. Schmitt and Schmitt (2020) remind us that what it means to know a word could fill a very large volume. If we can read and know words, we generally know how to use a dictionary and can understand words in context. When we know a word, we know its form (morphology), its meaning (semantics—linguistic meaning and how it is conveyed), and its use.

In morphology, we know what the word looks like, how to spell it, and how to pronounce it. We also know different forms of the word and how to form words. We can think about a word's parts (prefix, root/base word, suffix) and use resources—such as a dictionary or thesaurus—to determine the word's meaning. We are able to add affixes to words to change their form and know how these changes affect the word either grammatically or in meaning.

Semantics concerns not only meanings of words but also "how word meanings combine to produce the meanings of larger phrasal expressions" (Dawson & Phelan, 2016, p. 246). Schmitt and Schmitt (2020) defined semantics as the study of meaning relationships; they categorize meaning relationships as sense relations (p. 42), which include "oppositeness and similar meaning" (p. 42) but are more precisely referred to as things like synonymy (closely related meanings), antonymy (opposite meanings), and hyponymy (e.g., a Scottish terrier is a dog; it is part of the set of all things that can be referred to as a dog).

When we know how to use a word, we know when it is appropriate to use the word, what Schmitt and Schmitt (2020) referred to as an appropriateness decision (p. 84). We ask questions such as *Should I use this word? Is it too common? Too informal? Too much jargon?* The authors noted that learners must develop rough intuitions about the appropriateness of a word, but Schmitt and Schmitt worry that L2 learners might never receive enough input and therefore need to be explicitly taught in order to develop intuition.

Another question that is often asked when considering vocabulary is *How many words should we know in another language?* Goulden, Nation, and Read (1990) suggested that native speakers of a language know approximately 17,000 base words. Gonzalez (2017) researches vocabulary in second language writing, what we should teach in our writing classes, and how we might teach vocabulary. She has noted that "lexical diversity has a greater impact on writing achievement than lexical frequency; however, frequency does initially help increase writing scores at the lower proficiency levels" (p. 915). She recommends that simply teaching a list of vocabulary in our writing classes is inadequate; we must also "guide learners in how to employ these words in a diverse manner during the composition process in order to achieve a richness of lexical usage for proficient second language writing" (p. 915). This same philosophy can translate to assessment; our aim is diversity of vocabulary use.

Vocabulary Assessment Standards

WIDA

We will once again use the example in the performance definitions for listening and reading from PreK–12. According to WIDA, vocabulary usage considers discourse, sentence/phrase, word/phrase level discourse focused on vocabulary usage, with the following features: "General, specific, and technical language; Multiple meanings of words and phrases; Formulaic and idiomatic expressions; Nuances and shades of meaning, and collocations" (p. 7). Here are the expectations at various levels:

At Level 1 Entering

- General content-related words
- Everyday social and instructional words and expressions
- Common social and instructional forms and patterns

At Level 2 Emerging

- General and some specific content words and expressions (including cognates)
- Social and instructional words and expressions across content areas

At Level 3 Developing

- Specific content words and expressions
- Words or expressions related to content area with common collocations and idioms across content areas

At Level 4 Expanding

- Specific and some technical content-area language
- Words and expressions with multiple meanings or collocations and idioms for each content area

At Level 5 Bridging

- Technical and abstract content-area language
- Words and expressions with shades of meaning for each content area

Clearly, these descriptions can be used by classroom teachers as a set of can-dos; once teachers see what their students can and can't do, the level descriptors can also be used to plan curricula.

Further help for teachers can be derived from the Expanded Strands in WIDA (2020) to support curriculum development and thereby assessment. For example, ELD standard 1 is Social and Instructional Language (p. 23). The cognitive function is "Students at all levels of English language proficiency REMEMBER how to work collaboratively with their peers" (p. 22) The Topic-Related Language: "Students at all levels of English language proficiency interact with grade-level words and expressions, such as: taking turns, cooperation, job, today, tomorrow" (p. 22). The example language features for vocabulary usage (word/phrase level) are shown in Table 7.1.

TABLE 7.1
Example language features for vocabulary usage

Levels 1–3	Levels 2–4	Levels 3–5
Yellow	Job	Center
Green	I can	Work together
Red	Help	Everyone
Blue	Leader	My turn
Group	Lunch count	Line leader
Help	Calendar	Share time/show and tell
Clean up	weather	

CEFR

While CEFR (2011) mentions of vocabulary are largely intertwined with the four skills of reading, writing, speaking, and listening, CEFR provides some sets of standards under the Linguistic aspect of Communicative Language Competence with references to vocabulary range and vocabulary control.

Under vocabulary range:

A1 Has a basic vocabulary repertoire of isolated words and phrases related to particular concrete situations.

A2 Has sufficient vocabulary to conduct routine, everyday transactions involving familiar situations and topics. Has a sufficient vocabulary for the expression of basic communicative needs. Has a sufficient vocabulary for coping with simple survival needs.

B1 Has a sufficient vocabulary to express him/herself with some circumlocutions on most topics pertinent to his everyday life such as family, hobbies and interests, work, travel, and current events.

B2 Has a good range of vocabulary for matters connected to his field and most general topics. Can vary formulation to avoid frequent repetition, but lexical gaps can still cause hesitation and circumlocution.

C1 Has a good command of a broad lexical repertoire allowing gaps to be readily overcome with circumlocutions; little obvious searching for expressions or avoidance strategies. Good command of idiomatic expressions and colloquialisms.

C2 Has a good command of a very broad lexical repertoire including idiomatic expressions and colloquialisms; shows awareness of connotative levels of meaning.

Under vocabulary control:

A1 No descriptor available.

A2 Can control a narrow repertoire dealing with concrete everyday needs.

B1 Shows good control of elementary vocabulary but major errors still occur when expressing more complex thoughts or handling unfamiliar topics and situations.

B2 Lexical accuracy is generally high, though some confusion and incorrect word choice does occur without hindering communication.

C1 Occasional minor slips, but no significant vocabulary errors.

C2 Consistently correct and appropriate use of vocabulary.

Types of Vocabulary Activities

Controlled Vocabulary Activity

Traditionally, vocabulary is assessed through multiple choice and fill-in-the-blanks activities. As mentioned earlier, authentic assessment of vocabulary is painstakingly difficult. It can be done, but it demands inordinate amounts of teacher time that might be better spent working with students.

A multiple choice question will look something like this:

1. It's a great place to live apart from the increasing volume of ________ that passes under my window every day.

    a. traffic

    b. vehicles

c. circulation

d. transport

Matching is always a great choice for beginning vocabulary lessons, activities, and assessments. Because there are a limited number of choices, there is a better chance for success, always a plus when considering affective issues. For very low proficiency students, word/picture matching is a great help.

Teachers need to be reminded of a very important take-away when considering the use of pre-made materials, especially when we can find quality worksheets online: one can spend inordinate amounts of time creating worksheets such as the one above—this creation exercise is massively time consuming. Instead, a busy teacher can go to the Internet and find thousands of helpful worksheets of this type to engage students and help the acquisition of vocabulary. It's an issue of practicality, as we have mentioned many times in this book: teacher burnout is real, and we need to take practical measures to combat it.

Using worksheets as assessment tools can be practical and provide positive washback for students. Grading is quick and relatively easy for the teacher because there is only one answer; quick grading is good as students can receive feedback quickly.

Guided Vocabulary Activities

Here are two activities that can encourage students to define unknown vocabulary they come across in their reading.

Personalized Vocabulary Lists

Students can create their own personalized vocabulary lists, which would empower them and help them to build their vocabulary. While students read, they often come across words they don't know. If they choose their own words to look up, they are more motivated to learn.

Teachers can provide charts like the one in Figure 7.3 to use as personal vocabulary logs. The chart below asks students to include information about the words so that they can go back and find the word, read it in context, and guess the meaning.

Students might also share words from their lists with other students in the class; they can share words that they were most surprised to learn or words whose definitions are quite different from what they thought they'd be. To extend this activity to assessment, students can each pick two to three words from their personal vocabulary lists; the teacher can use those words to create a vocabulary quiz for the entire class.

FIGURE 7.3
Personal Vocabulary Log

New Word	Definition	Date	Source	Page #

Context Clues

Using the context clues approach, the teacher provides reading passages or sentences with new vocabulary words embedded in them. Students then attempt to guess the definitions. Teaching vocabulary through context clues encourages critical thinking skills and helps students make connections to words, ultimately helping them remember meaning.

It's important to remember that when students can identify and determine meanings of words, they can more clearly see the value of reading as a path to knowledge. Even if students miss a word, they are still increasing their awareness of and interest in words and their meanings.

A sentence activity might look something like this. Possible vocabulary words are italicized and underlined.

1. The sunset *hovered* for just a moment on the horizon before it set.
2. The woman slowly *sauntered* into the restaurant.
3. *Dinosaurs* roamed the earth millions of years ago.

The students can attempt to guess the meaning of the words from the context of the sentence. They can be asked to write definitions for the words. They can also be asked to point out any other words in the sentences that might be unfamiliar. The teacher can provide feedback and the correct definitions. The sentence activity can then be converted into an assessment, which could take many forms. One form could provide a word bank of the new vocabulary. The students would be asked to write a story using the words from the word bank. The teacher would read each story and assess the students' vocabulary knowledge and ability to use the new words correctly.

Students can use context clues from a reading passage to determine word meanings. Below is a passage at the 5th grade level; because it is important not to cognitively overload students, limit the number of words to be defined in a passage. Vocabulary words that could be highlighted in the passage below are *accomplish*, *success*, and *frustrated*, words that might easily be defined from the context.

Fitness Goals Can Help You Find Success

When you watch skateboarders or snowboarders perform daring jumps and spins, you might wonder how they became so good. You can bet it took more than courage. "The kids who do these tricks have strength, stamina, and excellent balance," says Kathy Kaehler, a fitness trainer who created the kids' exercise programs Schoolhouse Workout and Fitkids. "They've also practiced so much that their skills look easy." At one time, those boarders only dreamed of doing those tricks. But they made it happen.

Any accomplishment takes time and effort—but it starts with setting a goal. Here's some great advice for tackling even your biggest challenges.

Get Goaling

1. Figure out what your goal is. Setting a goal provides focus so that you can make a plan and stick to it. Make your goal as specific as possible by understanding why it's important to you and when you want to accomplish it. For example, you might say to yourself, "I want to improve my karate skills so I can earn a new belt by the spring."

"You don't want the goal to be too hard so that you get frustrated and quit," says Kaehler. Maybe you want to run the 100-meter dash for your school track team. Breaking your goal into small steps that are easier to reach can make the process seem a lot more doable. "Instead of focusing on the end goal—the race—set up a monthly goal," Kaehler says. Each month, gradually increase the speed and distance of your runs until you are ready to run a 100-meter dash.

[Excerpted from Tecco, 2012.]

For an assessment, the teacher can write a series of multiple choice questions:

1. As used in the sentence, what does the word *frustrated* mean?
   a. upset or angry
   b. proud or happy
   c. excited
   d. reaching your goal

2. In the story, the author uses the word *success* ("Fitness Goals Can Help You Find Success"). What does the word success mean in this context?
    a. victory or triumph
    b. defeat
    c. sadness
    d. crankiness
3. Find the word *accomplish* in the paragraphs above. What does the author mean when using this word?
    e. give up
    f. achieve
    g. jump
    h. frantic

It is also important to present examples to students where context does not work effectively. By encouraging flexible thinking and persistence, you are helping your students develop habits of mind that will benefit them beyond the walls of the classroom. Exposure to vocabulary in context is critical to the development of language and literacy, yet empowering students to figure out the meaning of unfamiliar words by using context clues is just one element of vocabulary instruction. Students "own" words that they can:

- Read or hear in multiple and repeated rich contexts
- Define and determine in relation to other words
- Connect to known information or personal experience
- Use and manipulate in expressive language activities

Free Vocabulary Activity

Folse (2020) has reminded us that it can be incredibly difficult to create wholly communicative assessments, especially with grammar and vocabulary. Again, as we mentioned for grammar, in vocabulary, it's also so incredibly hard to get a *truly* free activity.

The closest we can come might be to ask students to write a story using vocabulary that they have learned in a certain time period. For example, the students might have learned the words *success*, *accomplish*, *frustrated*, *goal*, *support*, and *action*. The teacher could write a prompt such as the following:

> Have you ever set a goal to do something like run a race, lose weight, build a backyard shed, or plant a garden? Using the vocabulary list from this week, write a story about such a time in your life.

Assessment: As we mentioned above, it's very difficult to assess vocabulary without including other skills. The rubric in Figure 7.4 includes organization,

FIGURE 7.4
Story Rubric

	0 Missing	**1 Inadequate**	**2 Developing**	**3 Proficient**	**4 Exemplary**
Organization	No clear thesis, no focus, unity, coherence	The lack of a clear thesis interferes with comprehensibility	Writer is developing ability to produce a clear thesis with focus, unity, coherence	Writer is able to develop one idea, link it to rest of paper in logical manner with transitions	Exemplary development with single focus, unity of ideas throughout, clear transitions
Vocabulary	No vocabulary words were used	Correctly used only one new vocabulary	Correctly used two to three new vocabulary words	Correctly used 4 new vocabulary words	Correctly used ALL new vocabulary words
Development	No evident development	Ideas explored using relevant details and evidence to support the thesis?	Ideas explored using relevant details and evidence to support the thesis?	Ideas explored using relevant details and evidence to support the thesis?	Ideas explored using relevant details and evidence to support the thesis?
Conventions	Writer is unable to use conventional spelling, punctuation, paragraphing, capitalization, and grammar correctly	Writer is only marginally able to use conventional spelling, punctuation, paragraphing, capitalization, and grammar correctly	Evidence of development of the conventions of English	Writer uses correct spelling, punctuation, paragraphing, capitalization, and grammar competently with few errors	Writer displays nearly complete competence in the conventions of English

FIGURE 7.5
Primary Trait Rubric Example

	Primary Trait: Vocabulary Use in Writing
0	Shows no control over vocabulary taught in class; not enough writing to evaluate
1	Shows limited control of vocabulary taught in class; appropriate use is infrequent
2	Shows control of an adequate range of the vocabulary taught in class and most often uses this vocabulary appropriately
3	Shows control of a wide range of the vocabulary taught in class and always uses vocabulary appropriately

Adapted fromhttp://www.carla.umn.edu/assessment/vac/Evaluation/rubrics/types/interpersonal.html

conventions, and development in addition to vocabulary for this very reason; of course, teachers can eliminate all criteria except vocabulary if they choose. We've just provided a rubric for more than vocabulary in case teachers would like to assess more than vocabulary. As long as students are aware of the criteria upon which they will be assessed, it is fine to include other categories, but if we want to focus on vocabulary exclusively, we can do that as well.

A vocabulary-focused rubric might look something like Figure 7.5 and would be classified as a primary trait rubric:

Activities and Questions

Activities

1. Using the information provided in the introductory sections of the grammar part of the chapter ("Why Is Grammar Important?" and "Basic Considerations in Teaching Grammar") and the flow of assessment examples (controlled to guided to free), design a grammar assessment for your students. Keep in mind students' proficiency levels, where they might fall in relation to particular standards (e.g., WIDA or CEFR), and how that assessment can inform your teaching. What do you want to know about what your students can or cannot do?

2. Create a vocabulary assessment following similar guidelines to those used in #1, considering the information provided in the introductory sections of the vocabulary part of the chapter ("Why Is Vocabulary Important?" and "Vocabulary Assessment Standards") and the flow of assessment examples (controlled to guided to free).

Discussion Questions

1. We write in the introduction to Chapter 7 that "evaluation must reflect contextualized real-life uses of grammar." Discuss the problems with decontextualized grammar drills and how you might design activities that "reflect contextualized real-life uses of grammar."
2. In pairs, discuss three key take-aways from this chapter and how they might influence your grammar and vocabulary assessment practices.
3. You were asked to develop a grammar assessment and a vocabulary assessment. In pairs, discuss the rationales behind the assessments you created and how they support learning. What are the specific difficulties that students are likely to face in completing the assessment task, and how might a teacher support learning, before or after the assessment?

8

High-Stakes, Standardized Assessments

High-stakes standardized testing has played an increasing role in education systems around the world over the past few decades, including in the U.S. and the UK. The U.S. has seen ongoing discourses about an education crisis with the publication of books like *Why Johnny Can't Read* in the 1950s (Flesch, 1955), the *Newsweek* article "Why Johnny Can't Write" in the 1970s, and the publication of a Department of Education Report in the 1980s titled *A Nation at Risk*. The latter described an education system that was leaving students and the U.S. as a whole behind in the broader global economy, lamenting that "the educational foundations of our society are presently being eroded by a rising tide of mediocrity that threatens our very future as a Nation and a people." Since the 1980s, the use of high-stakes standardized tests has expanded widely in the U.S., with increasing consequences for students, their teachers, and their schools. With increasing frequency, schools and teachers are evaluated on the testing performance of their students, including how quickly teachers are able to deem students proficient in English. Over the years, states have developed various iterations of tests, which typically focus on core subjects like math and English, and language learners are required to take them. As discussed in earlier chapters, there have been efforts to develop nationwide tests, with the PARCC and Smarter Balanced tests being relatively recent attempts that have declined in recent years. The WIDA (2020) ACCESS is a more successful example of a test used by more than 40 U.S. states and territories (https://wida.wisc.edu), albeit one focused specifically on testing students out of the English language learner designation and not targeted to PreK–12 students in general.

With the emergence of more systematic testing in the 1940s, standardized language assessments have played an important and increasing role throughout the 20th century. According to Farhady (2018), language testing has progressed through a few different eras that have aligned with shifts in language instruction. During the structuralist era in the 1960s, test designers increasingly paid attention to reliability and validity. To improve reliability, tests included increasing numbers of multiple choice items. To improve validity, tests included questions about "as many elements of language as possible" & (7). With the arrival of the communicative era in the late 1970s, tests increasingly attempted to assess learners' abilities to communicate in real-world contexts rather than just measure their knowledge of specific aspects of language.

The TOEFL (Test of English as a Foreign Language) was initially developed "to assess the English proficiency of second language speakers of English who intend to study in institutions where English is the language of instruction" (ETS, 2020, p. 4)—as evident from this description, it has always had an academic focus by assessing whether or not students are prepared to study in English. The test itself has been refined over the years, originating as a paper-based test, moving to a computer-based version, and, most recently, in 2005, to an Internet-based test, hence the name TOEFL iBT. It has evolved along with research trends as well, with the ETS (2020) noting that the first test focused on assessing skills discretely and later iterations on responding to research that demonstrated how the four skill areas of reading, writing, speaking, and listening are integrated and should be assessed that way. Similarly, the 1990s saw the redesign of the test to focus more closely on communicative competence, although speaking was assessed separately until the creation of the TOEFL iBT.

The International English Language Testing System (IELTS) was developed with a similar goal to the TOEFL but emerged out of the UK and was intended to evaluate international students' abilities to study at UK universities. Earlier versions were introduced in the 1960s under the name English Proficiency Test Battery (EPTB). The IELTS was developed in the 1980s by the British Council, Cambridge English Language Assessment, and the International Development Program of Australian Universities and Colleges. The first students took the test in 1989. Like the TOEFL, it has traditionally focused on students' understanding of academic discourse and has tested the four skill areas. A more recent offshoot of the IELTS is the IELTS Life Skills test, which is a shorter test focused on everyday language that tests only speaking and listening skills. As will be referenced below, a key difference between the TOEFL and IELTS is the former tests speaking via computer while the latter involves a conversation with an examiner.

While the TOEFL and IELTS are focused on evaluating language learners' readiness for postsecondary studies, the next test we discuss is targeted toward language learners in the PreK–12 context. According to the WIDA website, WIDA was created in 2003 in response to the increased focus on testing language learners as part of the 2001 No Child Left Behind Act. WIDA was originally created through a grant awarded to the Wisconsin Department of Public Instruction but quickly adopted by additional member states. The WIDA mission states that "WIDA advances academic language development and academic achievement for children and youth who are culturally and linguistically diverse through high quality standards, assessments, research, and professional learning for educators" (WIDA, 2020 https://wida.wisc.edu). The WIDA primary assessment for ELs is the ACCESS.

A number of U.S. states have decided to use their own language proficiency tests for various reasons. Some of these are political, with some states reluctant to adopt a test because it may not reflect their values or simply because they want to assert state-level rights. Some of the largest states have chosen to opt out of WIDA ACCESS perhaps because their sheer population numbers makes it more efficient for them to develop their own tests—California (English Language Proficiency Assessments for California-ELPAC), Texas (Texas English Language Proficiency Assessment System-TELPAS), and New York (New York State Identification Test for English Language Learners-NYSITELL) come to mind for the latter. Texas is also a unique case because it was one of the early pioneers of high-stakes standardized testing and also has a fiercely independent streak. Like the ACCESS, these tests and their predecessors were developed with the arrival of No Child Left Behind in 2001, with the TELPAS a few years before in 1999.

Problems

A variety of researchers have documented problems and limitations with high-stakes standardized assessments over the years. While these tests are largely here to stay in some form and serve important purposes in our education system, such as helping ensure that students get the supplemental instruction that they need, it is important to know about these limitations so that teachers can find room for agency within the existing system.

Test Is Acontextual

By its very definition, a standardized test aims at testing large numbers of students studying in different contexts with different teachers and goals. This comes with the benefit of comparing performance across states, institutions, and international boundaries—information necessary in higher education, for instance, where institutions have students applying from all over the world to study at advanced levels in English. With this broad aim comes the limitation that none of these tests can really achieve what we've emphasized in earlier chapters: the most useful assessment work is tied to the local context. Large-scale assessments can never fully account for the breadth of cultures and languages present in different contexts and reading passages and other questions may contain information that may be familiar to a student in New York but unfamiliar to a student in New Mexico. In another example, a question that draws on knowledge of U.S. football may pose challenges to a student from a country where this game is not commonly played.

One of the largest problems with the acontextual nature of standardized assessments is the fact that they aren't responsive to local curricular decisions and needs. Either the curriculum has to adapt to the test (which we see with the prevalence of teaching to the test) or there exists a disconnect between what is locally taught and valued and that which is assessed. For instance, while teachers might like to bring in regional authors (say Chicanx or Native American authors in the U.S. Southwest), standardized tests may draw on traditional literary canons (e.g., Shakespeare) or on generic texts written for the tests themselves that may have some inherent bias based on who is writing them and where that person is based. Because standardized tests aren't tied to local curriculum, they'll never provide the same level of information for teachers as a locally designed assessment.

Narrow Focus on One English

Teachers and scholars are increasingly recognizing that their students bring a variety of linguistic resources to the classroom and advocating for curricular shifts that invite students to move fluidly between their L1 and L2 in their writing and other work. Alongside this trend, the last few decades have seen the growth of the World Englishes field, which recognizes that English does not belong to just a few countries but is widely used by people around the world. According to the British Council (2013), the number of speakers of English as a second or additional language outnumbers English L1 speakers four to one. The majority of many learners' interactions may occur with L2 users using a variety of English tied to their specific context, whether Hong Kong English, Indian English, or Spanglish used in the U.S.–Mexico border region. Despite these shifts, tests still largely reflect the status quo—users are expected to master a particular variety of English in many academic and professional pursuits. Tests still expect students to use either a U.S. or UK variant of English, and academic journals typically expect authors to publish and be consistent in the use of one of these forms. As long as high-stakes, standardized assessments and other professional spaces are driven by standard language ideologies, the more fluid approach to teaching language that some scholars have advocated will remain constrained.

Inauthentic Writing Assessment

As we have noted elsewhere (Crusan & Ruecker, 2019; Ruecker & Crusan, 2018), standardized high-stakes tests typically assess writing under timed conditions, which doesn't enable test takers to demonstrate their best writing abilities. For instance, most writing classrooms now take a social process-oriented approach to writing, which involves pre-rewriting, drafting, feedback, and revision. In the 20–30 minutes provided in many test-based writing tasks, takers are not able to engage meaningfully in these various stages—generally, they'll just have time to make a quick outline before starting.

Another concern surrounding standardized writing assessment is the increased use of automated scoring—that is, the use of computers to assess one's writing ability. Various scholars (Condon, 2013; Crossley et al., 2014) have shown how these programs often focus on grammatical accuracy and writing complexity and fail to assess the rhetorical effectiveness of a piece, which is often the trait most valued in writing classrooms. While IELTS and TOEFL still include a human rater alongside a computer rater, future cost pressures and advances in technology may eventually erase the human element entirely. It is important to note that this is a concern for other skill areas as well, with ETS noting that they have used an automated scoring engine for online speaking practice tests since 2006. The WIDA ACCESS responses are fully human scored.

Pressure/High Stakes

While exemption options are commonly available, many states require testing for students to meet graduation requirements. Colleges and universities depend on scores on tests like the TOEFL for admission and placement in their programs. These policies put immense pressure on language learners and their teachers and can narrowly constrain the curriculum to focus on what is valued by a particular test and also lead to more teacher-centered pedagogies (Au, 2007). While a certain amount of pressure can motivate students to learn as they strive to meet high expectations, research has shown that too much stress can overwhelm students and lead them to perform more poorly on tests than they would have if they were more relaxed (e.g., Salehi & Marefat, 2014).

Testing Prep Industry

A number of researchers have found that standardized test scores often correlate with a test taker's socioeconomic status. Upper-income students often have access to better educational opportunities and smaller classrooms, including private language schools. As researchers have documented elsewhere (e.g., Ruecker, Chamcharatsri, & Saengnogoen, 2015), this disparity may be because test items are written to a white, middle- and upper-class norm. Perhaps the clearest connection between socioeconomic status and success can be drawn by looking at the prevalence of testing prep schools and tutors. For instance, Manhattan Review (2020) advertises seven-week TOEFL prep courses in Seoul for $1,600. Their website tells prospective students that "Your high TOEFL score can help you get accepted into the best schools around the world…Don't waste your time or have the hassle of studying for this exam blindly. Before you enter the TOEFL exam room, you will be prepared to maximize your points" (https://www.manhattanreview.com/). Those who can afford to pay can essentially buy their way to higher scores.

Technology

For convenience, security, and ease of scoring, large-scale tests are increasingly being offered on computers. As scholars of the digital divide have long said, our students come to our classes with a wide range of experience with technology, in part shaped by their social class growing up. Also, the types of devices students may use for testing can vary widely: a student taking a test on a small tablet or slow laptop computer will be at a disadvantage to a student taking a test on a desktop computer with ample Internet speed and a large screen. Todd has seen in his own research how schools, especially in rural areas, can struggle to build sufficient Internet bandwidth to enable smooth testing with large numbers of students. He has also seen computer labs devoted mostly to testing at certain times of the year, limiting the amount of classwork students can do online, such as researching and writing.

Question Types

In order to better prepare their students for tests, teachers need to be aware of the different types of questions that students will encounter. Here, we will briefly review the structure of common tests and the types of tasks they ask students to do.

TOEFL®

The TOEFL iBT® (2020) includes sections based on the four skills covered in previous chapters: reading, writing, speaking, and listening (https://www.ets.org/toefl). The reading portion, lasting 60–100 minutes, consists of a short passage followed by a variety of multiple choice questions asking about different aspects of the text, including the definitions of particular words, what can be inferred from particular paragraphs, and the most appropriate sentences to summarize the most important ideas in the passage. The listening portion, lasting 60–90 minutes, has students listen to a short exchange or a lecture and answer multiple choice questions that ask them to do a variety of tasks, such as identify the focus of the recording or the intention behind mention of a particular detail. Students are allowed to take notes while listening. The speaking section is 20 minutes long and has several tasks, beginning with a couple questions that ask test takers to speak about a familiar topic, such as a memorable event. Other tasks have test takers read a passage and then summarize and/or respond in some way to what they read. Additional tasks have them listen to a conversation or lecture and respond orally. After reading each stimulus (i.e., text), test takers have a short time, ranging from 15–30 seconds, to prepare to respond; the time allotted for their response is anywhere up to 60 seconds. It is important to note that test takers do not interact with an examiner during this time but speak into the computer, which records them. The writing section lasts 50 minutes and has two tasks. One is an integrated writing task that has test takers read a few texts and integrate them into a response. The second task, more common on traditional standardized exams, asks test takers to state their opinion with supporting evidence on a particular topic or issue.

IELTS®

While the TOEFL focuses primarily on academic discourse, IELTS (2020) includes two testing options: Academic and General Training—we will focus on the Academic option here (https://www.ielts.org/). An important difference between IELTS and TOEFL is that IELTS is paper based, while 95% of TOEFL takers take the iBT, or Internet-based test version. Like the TOEFL, IELTS is divided into the four skills. The listening portion lasts 30 minutes and has takers listen to four recordings, both monologues and conversations, and answer a variety of question types, including multiple choice, matching, diagram labeling, form/table completion, sentence completion, and short answer. As evident from this list, IELTS includes a wider variety of open-ended answer options than the TOEFL and fewer multiple choice questions—with these open-ended questions, IELTS provides specific guidelines for word count, restricting takers to two words, for instance, in a particular response. The reading section is 60 minutes long, has test takers read three short passages, and has the same variety of question types as the listening section does, including traditional multiple choice and activities such as matching items and picking the best sentence ending from a list. It also includes open-ended options like completing a sentence with a set number of words or the completion of a table or flow chart. The writing portion is 60 minutes long and has two tasks—test takers are encouraged to spend 20 minutes on one and 40 minutes on the other. The first task has students look at a chart or table and describe it. The second has them respond to a point of view, argument, or problem—unlike the TOEFL, takers don't have to read passages for either task. The speaking portion, 11–14 minutes, involves a conversation with an examiner and focuses on three areas: answering questions about oneself and one's family, speaking about a topic for 1–2 minutes, and then having an interactive conversation on the same topic.

WIDA

As mentioned above, the ACCESS test is the most commonly used exam to pass students out of the English language learner designation in the U.S. PreK–12 context. WIDA has a variety of test types based on grades and on whether the school chooses an online or paper version, although the online version is most common (https://wida.wisc.edu). As the test is generally oriented to younger learners, there are a lot more visuals throughout the test than in the counterparts described above. While WIDA itself recommends that students be given as much time as they need to complete the ACCESS, states and schools may set more restrictive times. The time estimates WIDA provides include "convening students, material distribution, directions or embedded test practice." With this administrative work included, the ACCESS site notes that the reading portion typically lasts up to 60 minutes and does not have a fixed structure, varying widely by grade level. An example question might have students look at a picture with text and determine the answer. The listening section typically lasts up to 65 minutes and similarly uses images with an example activity having the student listen to a description of an image and asking the student to select the image that is described. Speaking typically lasts up to 50 minutes and a sample activity has students listening to recorded speakers and responding to their questions. Writing typically lasts up to 90 minutes and also can involve images, such as this example of a writing prompt: "Look at the diagram showing the assembled equipment. Write a paragraph of at least 8 sentences explaining how Camila will use the equipment to find out which of the liquids has the highest boiling point" (Gottlieb, 2016, p. 214). ACCESS prompts tend to connect to grade-appropriate academic activities since it strives to measure students' readiness to undertake those tasks in English.

TELPAS

Let's take a look at one of the larger state language tests, the TELPAS. The reading, listening, and speaking portions are typically offered online and no time limit is specified in the guide for educators (TEA, 2019). The sample tests we viewed paired the speaking and listening assessments together and had 20 questions (Testnav, 2020, https://tx8.testnav.com/). The listening portion may include short recordings asking students to point to a particular picture based on what they hear. A sample speaking activity shows a series of four pictures and invites students to tell a story about them; another invites students to describe the ways two pictures are similar and different. The reading test we viewed had 60 questions and included a mix of activities, ranging from multiple choice based on what was depicted in a picture to a short academic text with drop down choices for missing words to reading passages of various lengths. While the WIDA ACCESS tends to be more consistently focused on academics, the TELPAS samples include a mixture of items focused on both everyday life and more academic topics. The TELPAS writing section is pretty unique and innovative compared to the rest of the test—students are assessed by their own teachers based on a portfolio of their work, which the TELPAS refers to as a writing collection. These collections are required to include five writing assignments, at least one of which must use the past tense and two of which must be based in the mathematics, science, or social studies content areas.

Scoring Reports

In addition to including a total score, TOEFL and IELTS score different skill areas: reading, listening, speaking, and writing. Scores on the traditional paper-based TOEFL go up to 677; they only go to 120 on the online version. A typical requirement for graduate admissions is 79/120 on the online version—institutions don't typically have requirements for specific skill areas (with occasional exceptions such as the speaking portion being used for international teaching assistant placement at some institutions) and instead focus on the overall score.

TOEFL score reports have a useful addition that provides more clarity—explanations of a test taker's performance level that can provide more guidance on how to improve in subsequent attempts. For instance, someone who scores between 15 and 21 on the reading portion is considered intermediate and given this descriptor on the scoring report:

> Test takers who receive a score at the INTERMEDIATE level, as you did, typically understand academic texts in English that require a wide range of reading abilities, although their understanding of certain parts of the texts is limited.
>
> Test takers who receive a score at the INTERMEDIATE level typically
>
> - have a good command of common academic vocabulary but still have some difficulty with high-level vocabulary;
> - have a very good understanding of grammatical structure;
> - can understand and connect information, make appropriate inferences, and synthesize information in a range of texts but have more difficulty when the vocabulary is high level and the text is conceptually dense;
> - can recognize the expository organization of a text and the role that specific information serves within a larger text but have some difficulty when these are not explicit or easy to infer from the text; and
> - can abstract major ideas from a text but have more difficulty doing so when the text is conceptually dense.
>
> (TOEFL, 2020, https://www.ets.org/toefl)

While necessarily generalized, this description provides some useful information that can guide additional study. For instance, we see multiple references to "difficulty with high-level vocabulary" as well as references to difficulty understanding more complex texts where some ideas may be inferred. It is evident that additional reading practice of more complex tests with comprehension activities followed by more systematic recording and studying of vocabulary from these texts might help an intermediate student improve their performance on future TOEFL attempts—of course it is important to note that, as we discussed in Chapter 2, language acquisition occurs over time and one should have realistic expectations about the time and work needed to acquire additional vocabulary.

WIDA ACCESS scores are on a six-point scale, with many states labeling students proficient and no longer in need of regular language support services at a five (https://wida.wisc.edu). Scores are similarly reported in the four skill areas, although the test provides additional composite scores in combined skill areas: oral language (50% listening and 50% speaking), literacy (50% reading and 50% writing), and comprehension (70% reading and 30% listening). The overall score values certain areas more than other (35% reading, 35% writing, 15% listening, and 15% speaking), likely because reading and writing are generally more valued in school settings. As discussed elsewhere (Chapman et al., 2018), WIDA takes a Can Do approach to its scoring—preferring to focus on students' abilities rather than their deficits: "By focusing on what language learners can do, we send a powerful message that children and youth from diverse linguistic and cultural backgrounds contribute to the vibrancy of our early childhood programs and PreK–12 schools" (WIDA, 2020, https://wida.wisc.edu). For instance, a student who scores a three out of six is given the following information:

> Students at this level can generally understand written language related to common topics in school and can participate in class discussions, for example:
>
> - Classify main ideas and examples in written information
> - Identify main information that tells who, what, when or
> - Identify steps in written processes and procedures
> - Recognize language related to claims and supporting evidence where something happened

Compared to the TOEFL, the ACCESS scoring report doesn't provide guidance on where a student might improve—however, it helps students have a positive impression of their abilities. Educators have access to other WIDA resources that can help them make sense of students' scores and how they might help students reach new levels. For instance, WIDA (2020) publishes Can Do descriptor guides for different grade levels that show what students at the different levels should be able to do (https://wida.wisc.edu). Table 8.1 shows what readers in grades 4–5 can do at different proficiency levels.

TABLE 8.1
WIDA Can Do Example for Grade 4–5

	Level 3 Developing	**Level 4 Expanding**	**Level 5 Bridging**
Readers	Process recounts by ▪ Sequencing events in stories or content-related processes ▪ Identifying main ideas in narrative and informational text	Process recounts by ▪ Connecting details to main ideas or themes ▪ Identifying conclusions in multi-paragraph text	Process recounts by ▪ Becoming familiar with the language of related genres (e.g., news reports, historical accounts) ▪ Summarizing information from multiple related sources

Comparing these levels side by side helps illustrate the kinds of skills teachers can work with to bring their students to the next level.

Accommodations

Test makers and states have developed a number of accommodations to make tests a fair and valid measure of students' abilities. For tests of students' language proficiency, the use of these accommodations may be limited to students with a particular disability, such as those who are deaf or hard of hearing or blind or have visual impairments. However, language learners in U.S. schools are also expected to take high-stakes state assessments aimed at all learners across different subjects—accommodations become particularly important to a wide swath of language learners on these tests. It isn't fair to conflate students' language and math abilities on the math portion of tests, for instance.

Abedi et al. (2004) discussed research exploring the most common accommodations:

- Tests in students' native languages
- Linguistic modification of test items
- Extra time
- Published dictionaries
- Glossaries and customized dictionaries
- Oral administration

When deciding which accommodations are appropriate, Abedi et al. (2004) noted that it's important to consider factors such as their effectiveness to help students overcome language barriers, the validity of the accommodation (e.g., it must help the target group but not impact other students), differential impact, and feasibility. He advised against a uniform approach for all students, because each student might need different supports to be more successful on these tests—for instance, students who haven't studied the academic content in their L1 will likely not see a benefit from translating test items into their L1. Abedi et al. (2004) argued that some accommodations could be useful for all students: "There is no reason why all students should not have content-area assessments that use clear language and provide sufficient time for them to show what they know. In addition, customized dictionaries or glossaries can be provided for all students, regardless of their level of English language proficiency" (p. 17). In general, he felt that simplifying the language on assessments was one of the most promising forms of accommodation but was rarely considered.

State/Federal Policies and Advocacy

Policies at the state and federal level are always changing as new leaders transition in and out and bring with them their own "great" ideas, often involving high-stakes testing, for improving the educational system. For instance, under the previous governor, New Mexico developed one of the most stringent teacher evaluation systems in the U.S. It tied 50% of a teacher's evaluation to student results on the PARCC exam; responding to broad public outcry, the latest governor scrapped this system and the PARCC exam. It is important for educators to learn about these shifts and how they'll impact both teachers and their students. Policy information is typically found on state department of education websites. For instance, many states are increasingly tying teacher evaluations to how well their students score on particular tests—the calculations for these evaluations often use complicated models called value-added modeling that ostensibly account for factors such as student demographics and growth over time. States are often grading schools on A-F scales, with information about the calculations for these grades available as well. A quick Internet search with the name of the education agency and the topic you're interested in learning about can help you find this information: for example, for Texas you could search "Texas Education Agency school report cards."

Testing requirements for language learners, such as how many years new immigrants can take a test in their first language (if available) and which tests are offered in which languages, are typically spelled out at the state level. Armed with this information, teachers can advocate for their students to ensure they get the accommodations they need. One language teacher in Todd's research detailed how the school counselors weren't familiar with the accommodations available to ELs and explained how she had to advocate for her students and arm herself with knowledge about state policies.

Testing Strategies

As referenced earlier, there is a large test preparation industry that focuses on teaching students test-taking strategies—being familiar with the question types and tools offered by a particular test as well as having strategies for answering questions gives students an advantage.

Previewing Test Items

This is perhaps the most obvious approach to preparing students for tests—letting them know what types of questions to expect and running them through practice tests. There are a variety of resources out there—hard copy and online options by third-party vendors as well as practice tests provided typically free of charge by the vendors themselves. The more familiar students are with the different tasks they face, the less time they will have to spend reading instructions during a timed testing period—and the less likely that ELs will be confused by the instructions they encounter.

Using Multiple Choice Strategies

A quick online search reveals many sites offering advice on how to do better on multiple choice questions, ranging from how to approach the question better to how to make the best guess when one is really unsure. We recommend taking a look at some of these sites and thinking about what might be most useful for your students. Some common pieces of advice we came across:

- Answer the questions you know first. Then you know how much time you have to figure out the more difficult ones.
- When in doubt, stick with your first instinct.
- Pay attention to specific words such as "always" or "best answer" as some answers may often or arguably be true, but they may not be the best fit and will consequently be marked wrong.
- Read the whole question before looking at the options—if you jump to the answer that you think is correct, then you may have missed a nuanced point in the question. Along these lines, it can be useful to predict the answer based on your reading of the question before looking at the options.
- Use a process of elimination—decide which answers you know are incorrect so you can then decide among fewer options.
- Don't choose an answer because you don't understand all the words in another answer. Look carefully at the answers you completely understand and decide if they are correct or not—if not, then you can narrow your guessing among the other options.
- Longer and more scientific-sounding options are often more likely to be correct.

Using Tools

It is important for students to be familiar with all the tools accessible to them. On paper-based tests, they may have scratch paper available for outlining a response to a writing prompt. One of their accommodations may be to have a paper-based dictionary.

In that case, it's important that students gain practice in class on how to use one—they may be used to looking up definitions online on their phones or on another device, which may not be allowed during testing.

As tests are increasingly taken on computers, the use of particular tools may be less obvious, so explicit guidance is all the more important. For instance the ACCESS has "Universal Tools" available to all test takers in its online test: options to change the color combinations for better visibility, the ability to highlight text, the ability to use the keyboard to navigate the test screen, a line guide to facilitate easier reading, a magnification tool to make text larger, and sticky notes to outline responses for the writing test. Chapman et al. (2018) reported that only 11% of test takers use at least one of these tools and suggested that age and grade level, as well as familiarity, have a factor in tool use. It is evident from this low number that more students might be encouraged to use one or more tools while testing online, which can often be more challenging than taking a paper-based test.

De-Stressing

It is common for students to say they aren't good test takers, and it's true that their scores may not reflect their true abilities to their teachers. While low performance on tests might be caused by a variety of factors, stress is certainly a common one. Testing in general can be a stressful experience. Many students suffer from test anxiety, which is only exacerbated by the additional pressures that students are increasingly aware of: their score can determine their admission to and placement at a university, their graduation from high school, or whether or not their teacher or school is evaluated positively or negatively. Thus, helping students relax in stressful testing situations can help improve their performance.

The techniques discussed in this section so far certainly help reduce stress—the more comfortable a student is with the test structure, the timing, and the kinds of questions they'll face, the less stressed out they'll likely be. If they are taking a test on a computer, familiarity with the computer, the online testing interface, and the tools available will certainly help. Other techniques include:

- Prioritizing questions: as referenced during the multiple choice discussion, it's best for students to complete the questions they know first. Then they'll know how much time they have to finish the more challenging ones, which can decrease pressures associated with time limits.

- Moving around during breaks: during break times, it's important to get up and move around, use the restroom, and drink some water. This can distract a student's mind from the test, which can be hard to forget about when one remains sitting in in the same spot.
- Stretching: students can lift their arms up and stretch them to the side—the movement and stretch can help relax them. Another approach is to push their feet against the floor while pulling down on their chair, holding that for a few seconds, and then releasing before doing it again.
- Meditating/Breathing: a class-wide meditation session before testing can help clear everyone's mind. During the test, students can be taught how to pause between sections and do breathing exercises. A simple one is to slowly breathe through one's nose, fill one's lungs from the bottom up, hold for a few seconds, and then slowly release through the mouth before repeating.
- Encouraging positive self-talk: it is important for teachers and others to help students feel confident about an upcoming test. Positive reinforcement can help the students see their abilities more positively and avoid negative self-talk that can add to stress.

Final Thoughts

As much as students, teachers, and administrators complain about the prevalence of standardized, high-stakes testing (we're no exception to this—see Ruecker and Crusan, 2018), it appears that these tests are here to stay. While we can continue to hope that concerns about over-testing are taken seriously and that the number of tests students have to take are consolidated and reduced, these tests can and do serve an important purpose. As a number of civil rights groups have pointed out (Leadership Conference, 2015), they help draw attention to disparities in our education system—of particular interest to the audience of this collection, well-designed tests can let us know when language learners are ready to tackle mainstream classes without additional language support. We hope that this chapter has given you an understanding of some of the various language tests out there and what features of the tests are important for you to know.

Activities and Questions

Activities

1. Take a closer look at a standardized test (both the test itself and the information provided by the test maker about administration and use) used in your current or anticipated future teaching context and analyze it with some of the issues discussed in the problems section (acontextual, narrow focus on one English, inauthentic writing assessment, pressure/high stakes, testing prep industry, and technology). A quick Google search will list many websites where copies of disclosed tests as well as practice tests can be found.
2. Review the suggested testing strategies and develop an additional strategy or technique you might teach your students to help them do better on a standardized test they may encounter.

Discussion Questions

1. What have been your own experiences with standardized tests, either as a test taker or a test administrator? How might you draw on these experiences to help your students?
2. What are the advantages/benefits and disadvantages/problems of standardized testing?
3. Due to the pressures surrounding standardized tests, students can often be upset when their scores are lower than they would like them to be. How can you encourage or support students who are disappointed in their scores?

9

Conclusion: Developing an Assessment Philosophy

Effective classroom assessment involves a great deal of decision making and is shaped by a teacher's individual values and attitudes toward teaching and learning and particularly by the needs of the students she works with. This final chapter will lead teachers through the process of articulating their ideas, knowledge, and values surrounding assessment and incorporating them into a philosophy that will shape the work they do. As they ready themselves to enter the job market, many teachers are asked to write a teaching philosophy. This assessment philosophy is related and can be incorporated into a larger teaching philosophy; it is important on its own because it highlights an often-forgotten piece of the teaching puzzle—assessment.

We will discuss the importance of the theory-practice link, summarizing some of the major approaches to assessment described earlier in the book. We will also consider different philosophies and provide activities around brainstorming the creation of an assessment philosophy.

Importance of the Theory-Practice Link

Crusan (2010) noted, "Objectively or subjectively, we base everything we do on a theory—a principle, a philosophy, a value, the way we believe—and this stance is clearly visible in our pedagogy" (p. 18). Todd and Deborah both learned very early that a deep understanding of why we do what we do in our classrooms is vital to our work as teachers and researchers (Johnson, 1999). When we profoundly reflect on our practices, we often realize why we do what we do and how to change if change is warranted. We can and should improve our practices. Embedded in every chapter of this book is the notion of teacher reflection and improvement of pedagogy.

Some may find the word *theory* a bit off-putting, but a theory is simply a set of connected ideas intended to help explain something; a theory provides a framework for explaining observations; a theory is an idea about the way the world works that allows you to predict what will happen if you do something.

Practice is doing; it is what happens when you do that something. The better the theory, the better the match between your thoughts and predictions (your theory) and what occurs in practice. Scientists can test a theory through empirical research and gather evidence that supports or refutes it. The same goes for teachers; we can test our theories in our classroom practices. Clearly then, we recognize the role theory plays in teacher education practice.

During her graduate education, Deborah always felt fortunate to have the opportunity to be teaching English learners at the same time she was studying second language acquisition theories and noticed that some of her fellow students did not have that opportunity. While she might not have been able to articulate fully what was happening to her pedagogical and assessment philosophies during her graduate school experience, she watched those theories and philosophies come to life in her classroom practice. Her understanding now makes it imperative that her prospective teachers interact with language learners as often and in as many different avenues as possible so that they test the theories they've been learning.

Deborah has long believed, "One of the primary responsibilities of teacher educators is to demonstrate and model for their students what it means to practice from a theoretical stance. Again, what we *do* (in this case with regard to assessment) exemplifies our theoretical stance much more than what we *say*. We need to be cognizant of assessment theory and history and the ways in which we represent them in our pedagogy" (Crusan, 2010, p. 19). It is also important to be cognizant of that practice-what-you-preach expression; in other words, it's important to do (in our assessment practices) what we say (about assessment). Of course, theory and practice don't always meet since we live in an imperfect world. Sometimes teachers are pressed for time and might have to use prepared tests, rubrics, and activities that might not be as authentic as we'd like, but they could possibly be the most efficient, effective, and practical materials to use at that moment. It's at these times that we realize the importance of practicality in our assessment practices.

Major Approaches to Assessment

As we have indicated throughout this book, we see a place for both summative assessment and formative assessment in the classroom, but we find formative assessment—ongoing assessment that consistently and continuously assesses our students—more helpful for student learning and teacher planning. We adopt integrated assessment (the assessment of the four skills of reading, writing, speaking, and listening together) whenever possible; we strive to model good assessment practices for our students that they can carry with them into their own classrooms or into whatever venue they find themselves at work. The ethics of good assessment—concern for the test taker, notions of practicality, the concepts of reliability and validity—can inform many fields.

In preparation for developing a philosophy of assessment, we thought it might be instructive to examine a few assessment scholars' philosophies.

Deborah Crusan

In her 2010 book, Crusan makes her philosophy of assessment very clear. She has long been on a "quest for justice, fairness, and individual students' needs" (2010, p. ix), which has driven her to explore "the political motivation and economic and social consequences of assessment" (p. ix). Through that exploration, she has discovered that there are many stakeholders in assessment, all with valid positions; that recognition has tempered her philosophy. Further, she understands that a great many teachers are unprepared to systematically establish and use criteria to assess the work their students do. In order to rectify this situation in her own classroom, Deborah's students read about the history and theory surrounding assessment and explore assessment strategies through individual and group activities. She also introduces students to the tools of assessment, having them create and implement various assessments. Finally, she believes that her students need to understand that assessment is within their purview and that they should be informed about politics outside their classrooms that determine everything from how much money schools are allotted to how many standardized tests their students will be required to take. Teachers need to understand the proper use of such tests and they need to be able to intelligently articulate objections to the misuse of these tests. She teaches her students to be critical of assessment and its ramifications and the ways that some students, particularly English learners, are marginalized by assessment.

Douglas Brown and Priyanvada Abeywickrama

While they present the four skills individually, Brown and Abeywickrama (2019) advocate a philosophy of integration and fairness. Their philosophy is best encapsulated in their five principles of language assessment: practicality, reliability, validity, authenticity, and washback. While other assessment specialists focus on reliability, validity, authenticity, and washback, Brown and Abeywickrama are unique in their focus on practicality. They contend that a test is practical when it "stays within budgetary limits, can be completed by the test taker within appropriate time constraints, has clear directions for administration, appropriately utilizes available human resources, does not exceed available material resources, and considers the time and effort involved in both design and scoring" (p. 28).

Practicality is especially important when considering teacher burnout. Deborah remembers a former student who, for a required test creation final project, decided to assess her students' speaking proficiency through a recorded task that she would later listen to, using a rubric that she had created for the assignment and shared with her students (both good assessment practices). Unfortunately, she didn't place a limit on the length of the recordings, so she ended up listening to approximately 20 minutes of recorded speech from each of her 17 students (!). In that test creation assignment, students were asked to present various aspects of the test they created. They had to address the following questions:

- Briefly discuss the success or failure of your assessment, the purpose, the rubric.
- Report on the actual administration of the assessment.
- **What did you learn from completing the project**?
- What might you do differently if you were starting over?
- How might this knowledge help you in the future?

When addressing the *what did you learn* question, the student with the 340 minutes of recorded speech (for one assignment) was quick to point out how the concept of practicality was brought home for her as she listened to her students' recordings. She felt compelled to listen to all 20 minutes since her students had so sincerely completed their assignments and she had not established a time limit. She learned quickly that setting criteria for length is important, especially in regard to teacher engagement, the ability to assess, and "time and effort in...scoring" (Brown & Abeywickrama, 2019, p. 28).

Liz Hamp-Lyons

Primarily focused on writing assessment, Hamp-Lyons has long championed a philosophy of ethical assessment. She has had a tremendous impact on the field in terms of portfolio assessment, the assessment of language for specific purposes, language assessment, and teacher training. She believes that teachers are responsible for assessment as well as ethics in assessment and are certainly stakeholders in assessment (Hamp-Lyons, 2000). She has long held that "all assessment practices are political" (Hamp-Lyons, 2001, p. 117). By this she means that the many biases held by the decision makers affect which assessments are considered best. For example, large testing companies who earn millions of dollars in administration of language tests worldwide have a decidedly different view of testing—what's right; what's fair—than a classroom teacher might have. Additionally, Hamp-Lyons has long championed teacher assessment literacy, which, simply defined, means that teachers understand the principles of sound assessment, including scoring, grading, and making judgments about students. She further believes that teachers need to have the ability to create fair assessments that provide information about students' language ability and that teachers should be able to develop scoring rubrics and assessment criteria that clearly demonstrate how students will be held accountable.

Lia Plakans and Atta Gebril

Plakans and Gebril (2015) offer a look at the more technical side of language testing and refute eight myths, including:

1. Assessment is just writing tests and using statistics.
2. A comprehensive final exam is the best way to evaluate students.
3. Scores on performance assessments are preferable because of their accuracy and authenticity.
4. Multiple choice tests are inaccurate measures of language but are easy to write.
5. We should test only one skill at a time.
6. A test's validity can be determined by looking at it.
7. Issues of fairness are not a concern with standardized testing.
8. Teachers should not be involved in preparing students for tests.

A look at these myths shows clearly the stance of the writers as well-versed language testers familiar with the technical side of test development; however, the authors also show their concern for all those affected by tests, particularly teachers and students. The myths serve to reiterate language testing theory but do it in a way that is more palatable for teachers. One of the main concerns of many assessment researchers is that the field of language testing has been divided into two camps: teachers and test developers (Crusan, 2010; Hamp-Lyons, 1997; Shohamy, 1997; Shohamy, 2001). Scholars like Plakans and Gebril narrow that gap with their inclusive research.

Todd Ruecker and Deborah Crusan

In our 2018 *The Politics of English Second Language Writing Assessment in Global Contexts* collection, we described our assessment philosophy as follows:

> We feel strongly that well-designed, context-driven assessment is a force for good in improving classroom structure and student learning. Having clearly defined goals, focused criteria, and informal and formal assessments can help a teacher and student constantly gauge individuals' progress so that teaching can be adjusted as needed to focus on a particular topic or theme. However, when politicians, big-money organizations, and distant administrators get involved and create poorly designed assessments and impose uninformed or heavy-handed penalties for low performance, the value of assessment gets distorted and has real potential to harm students and teachers. (Ruecker and Crusan, 2018, p. 2)

This philosophy emphasizes some of the notions we value that have been articulated throughout this book: establishing clearly defined learning goals, and using a variety of formative and summative, informal and formal assessments to gauge student learning and adapt one's teaching. The collection the above quote comes from was focused particularly on the politics of assessment, a thread that has been present throughout our work and this book—we constantly articulate the value of local assessment expertise and decry the problems when people far removed from a particular teaching context dictate how learning proceeds and is measured.

Asao Inoue

Inoue's work focuses on writing assessment, particularly addressing what he has identified as racist assessment practices. Writing from a position that proactively values the variety of languages that students bring to the classrooms, he attributes biases in traditional assessment to judging student work by a unitary standard "because all grading and assessment exist within systems that uphold singular, dominant standards that are racist, and White supremacist when used uniformly. This problem is present in any grading system that incorporates a standard, no matter who is judging, no matter the particulars of the standard" (Inoue, 2019, p. 3). As we have noted elsewhere, adopting this philosophy wholeheartedly can pose a challenge in a language classroom where teachers need to prepare their students for classrooms or tests based around a less-tolerant attitude toward language variety or correctness; however, we definitely recognize the value of teaching our students about language variety and change and the politics surrounding ways in which certain languages become privileged over others. When grading writing, for instance, we also recognize the value of assigning less weight to language conventions and prioritizing other aspects of writing, such as rhetorical effectiveness.

Ultimately, Inoue (2019) believes that "designing fair and meaningful grading practices is about cultivating with our students an ecology, a place where every student, no matter where they come from or how they speak or write, can have access to the entire range of final course grades possible" (p. 3). Elsewhere, we have discussed the failure of standardized test makers to address issues of bias and give students equal opportunity to demonstrate their proficiency in a certain skill area—Inoue's philosophy helps emphasize for us the idea of being radically inclusive in our teaching practices and constantly striving to minimize racism and bias in our assessment practices.

Developing Your Assessment Philosophy

In Deborah's classes that focus on assessment—TESOL Assessment, a required course in all tracks of TESOL at her university (MA, BA, concentration, graduate and undergraduate certificates, teacher license endorsement), and Writing Assessment, a graduate seminar taught every other year—she uses a combination of readings, videos, and discussions to help her students build an assessment philosophy. In the writing assessment seminar, she invites leading scholars to videoconference with her class, which is an excellent way for students to learn about a variety of assessment practices and philosophies.

She also uses a series of prompts that her students write about and discuss. She uses those questions throughout the semester to consistently bring students to a philosophy that is ethical, informed by both research and practice, and practical. Here are those prompts:

1. **What is your best experience with assessment:**
   - ❑ as a teacher?
   - ❑ as a student?

2. **What is your worst/most difficult experience with assessment:**
   - ❑ as a teacher?
   - ❑ as a student?
3. **What experiences have you had with each of the following?**
   - ❑ devising instructions
   - ❑ devising prompts
   - ❑ devising scoring rubrics
   - ❑ the training of raters
4. **What do the following terms or concepts mean for you?**
   - ❑ direct testing
   - ❑ indirect testing
   - ❑ washback effects of tests
   - ❑ prompts
   - ❑ subjective scoring of writing samples
   - ❑ holistic scoring
   - ❑ analytic scoring
   - ❑ primary trait scoring
   - ❑ multiple trait scoring
   - ❑ rater training

Adapted from McNamara (2002)

Because Deborah believes that it is vitally important for her students to grapple with these questions, she devotes *at least* two full class periods to their discussion. As can be seen from the questions, a lot of assessment ground can be covered by merely addressing them.

Some activities that can be used to fashion one's assessment philosophy:

- Background knowledge probes (short, simple questionnaires such as the one above) can be used at the beginning of a course, at the start of a new unit or lesson, or prior to introducing an important new topic. Teachers can determine the most effective starting point for lessons and discovering what students know.

- Another technique to spark ideas is the partially empty outline in which the instructor provides students with an empty or partially completed outline containing her assessment philosophy, which she has just presented to the class. Students are given a limited amount of time to fill in the blank spaces. This activity helps students remember important points of the mini-lecture and also provides scaffolding upon which to hook new ideas about personal assessment philosophies.
- Quick writing can also help to solidify ideas. Ask students to summarize their developing assessment philosophy in one sentence. In terms of assessment, they should think about who does what to whom (e.g., test developers, teachers, politicians), when, where, how, and why, and how the answers to those questions might guide them in incorporating their assessment philosophy into their pedagogy.
- Teachers can ask students to write down at least one possible, real-world application for an important principle, generalization, theory, or procedure that they've learned. Through this, the instructor can determine how well students understand the possible applications of their developing assessment philosophies.
- In focused autobiographical sketches, students are directed to write a one- or two-page autobiographical sketch focused on a single assessment experience in their past—an experience relevant to the development of their assessment philosophy. This provides information about the students' self-concept and self-awareness as learners within a specific field.
- Students and teachers listen, reflect, and write. First students listen to short presentations of other students' developing assessment philosophies. Reflecting on their own philosophies, they then write down any insights they have gained and ideas that can be incorporated into their own philosophies. Students might also share and discuss what they've learned from presentations.

When All Is Said and Done

As we noted earlier in this chapter, it is vital to expand teachers' and future teachers' knowledge and values surrounding assessment. As this occurs, they can hone their assessment philosophies, incorporating what they have learned and read into a philosophy that shapes their pedagogy. This philosophy will be evident in everything they do in their classroom, for, as the aphorism goes, actions speak louder than words. What a person does is much more powerful than words and more clearly demonstrates the philosophy that a person ascribes to. In other words, a person's actions will tell you all you need to know.

Discussion Questions

1. Discuss some of the questions in the "Developing Your Assessment Philosophy" section. What is your best experience with assessment? What is your worst/most difficult experience with assessment? What experiences have you had with devising instructions, prompts, and scoring rubrics? Rater training? What do various assessment terms and concepts mean to you (e.g., direct testing, washback, holistic scoring)?
2. List three or four key words that define your assessment philosophy and explain them to a partner.

References

Abedi, J., Hofstetter, C.H., and Lord, C. 2004. Assessment accommodations for English language learners: Implications for policy based research. *Review of Educational Research*, 74, 1–28.

Abedi, J., Lord, C., & Plummer, J. R. (1997). *Final report of language background as a variable in NAEP mathematics performance* (CSE Report 429). Los Angeles: University of California at Los Angeles National Center for Research on Evaluation, Standards, and Student Testing (CRESST).

American Council on the Teaching of Foreign Languages (ACTFL) (2012). *ACTFL performance descriptors for language learners.* Alexandria, VA: American Council on the Teaching of Foreign Languages. https://www.actfl.org/sites/default/files/pdfs/ACTFLPerformance-Descriptors.pdf

Andrade, H., & Du, Y. (2005). Student perspectives on rubric-referenced assessment. *Practical Assessment, Research, and Evaluation, 10*(1), 3. DOI: https://doi.org/10.7275/g367-ye94

Au, W. (2007). High-stakes testing and curricular control: A qualitative metasynthesis. *Educational Researcher, 36*(5), 258–267. https://doi.org/10.3102/0013189X07306523

Bader, A. (2019a). A controlled speaking example [Class handout]. Department of English Language and Literatures, Wright State University, Dayton, OH.

Bader, A. (2019b). How good is your memory [Class handout]. Department of English Language and Literatures, Wright State University, Dayton, OH.

Bean, J. C. (2011). *Engaging ideas: The professor's guide to integrating writing, critical thinking, and active learning in the classroom.* New York: John Wiley & Sons.

Bond, L. A. (1996). Norm- and criterion-referenced testing. *Practical Assessment, Research & Evaluation, 5*(2). http://pareonline.net/getvn.asp?v=5&n=2]. https://doi.org/10.7275/dy7r-2x18

British Council (2013). *The English effect.* https://www.britishcouncil.org/sites/default/files/english-effect-report-v2.pdf

Brown, H. D., & Abeywickrama, P. (2019). *Language assessment: Principles and classroom practices* (3rd ed.). Hoboken, NJ: Pearson.

Brown, S. (2011). *Listening myths: Applying second language research to classroom teaching.* Ann Arbor: University of Michigan Press.

Brown, S., & Eisterhold, J. (2004). *Topics in language and culture for teachers.* Ann Arbor: University of Michigan Press.

Brown, S., & Larsen-Hall, J. (2012). *Second language acquisition myths: Applying second language research to classroom teaching*. Ann Arbor: University of Michigan Press.

Bunch, G. C. (2006). "Academic English" in the 7th grade: Broadening the lens, expanding access. *Journal of English for Academic Purposes, 5*, 284–301. https://doi.org/10.1016/j.jeap.2006.08.007

Burgess, K. (2017). New Mexico students' scores on PARCC exams rise slightly. *Albuquerque Journal.* https://www.abqjournal.com/1037602/parcc-results-shows-nm-barely-improving.html

Callahan, R. M. (2005). Tracking and high school English learners: Limiting opportunity to learn. *American Educational Research Journal, 42*(2), 305–328. https://doi.org/10.3102/00028312042002305

Celce-Murcia, M., Brinton, D. M., & Goodwin, J. M. (2010). *Teaching pronunciation: A course book and reference guide*. New York: Cambridge University Press.

Chamcharatsri, B. (2016). Student-generated rubric assessment: A meaningful literacy practice. *Journal of Assessment & Teaching of English Language Learners, 1*, 50–60.

Chamot, A. U., & O'Malley, J.M. (1987). The cognitive academic language learning approach: A bridge to the mainstream. *TESOL Quarterly, 21*(2), 227–249. https://doi.org/10.2307/3586733

Chapman, M., Kim, A. A., Wei, J., & Bitterman, T. (2018). Vignette: Challenging the deficit mindset: The WIDA Can Do philosophy in a second language writing context. In T. Ruecker & D. Crusan (Eds.), *The politics of second language writing assessment in global contexts* (pp. 216–222). New York: Routledge.

Chappuis, J. (2009). *Seven strategies of assessment for learning*. New York: Allyn & Bacon.

Chien, C., Kao, L., & Wei, L. (2008). The role of phonological awareness development in young Chinese EFL learners. *Language Awareness*, 17 (4), 271-288. DOI: 10.1080/09658410802146883

Chomsky, N. (1965). *Aspects of the Theory of Syntax*. Cambridge: MIT Press.

College Board (2016). *Extended time accommodation*. Retrieved from https://www.collegeboard.org/students-with-disabilities/typical-accommodations/time

Common Core State Standards (2015). English language arts standards. Retrieved from http://www.corestandards.org/wp-content/uploads/ELA_Standards1.pdf

Condon, W. (2013). Large-scale assessment, locally-developed measures, and automated scoring of essays: Fishing for red herrings? *Assessing Writing, 18*(1), 100–108. https://doi.org/10.1016/j.asw.2012.11.001

Council of Europe (n.d.). *Common European framework of reference for languages: Learning, teaching, assessment* http://ebcl.eu.com/wp-content/uploads/2011/11/CEFR-all-scales-and-all-skills.pdf

Council of Europe. (2011). *Common European Framework of Reference for Languages: Learning, teaching, assessment. Structured Overview of all CEFR Scales.* http://ebcl.eu.com/wp-content/uploads/2011/11/CEFR-all-scales-and-all-skills.pdf

Crossley, S. A., Kyle, K., Allen, L. K., Guo, L., & McNamara, D. S. (2014). Linguistic microfeatures to predict L2 writing proficiency: A case study in automated writing evaluation. *Grantee Submission*, *7*(1).

Crusan, D. (2010). *Assessment in the second language writing classroom*. Ann Arbor: University of Michigan Press.

Crusan, D., & Matsuda, P. K. (2018). Classroom writing assessment. In J.I. Liontas (Ed.), *The TESOL encyclopedia of English language teaching*. Hoboken, NJ: Wiley-Blackwell.

Crusan, D., Plakans, L., & Gebril, A. (2016). Writing assessment literacy: Surveying second language teachers' knowledge, beliefs, and practices. *Assessing Writing*, *28*, 43–56. https://doi.org/10.1016/j.asw.2016.03.001

Crusan, D., & Ruecker, T. (2019). Standardized testing pressures and the temptation of the five-paragraph essay. In N. A. Caplan, & A. M. Johns (Eds.), *Changing practices for the L2 writing classroom: Moving beyond the five-paragraph essay* (pp. 201–220). Ann Arbor: University of Michigan Press.

Cummins, J. (2016). Reflections on Cummins (1980), The cross-lingual dimensions of language proficiency: Implications for bilingual education and the optimal age issue. *TESOL Quarterly*, *50*(4), 940–944. https://doi.org/10.1002/tesq.339

Cummins, J. (2007). BICS and CALP: Empirical and theoretical status of the distinction. In B. Street & N.H. Homburger (Eds.), *Encyclopedia of language and education, volume 2: Literacy* (pp. 71–83). New York: Springer Science.

Cummins, J. (2000). *Language, power and pedagogy: Bilingual children in the crossfire* (Vol. 23). Clevedon, England: Multilingual Matters.

Cummins, J. (1981). The role of primary language development in promoting educational success for language minority students. In California State Department of Education (Ed.), *Schooling and Language Minority Students: A Theoretical Rationale* (pp. 3-49). Los Angeles, CA: California State University.

Cummins, J. (1980). The cross-lingual dimensions of language proficiency: Implications for bilingual education and the optimal age issue. *TESOL Quarterly*, *14*(2), 175–187. https//doi.org/10.2307/3586312

Dale, E. (1969). *Audio-visual methods in teaching* (3rd ed.). New York: Holt, Rinehart & Winston.

Dawson, H. C., & Phelan, M. (Eds.). (2016). *Language files: Materials for an introduction to language and linguistics* (12th ed.) Columbus: Ohio State University Press.

Drucker, P. F. (1954). *The practice of management: A study of the most important function in America society*. New York: Harper & Brothers.

Emanuel, R., Adams, J., Baker, K., Daufin, E. K., Ellington, C., & Fitts, E. (2008). How college students spend their time communicating. *International Journal of Listening*, *22*(1), 13–28. https://doi.org/10.1080/10904010701802139

Enright, K. A. (2011). Language and literacy for a new mainstream. *American Educational Research Journal, 48*(1), 80–118. https://doi.org/10.3102/0002831210368989

ETS (2020). *TOEFL® program history: Volume 6*. Retrieved from https://www.ets.org/s/toefl/pdf/toefl_ibt_insight_s1v6.pdf

Farhady, H. (2018). History of language testing and assessment. *The TESOL Encyclopedia of English Language Teaching*, 1–7. New York: Wiley.

Farnsworth, T. L., & Malone, M. E. (2014). *Assessing English learners in U.S. schools*. Alexandria, VA: TESOL Press.

Ferris, D. (2011). *Treatment of error in second language student writing* (2nd ed.). Ann Arbor: University of Michigan Press.

Fillmore, L.W, & Snow, C.E. (2000). What teachers need to know about language. Office of Educational Research and Improvement. http://files.eric.ed.gov/fulltext/ED444379.pdf

Flesch, R. (1955). Why Johnny can't read: And what you can do about it. New York: William Morrow Paperbacks.

Folse, K. S. (2020). Personal communication, March 4.

Folse, K. S. (2016). Keys to teaching grammar to English language learners: A practical handbook (2nd ed.). Ann Arbor: University of Michigan Press.

Folse, K. (2010). Communicative competence and grammar classes revisited: 1980 and 2010. *Contact, 36*(2), 7–19.

Folse, K. (2006). *The art of teaching speaking*. Ann Arbor: University of Michigan Press.

Freire, P. (1985). *The politics of education: Culture, power, and liberation*. Westport: Greenwood Publishing Group.

García, O. (2011). *Bilingual education in the 21st century: A global perspective*. New York: John Wiley & Sons.

Gilliland, B. (2015). Reading, writing, and learning English in an American high school classroom. *Reading in a Foreign Language, 27*(2), 272–293.

Gogglieb, M. (2016). *Assessing English language learners: Bridges to educational equity*. Corwin.

González, M. C. (2017). The contribution of lexical diversity to college level writing. *TESOL Journal, 8*(4), 899–919. doi:10.1002/TESJ.342

Goulden, R., Nation, P., & Read, J. (1990). How large can a receptive vocabulary be? *Applied Linguistics, 11*(4), 341–363. https://doi.org/10.1093/applin/11.4.341

Grabe, W., & Stoller, F. L. (2011). *Teaching and researching reading* (2nd ed.). Routledge.

Grant, L. (2014). Prologue to the myths: What teachers need to know. In L. Grant (Ed.), *Pronunciation myths: Applying second language research to classroom teaching* (pp. 1–33). Ann Arbor: University of Michigan Press.

Haladyna, T. M. (2004). *Developing and validating multiple-choice test items.* New York: Routledge.

Haladyna, T. M., Downing, S. M., & Rodriguez, M. C. (2002). A review of multiple-choice item-writing guidelines for classroom assessment. *Applied measurement in education, 15*(3), 309–333. https://doi.org/10.1207/S15324818AME1503_5

Hamp-Lyons, L. (2003). Writing teachers as assessors of writing. In B. Kroll (Ed.), *Exploring the dynamics of second language writing* (pp. 162–189). New York: Cambridge University Press.

Hamp-Lyons, L. (2001). Fourth generation writing assessment. In T. Silva & P. K. Matsuda (Eds.), *On second language writing* (pp. 117–127). Mahwah, NJ: Lawrence Erlbaum.

Hamp-Lyons, L. (2000). Social, professional, and individual responsibility in language testing. *System 28*, 579–591. https://doi.org/10.1016/S0346–251X(00)00039-7

Hamp-Lyons, L. (1998). Ethics in language testing. In C. Clapham & D. Corson (Eds.), *Encyclopedia of language and education* (Language testing and assessment, Vol. 7, pp. 323–334). Kluwer. DOI:10.1007/978-1-4020-4489-2_29

Hamp-Lyons, L., & Condon, W. (2000). *Assessing the portfolio: Principles for practice, theory, and research.* Hampton Press.

Harlen, W. (2006) .On the relationship between assessment for formative and summative purposes. In J. Gardner (Ed.), *Assessment and learning* (pp. 87–102). Sage.

Hausman, D. (2012). Ad analysis scoring guide [Class handout]. Department of English Language and Literatures, Wright State University, Dayton, OH.

Hinkel, E. (2006). Current perspectives on teaching the four skills. *TESOL Quarterly, 40*(1), 109–131. http://dx.doi.org/10.2307/40264513

Hitt, M., & Helms, E. C. (2009). Best in show: Teaching old dogs to use new rubrics. *The Professional Educator, 33*(1), 1–15.

Huang, J. (2005). Challenges of academic listening in English: reports by Chinese students. *College Student Journal,* 39(3), 553+. https://link.gale.com/apps/doc/A135842841/AONE?u=anon~c859124c&sid=googleScholar&xid=6e70ec80

Huot, B. (1996). Toward a new theory of writing assessment. *College composition and communication, 47*(4), 549–566. https//doi.org/10.2307/358601

Hyland, K. (2004). *Disciplinary discourses, Social interactions in academic writing* (Michigan classics ed.). Ann Arbor: University of Michigan Press.

IELTS. (2020). *IELTS for study*. https://www.ielts.org/about-ielts/ielts-for-study

Inoue, A. (2019). *Labor-based grading contracts: Building equity and inclusion in the compassionate composition classroom*. Boulder: University Press of Colorado.

Irizarry, J. G. (2012). Los Caminos: Latino/a youth forging pathways in pursuit of higher education. *Journal of Hispanic Higher Education* 11(3), 291–309. https://doi.org/10.1177/1538192712446322

Irujo, S. (n.d.). What does research tell us about reading to English language learners? *Reading Rocket*. https://www.readingrockets.org/article/what-does-research-tell-us-about-teaching-reading-english-language-learners

Irujo, S. (2007). What does research tell us about teaching reading to English language learners? *The ELL Outlook: News, research, and discussion on the education of English language learners (ELLs),* Jan-Feb, 1–6. Retrieved from https://pdfs.semanticscholar.org/febd/dfc51edff8d92167789f-2c02f5f9f5451044.pdf

Johnson, K. (2013). Beyond standards: Disciplinary and national perspectives on habits of mind. *College Composition and Communication*, 517–541. https://www.jstor.org/stable/43490769

Johnson, K. E. (1999). *Understanding language teaching: Reasoning in action*. Boston: Heinle & Heinle.

Krahnke, K. J. (1985) Review of the natural approach: Language acquisition in the classroom. *TESOL Quarterly, 19*, 591–603.10.2307/3586280, https://www-jstor-org.ezproxy.libraries.wright.edu/stable/3586280

Krashen, S.D., & Terrell, T.D. (1983). *The natural approach: Language acquisition in the classroom*. Prentice Hall Europe.

Lam, R. (2016). Assessment as learning: Examining a cycle of teaching, learning, and assessment of writing in the portfolio-based classroom. *Studies in Higher Education*. https://doi.org/10.1080/03075079.2014.999317

Lam, R. (2015). Language assessment training in Hong Kong: Implications for language assessment literacy. *Language Testing, 32*(2), 169–197. https://doi.org/10.1177/0265532214554321

Larsen-Freeman, D. (2014). Teaching Grammar. In M. Celce-Murcia, D. M. Brinton, & M. A. Snow (Eds.), *Teaching English as a Second or Foreign Language* (4th ed., pp. 256–270). Boston: National Geographic Cengage Learning.

Laurinavicius, T. L. (2017, Dec. 6). Reasons why writing remains a critical skill for success. *The Huffington Post*. https://www.huffpost.com/entry/reasons-why-writing-remai_b_12701380

Li, N., & Peters, A. W. (2016). Preparing K–12 teachers/or ELLS: Improving teachers L2 knowledge and strategies through innovative professional development. *Urban Education*, 1–18. https://doi.org/10.1177/0042085916656902

Lightbown, P., & Spada, N. (1993). *How languages are learned.* London: Oxford University Press.

MacDonald, M., & Smith, I. (2010). Every student wins: Using Team English with large multilevel classes in Thailand. In B. Baurain, & L. H. Phan (Eds.), *Multilevel and Diverse Classrooms* (pp. 51–68). Alexandria, VA: TESOL.

MacSwan, J., & Rolstad, K. (2003). Linguistic diversity, schooling, and social class: Rethinking our conception of language proficiency in language minority education. *Sociolinguistics: The essential readings*, 329–340.

Malone, M. (2011, October). Assessment literacy for language educators. *CAL Digest*, 1–2.

Manhattan Review. (2020). *Test prep & admissions consulting: TOEFL prep courses in Seoul.* https://www.manhattanreview.com/seoul-toefl-prep-courses/

Martinez, J. (2019). California itinerary activity [Class handout]. Department of English Language and Literatures, Wright State University, Dayton, OH.

McCarthey, S. J. (2008). The impact of No Child Left Behind on teachers' writing instruction. *Written Communication*, *25*(4), 462–505. https://doi.org/10.1177/0741088308322554

McNamara, T. (2002, June 29–July 13). *L2 writing assessment*. The Summer Institute in Applied Linguistics. The Pennsylvania State University, State College.

Messick, S. (1996). Validity and washback in language testing. *Language Testing, 13*(3), 241–256. https://doi.org/10.1177/026553229601300302

Michigan Assessment Consortium (Producer) (2014, May). Rick Stiggens on assessment literacy [Video file]. Retrieved from http://michiganassessmentconsortium.org/resource/video-conference/rick-stiggens-assessment-literacy

National Commission on Writing (2004). *Writing: A ticket to work…or a ticket out: A survey of business leaders*. College Board.

Norris, D. & de Oliveira, L. C. (2013). Preparing mathematics teachers for culturally and linguistically diverse students: What's language got to do with social justice. In L. C. de Oliveira (Ed.), *Teacher education/or social justice: Perspectives and lessons learned* (pp. 105 114). Charlotte, NC: Information Age Publishing.

O'Malley, J. M. & Pierce, L. V. (1996). *Authentic assessment for English language learners: Practical approaches for teachers.* Addison-Wesley.

Peachy, N. (n.d.). A framework for planning a listening skills lesson. Retrieved from https://www.teachingenglish.org.uk/article/a-framework-planning-a-listening-skills-lesson

Plakans, L., & Gebril, A. (2015). *Assessment myths: Applying second language research to classroom teaching.* Ann Arbor: University of Michigan Press.

Powers, D. E. (2010). *TOEIC compendium study: The case for a comprehensive, four skills assessment of English language proficiency*. Retrieved from https://www.ets.org/Media/Research/pdf/TC-10-12.pdf

Robinson, L., Segal, J., & Segal, R. (2020, June). Healthy eating. https://www.helpguide.org/articles/healthy-eating/healthy-eating.htm

Roediger III, H. L., Putnam, A. L., & Smith, M. A. (2011). Ten benefits of testing and their applications to educational practice. *Psychology of Learning and Motivation-Advances in Research and Theory*, *55*(1), 1–36. https://doi.org/10.1016/B978-0-12-387691-1.00001-6

Ruecker, T. (2013). High-stakes testing and Latina/o students: Creating a hierarchy of college readiness. *Journal of Hispanic Higher Education, 12*(3), 303–320. https://doi.org/10.1177/1538192713493011

Ruecker, T., Chamcharatsri, B., & Saengngoen, J. (2015). Teacher perceptions of the impact of the Common Core assessments on linguistically diverse high school students. *Journal of Writing Assessment*, *8*(1), http://journalofwritingassessment.org/article.php?article=87

Ruecker, T. & Crusan, D. (Eds.) (2018). *The politics of English second language writing assessment in global contexts.* New York: Routledge.

The Leadership Conference on Civil & Human Rights (2015). Civil rights groups: "We oppose anti-testing efforts." Retrieved from https://civilrights.org/2015/05/05/civil-rights-groups-we-oppose-anti-testing-efforts/

Tucker, J. (2014, April). Test specifications and item writer guidelines in a multilingual world: issues and solutions [conference presentation]. ALTE. Paris, France.

Salehi, M., & Marefat, F. (2014). The Effects of Foreign Language Anxiety and Test Anxiety on Foreign Language Test Performance. *Theory & Practice in Language Studies*, *4*(5). doi.org/10.4304/tpls.4.5.931-940

Savage, K.L., Bitterlin, G., & Price, D. (2010). *Grammar matters.* New York: Cambridge University Press.

Savignon, S. J. (2017, March 7). Communicative Competence. *The TESOL encyclopedia of English language teaching*. (J. I. Liontas & M. DelliCarpini, Eds.). New York: Wiley. doi:10.1002/9781118784235.eelt0047

Scarino, A. (2013). Language assessment literacy as self-awareness: Understanding the role of interpretation in assessment and in teacher learning. *Language Testing, 30*(3), 309–327. https://doi.org/10.1177/0265532213480128

Schleppegrell, M. J. (2004). *The language of schooling: A functional linguistics perspective*. Mahwah, NJ: Lawrence Erlbaum.

Schleppegrell, M. J. (2001). Linguistic Features of the Language of Schooling. *Linguistics and Education, 12*(4), 431–459. https://doi.org/10.1016/S0898-5898(01)00073-0

Schmitt, N., & Schmitt, D. (2020). *Vocabulary in language teaching*. Cambridge University Press.

Schmitt, N., & Schmitt, D. (2014). A reassessment of frequency and vocabulary size in L2 vocabulary teaching. *Language Teaching, 47*(4), 484–503.

Schumann, J.H. (1976). Social distance as a factor in second language acquisition. *Language Learning, 26*(1), 135–143. https://do.org/10.1111/j.1467-1770.1976.tb00265.x

Selber, S. A. (2004). *Multiliteracies for a digital age*. Carbondale: SIU Press.

Selinker, L. (1972). Interlanguage. *International Review of Applied Linguistics, 10*, 209–231. https://doi.org/10.1515/iral.1972.10.1-4.209

Shannon, P. (1987). Commercial reading materials, a technological ideology, and the deskilling of teachers. *The Elementary School Journal*, 307–329. https://www.jstor.org/stable/1001179

Shohamy, E. (1997). Testing methods, testing consequences: Are they ethical? Are they fair? *Language Testing, 14*(3), 340–349. https://doi.org/10.1177/026553229701400310

Shohamy, E. (2001). *The power of tests: A critical perspective of the uses of language tests*. White Plains, NY: Longman.

Siriwardana, L. G. (2019a). Listening dialogue activity [Class handout]. Department of English Language and Literatures, Wright State University, Dayton, OH.

Siriwardana, L. G. (2019b). Guided grammar activity [Class handout]. Department of English Language and Literatures, Wright State University, Dayton, OH.

Siriwardana, L. G. (2019c). [ð] and [θ] sounds [Class handout]. Department of English Language and Literatures, Wright State University, Dayton, OH.

Sjostrom, B. (2020). Grammar project. Unpublished manuscript.

Street, B. (1997). The implications of the "New Literacy Studies" for literacy education. *English in Education, 31*(3), 45.

Suárez-Orozco, C., & Suárez-Orozco, M. (2001). *Children of immigrants*. Cambridge, MA: Harvard University Press.

Tardy, C. M. (2019). Is the five-paragraph essay a genre? In N. A. Caplan, & A. M. Johns (Eds.), *Changing practices for the L2 writing classroom: Moving beyond the five-paragraph essay* (pp. 42–63). Ann Arbor: University of Michigan Press.

Tardy, C. M. (2016). *Beyond convention: Genre innovation in academic writing*. Ann Arbor: University of Michigan Press.

Taylor, L. (2005). Washback and impact. *ELT Journal, (59)*2, 154–155. https://doi.org/10.1093/eltj/cci030

Tecco, B. D. (2012) You can do it! https://www.readworks.org/article/You-Can-Do-It!/1c2d104f-16e2-4ee3-8127e0c9cd73a6cd#!vocabularySection:triumphant/articleTab:content/

Testnav (2020). Retrieved from https://tx8.testnav.com/

Texas Education Agency (2019). *Educator guide: Texas English language proficiency assessment system (TELPAS).* Retrieved from https://tea.texas.gov/sites/default/files/2019_TELPAS_Educator_Guide_FORWEB.pdf

University of Arizona (n.d.). *IEP Curriculum.* Retrieved from http://www.cesl.arizona.edu/iep-curriculum

Valdés, G. (2004). The teaching of academic language to minority second language learners. In Ball, A. F., & S. W. Freeman (Eds.), *Bakhtinian perspectives on language, literacy, and learning.* Cambridge University Press.

Vygotsky, L. S. (1978). *Mind in society: The development of higher psychological processes.* [Trans J. V. Wertsch] Cambridge, MA: Harvard University Press.

Weigle, S. C. (2002). *Assessing writing.* New York: Cambridge University Press.

Weissberg, R. (2006). *Connecting speaking and writing in second language writing instruction.* Ann Arbor: University of Michigan Press.

White, E. M. (1998) *Teaching and assessing writing: Understanding, evaluating, and improving student performance.* Jossey-Bass.

WIDA (2020). *WIDA English language development standards framework..* https://wida.wisc.edu/sites/default/files/resource/WIDA-ELD-Standards-Framework-2020.pdf

Yancey, K. B. (1999). Looking back as we look forward: Historicizing writing assessment. *College Composition and Communication*, *50*(3), 483–503. https://doi.org/10.2307/358862

Yancey, K., Robertson, L., & Taczak, K. (2014). *Writing across contexts: Transfer, composition, and sites of writing.* Boulder: University Press of Colorado.